Back Home

Back Home
Journeys through Mobile

ROY HOFFMAN

The University of Alabama Press
Tuscaloosa and London

9 8 7 6 5 4 3 2 1 • 09 08 07 06 05 04 03 02 01

Designer: Michele Myatt Quinn
Typeface: Galliard

∞

The paper on which this book is printed meets the minimum
requirements of American National Standard for Information
Science–Permanence of Paper for Printed Library Materials,
ANSI Z39.48-1984.

Library of Congress Cataloging-in-Publication Data
Hoffman, Roy, 1953–
    Back home : journeys through Mobile / Roy Hoffman.
      p.   cm.
   Imprint from data view; no publisher's statement in galley.
    ISBN 0-8173-1045-2 (alk. paper)
    1. Mobile (Ala.)—Description and travel. 2. Mobile
(Ala.)—History. 3. Mobile (Ala.)—Biography. 4. Hoffman, Roy,
1953—Childhood and youth. I. Title.

   F334.M6 H56 2001
   976.1′22—dc21
                                 00-010633
British Library Cataloguing-in-Publication Data available

To my parents, Charlie and Evelyn Hoffman,
who gave me stories to tell.

And to Nancy and Meredith, my wife and daughter,
who helped me get them told.

Contents

Illustrations

Back Home

Introduction

As children we take for granted the voices of our family, our friends, our teachers. As grown-ups we listen more critically to those voices, at the same time hearing new ones: colleagues at work, strangers at the store, newcomers from other parts of the world.

"Back Home: Journeys Through Mobile" echoes with voices from my childhood but focuses on those I hear now, listening as an adult.

I was born and raised in Mobile, graduated from high school in 1971 and from college, at Tulane University in New Orleans, in 1975. For the next 21 years I lived in New York, first Manhattan then Brooklyn, returning home for holidays, and keeping in close contact with my parents in Mobile wherever I roamed.

Along the way I got married—to a woman from Mobile—although I took her north, too. That I would ever go back, single or married, was a far-fetched notion to me. Home, by definition, was a place you left, pined for, anguished about, but never really returned to. It would be like taking out familiar clothes from high school and trying to wriggle into them again.

Looking back now, I guess I was brooding on a return long before I made it. In October 1993, I published this essay in the "Southern Journal" column of *Southern Living*:

DAUGHTER OF THE SOUTH

In a lively Brooklyn playground, crowded with children speaking Spanish, Arabic, Yiddish and every dialect of English, you can spot her by the bow. It is large, pinned at the back of her thick, sandy-blonde hair. She scurries up the slide, taking her place behind a boy in a New York Mets sweatshirt. Next to the others she looks ready for a party in her smocked dress. As she comes soaring down, she squeals and laughs like any five-year-old, then turns to neighborhood friends and shouts, "Come on, y'all!"

Meredith Amanda Hoffman, my daughter, sometimes refers to a Southern accent as a "Southern accident," but it is no accident her spunky New York elocution is brushed with long *i*'s and soft *e*'s. Though she was born in Manhattan's Lenox Hill Hospital and took her first steps in Greenwich Village, the South has never been too far away. Since my wife, Nancy, and I are both native Alabamians, Meredith was being spoon-fed grits while other babies were gumming Cream of Wheat, and though cheesecake is a neighborhood delicacy, pecan pie is still her favorite dessert.

With Mobile being the family home, the Gulf Coast holds dreamy appeal. It's the one place all airplanes seem to travel to, and whether it's Thanksgiving or Mardi Gras, it always feels like the Fourth of July. Wool hats stay securely in closets, and lawns invite you to go barefoot.

The people down there are different, too. First of all, they do like to go *on and on*. Mommy and Daddy are especially talkative, too, filled with tales of their own youths. And through her grandparents, all Southern born, Meredith hears stories of a more colorful South beginning with *their* parents and grandparents.

In New York, Meredith's hardly alone in her ties to a region two day's drive the other side of the Hudson—whether she's with pal Marisa, whose Swainsboro, Georgia, mom, Becky Ford, throws a yearly Kentucky Derby party in Brooklyn Heights; or with friend Isabel, who travels south on holidays with her Louisiana mom, Caroline Stewart, who grew up on a sugar cane plantation not far from Baton Rouge. Her buddy Joshua even has a soft spot for the banjo; his dad, Eli Evans, son of Durham, North Carolina, has visited Joshua's Manhattan class to pluck a few tunes and to tell about traveling as an author on the *Delta Queen*.

All these children are very much New Yorkers. As Meredith gets excited to hear the Alabama Crimson Tide is whipping an opponent, so she groans to find out the New York Mets are getting pummeled. She takes for granted the accessibility of the arts: Her favorite performer is Big Bird, but her favorite painter is Matisse. And though she's more sheltered than her Southern cousins, she takes in more, too. Walking with us everywhere, she comes face-to-face with our world's craziness, its humor and despair.

Growing up with a dual allegiance to North and South can bring with it the twin joys of ice skating in winter and water skiing in summer; or watching snow blanket the streets for Valentine's Day and enjoying sugar beaches, far from the madding crowd, in the heat of August. It is to seek out the more personable elements of urban life: a chatty relationship with the butcher; a picturesque place to walk. And it's to eye American culture—from its foods, to its ethnicity, to its social concerns—in a special, stereoscopic way.

But the grasp of the South's essence need not be quite so profound. It's enough that Meredith laughs heartily when she hears Hush Puppy's drawl on Shari Lewis's "Lamb Chop" or that when she sees they're serving grits at the local diner (which is run not by Southerners but by immigrants from the Dominican Republic) it still speaks to her, in whatever language, of a place called home.

It was during one of those summer vacations, in 1996, that we did return to live year-round—unexpectedly.

Bailey Thomson, associate editor of the Mobile Register—now an associate professor at the University of Alabama—invited me to the Register to meet Stan Tiner, editor-in-chief, Mike Marshall, managing editor, and Dewey English, associate managing editor. (Since then, Stan went on to head up the Sun-Herald in Biloxi/Gulfport, Mike took over the Register's helm, and Dewey became managing editor.) They offered me a free-roaming, full-time position as "Writer in Residence," enabling me to write non-fiction while employing narrative techniques I'd learned as a writer of fiction, essays, and political speeches and as a magazine journalist.

As my father, Charles Hoffman, a Mobile attorney, once said to me: in adulthood, one does not make decisions in life so much as choices. Take the job or not?

We called a moving van.

My hometown journeys were made by car, bicycle, and foot, carrying me to worlds tucked away near my own backyard. Like a dog sniffing through the brush I zigzagged from arts, to sports, to farming, to family, to snowstorms, to hurricanes, to politics, to personal reflections, then back to arts. What was this dog hunting, after all?

Ultimately, it was what Southerners, and Southern writers in particular, have waxed eloquent about for generations—a sense of place. That "place," however, is growing harder to locate. Nearly a century ago my grandfather, Morris Hoffman, arrived from Eastern Europe at the Mobile train station and walked up Dauphin Street, enveloped, right away, in the sense of place. Today, when I walk back down that same street, what's left to tell me where I am?

"Back Home" represents my sense of place. Rather than a continuous movie it is akin to a photo album. Like Erik Overbey's photographs of Mobile during the early 20th century, these pieces often focus on ordinary goings-on, and they exist because I was commissioned to make a record of what was in front of my lens—pad and pen.

Most of these pieces appeared originally in the Register, a few elsewhere, as noted in the list of permissions at the back of the book. I have made minor edits, mostly to avoid repetition, since a reader moves through a book according to his or her own pace, but enjoys pieces in a newspaper as they appear, sometimes with material reiterated from earlier publications. I have not tried to chase the clock by updating every piece.

"Back Home" is not meant to be definitive of anything except my own interests as a writer given the license—and sometimes, by my editors, the direction—to head to certain destinations for a long, second look. My research methods are simple: Given the choice between reading a document and listening to someone talk, I'll always pull up a chair to the human voice. Some of these voices, in the course of the past four years, have been quieted forever, but not to me.

When buildings are leveled, when land is developed, when money is spent, when our loved ones pass on, when we take our places a little further back every year on the historical time-line, what we still have are stories.

PART I

GOING DOWNTOWN

❖

If you drive downtown on a week-
day afternoon in the last years of the 20th century and the beginning
of the 21st you may find, at first, a quiet place where time seems to
have curved just beyond the boundaries. It even seems haunted in
places, the names of old stores faint signatures on peeling walls. There
are new places thriving, to be sure—a children's science museum
called the Exploreum, a high-rise Government Plaza, rock-n-roll em-
poria that do not begin to fill until 10 P.M.—but most stores and
offices have moved toward suburban west Mobile, out where Airport
Boulevard and I-65 cross amidst a sprawl of shopping centers and
American eateries.

Three centuries have passed since the French first settled upriver, got flooded out and moved down to the present site of downtown Mobile, at the mouth of the Mobile River. The flags that flew
over the realm changed through the eras—French, British, Spanish,
United States, Confederate and, of course, United States again. But
the site of Mobile's heart, close to the boats and the trains, stayed
the same until automobiles took it far away.

I start my journeys through Mobile like my grandfather—on Dauphin Street. My stories are 20th-century ones, and now that the century has astonishingly come and gone, we can see what we had, and
what we lost—many of our downtown family enterprises, the bakeries and drugstores and movie houses and retail stores that made "going downtown" a special event, one you got dressed up for. That's
what many people remember and long for—not out of nostalgia, I
don't think, but yearning to be somewhere distinctive, somewhere
that says it's truly your home.

To go downtown today can be a melancholic experience, since so much has vanished even after these pieces were written. But if you remember some of the businesses and lives that flourished there, and replay the stories of some storekeepers and families, it can be a rich, involving experience, too.

My Grandfather's World

❖

A Walk Down Dauphin

There have been all kinds of stories written about Mobile over the course of 200 years, but none more intriguing to me than the City Directory of 1909.

It shows a town in which residents are clearly demarcated by race: "C" for colored, "Cre" for Creole, "Chi" for Chinese.

It reminds us, in advertisements for travel on the Mobile and Ohio railroad, how transportation has changed. It recalls, in advertisements for Mobile Electric Co., how concerns about safety have not: "A lighted porch light is the best protection against burglars."

Most revealing, in block-by-block listings of residents and cross-listings by profession, the directory shows who were neighbors, and how people spent their days. At 512 Dauphin, for example, between Lawrence and Cedar streets, was "Mobile Poultry Farm: Dealers in Eggs and all kind of Live & Home-Dressed Poultry." Next door at 514 was a Cleaner's and Presser's run by a young couple who resided at the same address, and who appeared in the directory the first time that year—Morris and Mary Hoffman, my grandparents.

How Morris and Mary, as youths, left Romanian villages, traveled to New York, met and married there and had their first child, Louie, is a saga which speaks to a time when America, to Europeans, glittered with golden shores.

That they eventually made their way to Mobile, had three more children—Charles, Goldie and Rebecca—and reared them over a

Dauphin Street store, comes from a chapter in history in which some Jews, like other immigrants, made their ways to port cities and merchant crossroads throughout the South.

I do not know the stories of all the early Dauphin Street families, but I suspect that the long journeys their names suggest—Habeeb, from Syria; Naman and Zoghby, from Lebanon; Matranga, from Sicily; Kurkulakis, from Greece; Bitzer, from Germany—tell triumphs of their own.

In a way it saddens me that to walk Morris and Mary's original block today, with pages from the 1909 directory in hand, is to visit Pompeii.

Their storefront, which they soon turned into a general mercantile store, has long been replaced by a short row of one-story offices. Across the street, where David Pinkerson, a great-uncle on my mother's side, ran Pink's Music Store, there's now a vacant lot; part of the shop's ceramic tile floor still covers the ground.

Two blocks away, on Conti Street, is a parking lot that, in my grandparents' era, held the Orthodox synagogue where the Hoffmans and other families—among them Lubel, Friedlander, Prince, Kamil—strolled on Sabbaths to congregate and pray.

Despite the fact that this stretch of Dauphin is mostly inhabited by spirits of the past, I make a pilgrimage here whenever I return home. I like to recall a time when store owners were families who lived close by, and customer relations meant a rocking chair and an extra cigar.

The fact that a few family businesses still thrive on Dauphin—Morris and Mary's legacy, the furniture store, among them—cheers me; and that a new generation now comes downtown to amble in and out of music clubs, gives me heart that the battered street, buoyed by the adventurousness, and dollars, of America's youth culture, may revive still.

In the city's vast, temperature-controlled shopping complexes I lose my compass; downtown, close to the port, with tall windows and balconies the setting for countless lives gone by, I recall where I am.

As Morris Hoffman stands at the center of this 1925 family portrait, Mary takes her place in front with daughters Goldie (left) and Rebecca (right). On either side of Morris are sons Charles (left) and Louis or "Louie" (right) the eldest, with diploma in hand. The couple, both born in Romania, met and married in New York and began their life in Mobile in 1907. The occasion of the photo—taken at Erik Overbey's studio a few blocks from Morris's store—was Louie's graduation from Barton Academy. (Erik Overbey, Hoffman family collection)

Granted, I have a good guide in my father's stories about his own long life on Dauphin, both growing up and in many years of legal practice within footsteps of Bienville Square.

He takes me back to the streets of downtown at the time of the First World War: to the trolley cars he rode all over town; to the Lyric Theater where, for a few coins, he saw Eddie Cantor and Al Jolson; to the drugstores, from Van Antwerp's to Ortmann's, on nearly every corner; to the pool hall where the entry requirement was long pants and where young boys still wearing shorts schemed a way to borrow knickers.

He also takes me back to the days, unimaginable to me, before air conditioning. I have a picture of him and his brother, Louie, dragging their mattress onto the store balcony some hot summer nights, hoping to catch an unlikely breeze. On a rare vacation day from the store, the family walked to the foot of Dauphin and caught the Bay Queen for the ride to Fairhope, where they enjoyed a refreshing swim.

Keeping people cool was an aspect of business, too. I remember a radio jingle for my grandfather's store, something like, "We have ceiling fans and window fans, one-room fans and three-room fans, any old fan, even a baseball fan."

My father also helps transform old directory addresses into real faces peering from windows. Behind one is John Fowler, a clock repairer, who claimed to have invented the airplane and kept one, as a tourist attraction, at Monroe Park.

My father remembers an even more extraordinary invention Fowler demonstrated in his shop: a perpetual motion machine that had a ball running up and down a track day and night.

Behind another window is Dr. E. T. Belsaw, a dentist and, as a black man, one of the few non-white medical professionals in town early in this century. Joining them is F. D. Bru, a Cuban gentleman who rolled and sold cigars and who at one time, with his family, rented an over-the-store apartment from my grandparents. Then there's Gus Seiple, a locksmith, who referred to himself as a "keyologist."

Many Dauphin Street names have continued through generations,

Once vibrant with shops, many run by new Americans selling daily necessities—vegetables, dairy products, clothing—today's Dauphin Street livens up principally at night, catering to young people who amble the strip, listening to music, flocking to clubs. (John David Mercer, Mobile Register)

to weave themselves through the city's commercial and civic life. From Megginson's Drugs on the corner of Lawrence came a mayor of Mobile. From Eugene Thoss Jr.'s store close by came decades of sporting goods. When I played Little League baseball as a boy, my team was sponsored by Thoss.

It's as though yesteryear's Dauphin Street created its own family tree, relating the city's dwellers in a thousand different ways. It even provided romance. My mother, Evelyn, when single, worked as a bookkeeper at the Toggery, an elegant clothing store, and watched her husband-to-be strolling by the square.

The Dauphin Street I remember growing up in the 1950s and '60s—a street where we frequently rode the bus—was vibrant with store logos: Hammel's, Gayfers, Metzger's, Kayser's, Reiss Brothers, Raphael's.

If the street's department stores and fashion shops have not been gobbled up by national chains, many have moved to locations more practically situated in an economy where consumers like to drive, park, and shop until late in bright, secure malls.

While the city continues to sprawl farther out to what used to seem like wilderness, the surroundings of the airport, I doubt that big stores will ever return to the downtown.

The Dauphin Street of my youth was also one where Mardi Gras parades still rolled their way down the street, the snare drums rattling

In the 1920s, Dauphin Street between St. Joseph and Royal—with Bienville Square on the left here—was busy with commerce. Evelyn Robinton, a young woman who worked at "The Toggery," indicated by the sign, would watch Charles Hoffman pass by that corner. They married and had four children, the youngest of whom is the author. (Erik Overbey Collection, University of South Alabama Archives)

the windows, the floats seeming to touch the sides of the buildings. On the balcony of my grandparents' store, I stood with Alberta West, a wonderful woman who worked for my family, and my sister Robbie, and shouted to the masked men below. They hurled back boxes of Cracker Jack, rubber balls and candy.

I can still feel the throws raining down.

I wish the streets around today's Dauphin felt safer. When I turn a block away onto St. Francis and pass by silent buildings, a scruffy white man with a sack under his arm watches me closely. What does he want? Although I have paced the streets of New York City, where I live, many a late evening, I feel more vulnerable here, on blocks where no one else on foot is around. I relax only when I turn back to Dauphin.

As the evening wears on, and I visit social establishments that have sprung up in recent years, I realize that the collegiate-looking youths shooting pool don't know they are reviving a Dauphin Street tradition, except that now girls play, too; and that the waitress in a restaurant which displays cigars doesn't know that a Havana emigre once sat in a room nearby and rolled scores of stogies, perfectly, by hand.

In one club, Boo Radley's, named for the reclusive neighbor in Harper Lee's "To Kill a Mockingbird," I listen to a folk singer, on open-mike night, struggling with a Simon and Garfunkel number while a Jimi Hendrix poster looks on. I check the 1918 directory: a tailor, Max Fry, a friend of my grandfather's, and whose family I know, once had his shop at this address. Here, as effectively as anywhere in the region, a memory of the old South and a sense of the new are crushed together like songs from different jukeboxes.

What would my grandfather have made of all this? I envision him alive and young again, coming down the street in Panama hat and suspenders, puzzled at the vacancy of so many storefronts where his friends, starting out life in America, sold items that were practical: bottles of milk, loaves of bread, tables and chairs, shoes and jackets.

Yet I feel sure he would appreciate this picture of money still exchanging hands, of small business owners taking risks, of people walking the street past dusk.

Since it's Dauphin Street, tonight he might even stop in for a beer. I'd be happy to join him.

A Contract for Watermelons

Come summer, wherever I may be, when I see watermelons like vast blossoms on top of overturned crates or stacked in green mountains at roadside stands, I think of a story about my grandfather handed down to me from my father.

The story begins on a road that runs about 30 miles from Semmes, Ala., to Mobile, through flat piney woods and farmland. The road was still dirt and clay back in 1912 when, on a Saturday in July, a young farmer named John, tall, sunburned, his hair prematurely silvering, was hauling a load of watermelons to Mobile's large produce market—a building housing City Hall upstairs and refurbished after World War II to hold just City Hall. A storm struck, muddying the road and slowing his cart considerably. By the time he arrived in Mobile the sun was sinking and the market was closing for the day.

Stuck with his load of watermelons and surely vexed by the thought of a few going bad, John turned his cart up Dauphin Street and made his way by the cluster of stores lighted by flickering gas lamps.

In front of one store was another young man, Morris Hoffman, my grandfather: dark eyes, genial, a touch portly. He was setting out sale items—socks, hats, overalls—in front of what was principally his cleaning and pressing shop.

"Howdy," John said, joking, "I see I'm not the only one getting a late start today."

Morris smiled and said that he and his wife, Mary, did not work on the Sabbath.

"Sunday ain't till tomorrow," John said, then leaned forward and peered closely at Morris. "Where ya'll from, anyways?"

Morris introduced himself, offered his hand and said, "We come from Romania. We are Jews."

John pumped his hand, said his own name, and replied: "I'm a Baptist myself, from Semmes."

"You are selling these?" Morris asked.

"Yessir. I got near 'bout 50. You buy just one you'd be doing me a favor."

Morris looked over the wagonload. "I want to give you help, but I cannot buy all."

By the time John had climbed down from his cart and accepted a glass of water Morris offered, they had exchanged more pleasantries.

"For one melon," Morris suggested, "one sock?"

"I could sure use some socks," John answered and lugged down his fattest melon.

Morris admired the melon, looked over the cart again and said that, in his opinion, the best customer is a repeat customer. "I will buy your 50 melons to help you," he said, "if we can make a contract. I will buy one melon a year for 50 years." They shook on it.

The next summer, when John appeared with an enormous watermelon Morris gave him a handkerchief. This time they visited longer and talked about the hot 1913 summer, about the varieties and shapes of melons. In 1914, when the watermelon was exchanged for a belt, John told how his forebears had come over from Europe long before the Civil War, pushed down through the Appalachians and ended up as farmers in southern Alabama.

Came 1915, when the watermelon became a second pair of socks, and 1916, when it was traded for a hat, and Morris told John how he had left Romania as a boy to escape religious persecution, stowed away on a ship to America and spent two years in New York where he'd met and married Mary, also a Romanian Jewish immigrant.

Feeling locked into the big city, and tiring of the cold, Morris headed south while Mary with their newborn, Louis, waited in New York. He arrived in a large eastern seaboard city (Baltimore, or perhaps Richmond?), where he took out his travel money, handed it to the man at the ticket window in the train station and requested passage to a small seaside town in a hot climate. The man handed him a ticket to Mobile. Mary and Louis soon joined him.

When 1916 turned to 1917, 1917 to 1918, personal reminiscences were set aside for talk about the World War. Already the watermelon contract seemed an excuse for a yearly conversation on a hot afternoon. By the early 1920s Morris' two sons, Charles and Louis, my father and uncle, were big enough to visit John's farm and walked delightedly down rows of the watermelon patch. And by the mid-1920s, John was delivering his annual melon in a truck to Morris who, having expanded his shop into a general mercantile store, offered shoes one year, a coat the next.

If watermelons were excuses for talking, they were also, by now, like calendars, each marking another year gone by. The years brought prosperity until the Great Depression, when Morris could give to John, as in earlier days, only a handkerchief or a pair of socks.

Morris shook his head and lamented to John: "All I have in my store is now not worth so much as one watermelon." But the men talked, even joked bleakly. They still honored their contract, as though honoring it were now a yearly ritual that assured they would both endure one year longer.

Then, after the Depression, Morris' merchandise became valuable again, doubled, tripled in value. His exchange with John became a yearly gift: a pot-bellied stove for a watermelon, a battery-powered radio for a watermelon. The store became the exclusive outlet for Aladdin gas lamps, which could illuminate an entire room. When Morris gave John an Aladdin lamp, John said he'd been given the best present imaginable, for the farm still had no electricity and his sons were "killin' their eyes trying to read by kerosene lamp." Morris gave John a second lamp, an advance on next year's watermelon.

Watermelons. Watermelons. If Morris could stack them all up from over the years, surely they'd reach as high as the eaves of his new store (a furniture store, down Dauphin Street a block): surely they'd be as high as a Succoth booth, or as an altar onto which one could climb to survey the plentifulness of the land.

Morris' children had children, and by the 1940s, when the Second

World War came, Morris said a ritual prayer each summer upon seeing John arrive at the store with a fat watermelon borne on his shoulder. He recited the prayer to John and explained what the Hebrew meant to him: "Praised be Thou, O Lord our God, ruler of the world, who has granted us life, sustained us, and permitted us to celebrate this new and joyous season."

Yet, as the 1950s progressed, both men knew that new seasons, however joyous, were not innumerable. In 1955 Morris made a grand gesture of friendship to John, presenting to him, in trade for his watermelon, a bedroom suite. In 1956, though, when John arrived at the store, Mary met him sadly. He put his watermelon down slowly onto the floor as she told him of Morris' death that April. "My old, old friend is gone," John said quietly. "I always thought I'd be the first not able to honor our contract."

For two more summers John came with a watermelon, honoring the contract and honoring the memory of Morris. In 1959 he did not show up: Folks at the store heard he had died. The contract had lasted 47 years.

My father, a lawyer, has handled some legal matters for John's son over the years, and John's offspring have shopped periodically at Morris' store, now run by my cousin. But the ritual connection between families no longer exists. John's farm was sold, with only a small plot bought back recently by a son for his house trailer; a watermelon for a pot-bellied stove seems a mark of the past. For my grandfather and the farmer, though, a watermelon was enough to inspire a contract, to set going a friendship.

The Enduring Ring

To you it may be only a ring—wide-banded, 18-karat gold, burnished to a soft hue—but to me it tells of a hundred years' time. Even the initials, MH, engraved on its surface, delicate as a whisper, speak of

a long-ago afternoon—New York City, the Lower East Side, a young
man newly arrived in America.

Morris Hoffman, 21 years old, had left Romania and made landfall
in New York with the new century, stepping off the boat at Ellis
Island, blinking at the majesty and the opportunity that awaited the
first wave of 20th-century pilgrims, immigrants from Eastern Europe,
the Adriatic, the Mediterranean.

All alone in New York—he would not marry and venture South
to the Port of Mobile until 1907—Morris earned wages where he
could. He carved meats at a delicatessen, assisted a tailor, learned
cleaning and pressing. Nickel by dime he amassed a fortune—10
dollars—his savings stuffed inside his back pocket.

On that 1901 afternoon he took out his fortune and bought a
simple, gold ring. "Make my initials in it," he told the ring-maker
on the Lower East Side, speaking in Romanian, or Yiddish, or German, or French. He had only an eighth-grade education, but he could
converse with the world. The jeweler began to engrave and, when
finished, Morris had his bank account. Now it was the ring that was
his savings, his security. "If he didn't have food or a safe place to
sleep," my father tells me of my grandfather, "he could always take
the ring and get fifty cents or a dollar at a pawn shop—he had to,
once or twice—but he always went back and got the ring. It was his
security that he would never go hungry."

While still in New York, Morris would go on to take a bride, Mary
Weissman, also from his homeland. They started a life together in the
Deep South. As they had a family, rooted into Mobile's immigrant
blocks and prospered, my grandfather wore no other jewelry save that
ring. At his store, as decades wore on, he swept the walk at daybreak,
cranked open the awnings by breakfast, welcomed customers in his
rocking chair. Security meant an account at the First National Bank,
owning property on Dauphin Street, living over the store, investing
in education.

The ring was a reminder of where he had started, how far he had
come.

• • •

One day in 1956, his health in decline, Morris took off the gold ring and tucked it away somewhere in his house. It was to be the final year of his life. The ring was lost; soon, forgotten. Four years later, Mary was taking crystal goblets down from a back shelf. Her own health had become fragile, and she had entertained little with her fancy dinnerware since her husband had passed.

In one of those goblets she discovered Morris' gold ring. My father slipped the ring over his finger. The initials, MH, scrolled across the smooth, dark-gold surface. I was only a child at the time, and as I recall images of my father over the years—walking with my mother, swimming in the Bay, leaning back in his office chair with the vista of Mobile's port out his window—I detect the glint of the ring.

Since I can remember, I have never seen it off his hand.

• • •

Recently my father, still hardy at a monumental age, was admitted to the hospital to undergo surgery for blockage in his carotid artery. Prior to the operation, while I could still be with him, the doctor asked him to remove any jewelry. Procedure, we were told.

He coaxed the ring off and, from the gurney, handed it out toward me.

"Take care of it," he said. "One day you'll wear it."

I protected it as best I knew how. While my family and I sat anxiously in the atrium of the Mobile Infirmary, around us were hundreds of others awaiting news of their own loved ones. I wondered which pieces of jewelry in that lobby were heirlooms—bands, earrings, necklaces, lockets—tiny treasures, safe-keepings of the past.

As I touched the ring on my finger, turned it, brushed its surface, I summoned the pilgrim speaking little English and ready to take on the boisterous new world. His youthful hand, from 1901, reached out to take mine on the brink of the year 2000.

• • •

The surgery was a success and my father was soon home, recovering. "You wear it a couple more days," he said, admiring the swirling MH where the gold band hugged my skin. The ring stayed with me at the office, at home, and when I went to sleep it remained on my hand. As I wrapped my fingers around the steering wheel of my car or touched them to the computer keyboard, the ring became my own security—against forgetting the men who'd come before me.

After I had borne it long enough so that it remained there, in a phantom touch, I took it off and gave it back to my father to keep on wearing, I prayed, for a good long time.

Corner Drugstores, Moviehouses, and Bread

The Lost Counter Culture

Fall 1996

To many grown-ups the corner drugstore was a place to seek relief from a headache, sore throat, or arthritis, but to us kids it was an oasis.

With its marbletop counters, glass jars filled with peppermint swizzles, and soda jerks in white hats concocting banana splits like able bartenders, the drugstore promised unclocked pleasure.

The Albright and Wood on the triangle near the Loop was a long building with terra-cotta roof. In our Murphy High neighborhood we would cycle there, letting our bikes, unlocked, clatter to the wall.

Impatient connoisseurs, we'd hurry in to slurp up chocolate sodas and vanilla phosphates, then scout out the model airplane kits. At the news rack we'd marvel at the world brought to our Mobile corner by Look and Life, and peek at a magazine, if we could find one, showing girls who looked nothing like our moms.

There are still some family pharmacies in town where patrons over the years have explained their maladies to generations with the same last name.

George Widney, a writer in his 70s, goes to Cox Drug Store on Marine Street because his mother did, even though he lives far away in the Crichton neighborhood.

"I inherited it," he jokes on a crowded Friday evening when another regular, Minnie Lee Clark, rests on her walker while looking over gift items. Pharmacist Bubba Straub, who trades shifts with Billy

Cool, serene, and inviting, the counter of the Albright and Wood drugstore at the corner of Royal and St. Francis Streets practically beckons customers to take a seat, order a soda. Established by E. Roy Albright and I. V. Wood, the popular chain began in 1911 with the first store at the corner of Dauphin and Jackson, with sixteen stores in existence by the 1930s. These drugstores—along with others like Van Antwerp's and Molyneux's—were not only outlets for the sale of medicines but also havens where customers could visit, spoon up ice cream, and relax. (Erik Overbey Collection, University of South Alabama Archives)

Cox, is counseling a woman whose little boy has a rash on his arm. Longtime delivery man Roy Portlock is heading out with a call-in prescription from a housebound customer.

But there was a time in Mobile when nearly every downtown block had a family drugstore—Ebbeck, Braswell, Van Antwerp, Albright and Wood, Megginson, and Molyneux and Demouy, next to my grandfather's store—each one a place where medicines were dispensed, sodas were made, and talk freely flowed.

• • •

George Bauer runs Bauer's Drug Store on Dauphin Island Parkway, which like Cox Drugs is a longtime family enterprise, though not at this location. His grandfather, Dave Bauer, had several stores, among them Bauer Drugs, directly across from Bienville Square. George's father, Dave Jr., was a pharmacist, too.

George explains that soda fountains came about in drugstores for obvious reasons. Drugstore chemists, he says, frequently used flavorings like cherry, orange extract, or sarsaparilla in mixing compounds —flavors doubly useful in making sodas.

The early formula for Coca-Cola, for example, involved the extract of coca leaves, and "Give me a dope" was the request for the carbonated beverage. The popular drugstore drink, phosphates, utilizes a chemical salt mixed with ice cream and carbonated water.

Dave Bauer, George recalls of his grandfather, even made his own chewing gum, most likely from acacia and tragacanth—the same ingredients used in drug suspension agents.

No fountain in town was as popular as the one at Van Antwerp's on the corner of Dauphin and Royal. Van Antwerp's had gotten its start as a drug and seed store on that corner in the 1880s.

George Widney, the Cox Drug Store regular, says the sodas at Van Antwerp's were "incomparable." A youth during the 1920s and '30s, Widney's only consolation for a trip to the dentist (the Van Antwerp Building was the central location for doctor and dentist offices) was a soda at the fountain afterward.

Growing up, Margie Barrett had relatives who lived near the Van Antwerp farm on Wolf Ridge Road with its cows supplying milk for the fountain's ice cream. She became a Van Antwerp herself, marrying James, now a Realtor.

Before that, she would head to the fountain on trips downtown in high school, in particular enjoying the famous buttermilk ice cream.

She was not alone in her enthusiasms. "My grandfather would say, 'If I ever go for a Sunday drive to Spring Hill without going to Van Antwerp's first for an ice cream, I don't know what I'd do.'"

· · ·

What happened to all the old soda fountains?

Some were taken out because of competition from fast-food restaurants, some as a result of the take-over of chains, and some, as Jonathan Henderson of Stacey Drugs in Foley, Ala., says, "because of integration."

George Bauer was away at college during the 1960s, but surmises that changes wrought during the civil rights movement put drugstore soda fountains at the heart of controversy. His own father, he believes, took out the fountain rather than have to feel caught between groups of patrons.

Jim Stowe of Nixon Drugs on Old Shell Road—another of the last, remaining family drugstores—says the soda fountain at his establishment underwent a similar fate.

In both stores now customers of all backgrounds, some too young to remember the era of lunch counter protests, comfortably come and go. Bauer has thought about putting a counter back in but says it's just no longer cost-effective. Stowe, years ago, sold his to a man who turned it into a bar in his suburban home.

At Nixon Drugs, Stowe steps from behind his pharmacist's counter like a cherubic minister to give counseling about aches and pains. His mother works at the entrance. She watched the original Mr. Nixon build this establishment when she was a first-grader at Old Shell Road School in 1926.

Cox Drugs, on its Marine Street corner, has never had a lunch counter, but Eugene Cox says his father did have a pot-bellied stove in the back where men drank coffee. When he was 8 years old he'd watch men like Tatum, the barber, and Silent Jim, the policeman, sit there and converse.

When Eugene saw Silent Jim shoot a man to death on Dauphin Street, he was struck that he'd watched the policeman, not long before, drinking coffee in the back of the drugstore.

• • •

Actress Margaret Black has lived away from Mobile for over 30 years, but when she comes home to visit, friends sometimes introduce her by her maiden name, Margaret Albright.

Her grandfather, E. Roy Albright, whom she remembers as "looking like Santa Claus, round and with a bald head," was a founder, with I. V. Wood, of Albright and Wood.

The first Albright and Wood, established in 1911 at the corner of Dauphin and Jackson, expanded into a family chain, with 16 stores in existence by the 1930s.

Pharmacists enjoyed popularity in those days.

Roy Albright became a visible public figure in many ways, riding a steed as grand marshall during Mardi Gras several times during the 1930s. Ernest Megginson of Megginson's Drugs became mayor of Mobile.

To Margaret, whose own father died suddenly at age 39, "the world" of Albright and Wood was one that varied from store to store. There was the Park Store with its old-fashioned soda fountain and round tables with ice cream chairs. There was the world of the No. 16 store across from where she took dance lessons at Miss Hall's. She came to know its employees as friends. "I also got to know the world of No. 8, at Five Points, on Springhill Avenue."

Margaret was fascinated by the soda jerks but, she recalls, as a family member, and a girl, she was discouraged from trying that work. Like many who grew up in Mobile, she speaks of the old Albright and Wood stores as emblematic of an era gone by; but for her it is also a story of a father who died young and a grandfather who remains, in her memory, part of a magical time.

• • •

Forty miles away from the original Albright and Wood, Jonathan and Cathy Henderson bought Stacey Drugs in Foley in 1990, revived the old soda fountain, put in some board games, and now have been voted several times as "favorite hangout" by the students of Foley Middle School down the block.

On a recent after-school visit there, talking with sixth-graders playing checkers and drinking peanut butter shakes, I realized that it is
here, in a renovated drugstore in Baldwin County, that one comes
closest to the feeling of the old corner drugstores in downtown
Mobile.

The kids in Stacey's today are named Amber and Kirsten and
Tasha—"cool names, not '60s names like Mary Beth and Donna Jo,"
says middle-schooler Hollen Ayers—and when I start talking about
the corner drugstores of my youth they grow impatient.

"Yeah, my dad and granddad came here and started talking about
back then, too," one boy says. "They went on and on."

Of course the nostalgia is pointed here, even down to the "Old
Tyme" logo that refers to the soda fountain. There is an atmosphere
here akin to Disney World, replete with player piano and choo-choo
train.

But maybe that's where the old-time corner drugstores are to be
found these days—in replicas of the past brushed up for children of
the 21st century.

But there's no arguing with success. The counter is jammed and
the students are having fun. It is only I, a grown-up, who notices
what I never did way back when.

There is a man named Jim at the end of the counter who tells me
he comes here for medication at the pharmacy. He had a nervous
breakdown many years ago and has to visit a drugstore regularly.

"I like to come here to get it," he explains. "It's like on that TV
show, the one about the bar up in Boston. You know how the song
goes, 'It's a place where everybody knows your name.'"

Moviehouse Dreams

In 1927, thanks to technology, Mobile's Mayor Harry T. Hartwell
shared the spotlight with Broadway entertainer George Jessel at the

Crown Theater on Dauphin Street. The occasion was the Southern debut of the "Vitaphone," a contraption that churned out sound synchronized with moving pictures on the screen.

"I heard the Vitaphone in New York last August," stated H. B. Gayfer of Gayfers Department Store in the program, "and I think it's wonderful."

After Hartwell, in person, welcomed the audience, Jessel, in celluloid, performed. The New York Philharmonic, on Vitaphone, struck the first chords and John Barrymore, in "Don Juan," appeared. In

At the Crescent Theater on Dauphin Street—one of several movie houses in yesteryear's downtown—patrons line up at the window for tickets to "Gold Diggers of 1933." Before our day of multi-plex screens and home video rentals, the movie houses were eventful, indeed glamorous, destinations for a big night out on the town. (Erik Overbey Collection, University of South Alabama Archives)

the romantic film, according to Warner publicity, the dashing star proceeded to "kiss Mary Astor or Estelle Taylor 127 times."

Vitaphone, like mere kissing, is a relic of movies past, and the movie houses, too, are gone. One of the few old movie edifices remaining is the Crown, recently restored as a dance club.

The Empire, the Strand, the Crescent, the Bijou—their names suggest a mystique from grand to bawdy that is elusive to our multiplexes. Even the neighborhood houses, the Azalea, the Loop, the Roxy—all gone, too—were places where what you saw seems bound up in where you saw it.

Our old theaters, linked to neighborhoods or downtown streets, enriched cinema dreams in a way impossible for today's sleek chains. Going out to the movies, before TV brought movies indoors to us, was a grand occasion.

As I take Meredith to the restored Saenger Theater one night for an old-movie series, she helps me understand one reason why. As Gene Kelly tap-dances across Parisian cobblestones in "An American in Paris," she gazes up at the ornate columns and enormous chandelier, saying, "This makes me feel royal."

• • •

Not all the old movie houses were palaces, of course. One of the earliest was outside, at Arlington Pier, on the waterfront that became Brookley Field. Olga Melech, 17 in 1933, the daughter of a Russian immigrant, worked as a ticket-taker and remembers the pleasant, open-air pier with bathhouse and concession. She can never forget her boss, a Greek immigrant, Alexander Gounares. Just like in the movies, they fell in love and wed.

That marriage led to a life in the movie business. She helped run Gounares' three movie houses—the Roosevelt on Broad Street; the Rex in Prichard; and the Roxy at "Little Five Points," the theater named after the 6,000-seat Roxy in New York.

These movie theaters were great places to see friends and fantasize the life of singing cowboys or lovestruck starlets. Leading ladies were glamorous but mysterious, and gunslingers drew six-shooters but no blood. Monsters were frightening without their mayhem being graphic. Jay C. Bear, now an Atlantan in the timber business, leapt behind the seats at the Loop when "The Thing" loomed from the screen in the 1950s.

From the time he was 8, in 1948, until 1953, Ralph Holberg III, now a Mobile attorney, walked on Saturday mornings to the Roxy from his Springhill Avenue home with his brother Bob and friend Robert Fulton, now a Catholic priest. For nine cents they'd enjoy a cartoon, a serial cliffhanger like "Rocket Man" and a Western with Roy Rogers or Gene Autry. Thinking back on those long Saturdays, a screen cowboy's adventures his only worry, Holberg felt "pure euphoria."

Even when times were not so innocent the Roxy was a meeting place. I remember the debut of a Beatles movie, when the lobby was full of long-haired friends flashing each other peace signs.

Movie openings at the Roxy were often colorful. When "Gone With the Wind" premiered, Mrs. Gounares studied the publicity photos of Vivien Leigh and created four dresses worn by Scarlett. Lady ushers wore them opening night.

The Roxy now serves as a church.

• • •

"Movie work isn't work," believes Ella Costa, daughter of the late Charlie King, who owned the Crown. "It's romantic work."

Mrs. Costa, who grew up over the Crown, was 2 years old in 1911 when her mother was giving her a bath but left the room a moment. Ella toddled downstairs. "The music conductor—movies had orchestras in those days—took his cape and bundled me up. He liked to say, 'At 2 years old Ella made her debut at the Crown.'"

Part of a promenade of Dauphin Street houses, the Crown showed big studio releases and often drew a fashionable crowd. "The Empire," she explains, "was not as fancy."

The Crescent, later refurbished as the Century, appealed to families, children, and laboring men, some of whom worked at the paper mills. Clarence Frenkel, a retired banker, describes how the owner, his late uncle Ed Frenkel, leaned on the parking meter out front and visited with patrons. Years later, when Clarence worked in business relations for a Mobile bank, older customers reminisced to him about his uncle Ed and evenings at the Crescent.

Ella Costa's uncle, John Heustis King, went so far as to drum up business for the family-owned Azalea, at the Loop. An old photo shows her uncle dressed up as a cowboy, standing in a cart pulled by billy goats. Behind him are wide-eyed urchins and a poster for the Saturday special: "Pistol Packing Mama."

Mobile native and writer Tom Atkins, a theater professor at Florida and Atlantic University, relished "the ritual" of Saturday afternoon triple features at the Azalea. In his introduction to a book on science fiction film he refers to the boyhood hours he spent there enthralled by spaceships and aliens.

Charlie King owned another series of theaters, several on Davis Avenue—the Pike, the Lincoln, the Ace, the Booker T., the Harlem —where black patrons lined up to watch the same John Wayne movie white filmgoers watched a mile away. The grandest venue was the Pike, which served as a vaudeville theater upstairs and a picture show downstairs. Legendary entertainers such as Billie Holiday and Cab Calloway performed there.

From the concessionaires to the projectionists, Mrs. Costa says, employees at these theaters were black—but the projectionists were not accepted by the union in Mobile. "My father sent them to New Orleans to join the union," she says. "And that's where the projectionists got training."

Weldon Limmroth, who was general manager of Giddens & Rester Theaters, which owned the Brookley, the Downtown, and the Loop, attributes the peaceful desegregation of movie houses to wise planning by community leaders, among them Dr. Robert W. Gilliard and John LeFlore.

Gilliard, a retired dentist and formerly chapter president of the National Association of Colored People, remembers meetings he and Bishop William Smith held around 1960 with Giddens & Rester management. Desegregating white-only movie theaters was a key part of the "package of initiatives" by the black community.

As a first step in bringing the two communities together—"without riots, without fisticuffs," he explains—movies shown in the all-white houses were immediately shown at the all-black houses as well. One of the first, which he remembers viewing at the Booker T., was "To Kill a Mockingbird." Then black patrons began to buy tickets at the Downtown. There was no violence that he can recall.

"People have to be educated out of attitudes," he says.

• • •

Weldon Limmroth fell in love with the movie business growing up in the 1920s in Trickham, Texas, where movies were shown in traveling tent shows during cotton picking season. In Mobile, Limmroth managed not only the Downtown and other theaters, including the first suburban complexes, but also that relic of the free-wheeling, tail fin–'50s: drive-ins. Although places like the Air-Sho and Do Drive-In were whispered to be, as one woman in her 40s reminds me, "passion pits," Limmroth explains that drive-ins were constructed to be family affairs, some even had playgrounds.

Patrolmen, though, were known to walk the lanes, making sure heads were visible. The drive-ins also were prime for teen hi-jinks. If cars dragged low in the back, trunks were checked to make sure friends were not being sneaked in.

"We'd run special promotions," Limmroth recalls, "such as prizes for the most people in a car. People would be hanging out the windows and onto the sides. Some cars managed as many as 30 or 40."

• • •

Not much is known of those New Orleans brothers, the Saengers, except that, throughout the South in the 1920s and '30s, they built more than 120 theaters. There are Saengers in New Orleans, Biloxi, Pensacola and Shreveport. The Saenger in Texarkana, owned by a famous tycoon, is "the Perot."

"All the Saengers are movie palaces," explains Bruce Morgan, manager of Mobile's Saenger for the University of South Alabama, owner of the theater (it would later be sold to the city of Mobile).

Murals above the staircase, painted by Susan Downing for the restoration, show scenes of Dog River, the Causeway and the Gulf of Mexico. Along the walls are profiles of a soldier in winged helmet, possibly Ben Hur.

Up the stairs, past the rotunda we go, into the high balcony once reserved for "colored." We look out the window at a parking lot, where the Lyric, a vaudeville theater, once hosted Al Jolson and Eddie Cantor. We wind back down, through corridors where the phantom of the opera would feel comfortable.

Morgan describes as "magical" a showing of Gene Kelly's "Singin' in the Rain." "People applauded after every musical number and they were laughing out loud. That wouldn't happen in a modern movie house."

Of course, old movies play every night on cable TV and some video outlets rent classics for under a buck. But to Morgan it's hardly the same. "When Vivien Leigh's face is 25 feet tall, she's gorgeous."

And that makes us feel the way movies used to make us feel—royal.

Our Daily Bread

4:30 A.M.

Long before dawn on Government Street, the traffic lights blink yellow, and lone men sit hunched over coffee in all-night food joints.

Turning south on Broad Street, I drive toward a brick building whose front panes are darkened. I park, rap on the door. No one answers. Suddenly the handle turns and a stranger ushers me down a corridor toward a pool of light. I step through the door. Elves are working.

"You made it," says Charles Pollman, 76, glancing up at the clock. "Not bad."

Pollman has been here half an hour already, mixing, kneading, rolling, punching, shaping, and cutting. From the time he was 5 and hitched a ride on his father's bread wagon on Royal Street, until this morning at 5, readying Thanksgiving delectables, he has spent a life in the family bakery.

"I'm not a baker," he says wryly, shuffling alongside a 10-foot table, rolling out dough for coffee rolls. "I'm a doctor of fermentology."

Bruno Klevins, 71, is flattening dough on the other side of the table. He learned his trade at his father's pastry shop in Latvia in eastern Europe. "The young people," he tells me, sprinkling cinnamon like fairy dust, "they are coming home at this hour from parties."

"I don't go to parties, I go to church," says Albert Davis, 63, who presides over the wall-sized ovens, starting daily at 1 A.M. He is shoveling out dozens of bread loaves.

"If it can be baked, Mr. Albert can bake it," says Simmie Brown, the dough man, a generation younger than the others.

5 A.M.

Albert Davis holds up a loaf of crisp French bread. "This is beautiful," he exclaims. "It takes hard work. The Good Lord doesn't just drop it from the sky."

Perhaps he has sensed that my baking wisdom is limited to fixing ready-made waffles in a toaster oven. During all the years that I relished Malbis breads, Smith's cookies, Pollman's cakes and Marshall's Electrik Maid biscuits, I never considered that they did not, like manna, rain from the sky.

I certainly never rolled over in bed at 4 A.M. and thought men and women were already alert, toiling to fill our bread baskets.

If anybody, Charles Pollman is our link to an American baking past. With his son Fred, 37, ready to take over as a third-generation baker, why does he keep on? "I feel like I can contribute," he says, sowing raisins across flattened dough like a Johnny Appleseed. "I read in a magazine about a baker in his 90s. I'm only 76."

5:30 A.M.

Into the bakery room at Pollman's comes Marcellus McDowell. "Mac" tells me he has been driving Pollman's trucks for 50 years. He worked for the original Fred Pollman, a Dutchman from New Orleans, who founded this business in 1918. Fred Pollman's sister Mary married another New Orleanian, Gordon Smith, who had come to Mobile and started the Smith Bakery in 1900.

Trish Meservey and Pam Gandy, the cake decorators, occupy chairs in their colorful room, squeezing sugary art onto the day's orders: soccer team cakes, bank building cakes, Thanksgiving gobbler cakes. For 30th birthdays they sometimes draw the celebrant going downhill; for the 40th, a tombstone. They even get requests to make what Charles Pollman calls "bikini" cakes—ones with icing designs of sexy women.

"We don't do that," he says.

Surely that must be the only baked item not created at Pollman's early this morning, when the fruit cakes are stacked high in bright canisters, pecan pies are cooling, pocketbook rolls are plumping in Albert's oven, and Bruno is rolling up strips of dough for mini-danishes.

As Charles Pollman moves his hand rapidly as a casino card dealer's over the tiny danishes, squirting each with flavored topping, he glances again at the clock.

"Tempus fugit," he says, picking up the pace. "Time flies."

6 A.M.

Alone with talk radio, Tom Janeroux, 55, is hard at work at Toni-el Boulangerie at the Loop. He has been baking since 4 A.M., too, mixing and proofing dough for 24-inch baguettes and 7-inch-long pistolettes and round, sandwich-sized muffulettas.

"I'm a frustrated artist," admits the strong, dark-haired Brooklyn native who came south to study at Spring Hill College. He tells me how his father, from Italy, once sang behind Caruso in the chorus of the Metropolitan Opera.

"The Lord didn't see fit to give me a voice," he says while making liquid sugar for brownies, using eye, hand and an ancient tabletop scale to achieve perfection. "Hopefully, he gave me a little creativity."

I scan the shelves of flours and flavorings and dried fruits and sugars and liquor bottles.

"People come in a bakery and think you're a drunk," he laughs. Bourbon for bourbon balls, rum for rum cake and truffles, cherry brandy for black forest cake. "I go by what I need."

He never set out to be a baker, he explains, once having run some restaurants. The bread he made for sandwiches was being sought out by other restaurateurs; he soon made his business strictly baking.

One of Janeroux's inspirations became Lafayette, La., baker Francois Poupart, who also passed on some recipes to Ann Knoderer, bread-maker at Andree's Wine and Cheese in Fairhope.

During the holiday season, as bakers wear out their backs filling the crush of demands, Janeroux needs all the verve he can muster. In addition to regular business he prepares German stollen bread for holiday tables. To get an edge in the pumpkin pie market, he creates pumpkin pie chiffon.

"Forget home life," he says.

There is a banging at the back door—a doctor, eager for croissants. Since the bakery does not open until 9 A.M., the croissants are not ready. Janeroux tells him to come back in a little while, he will do what he can.

By 11 A.M. Janeroux is also preparing for the lunch crowd who will occupy his cafe tables. Pulling Italian flat bread, foccacia, from the oven, he bends over, anointing it with olive oil.

He breathes in the aroma. "Makes you want to run out and hug an Italian."

1 P.M.

Sam Marshall, 82, got his start in his father's business, Marshall's Electrik Maid, at an early age. "I used to stand on a soda-water box to get up to the work table to help make rolls," he says to me after a Lions Club luncheon, a view of the Mobile docks out the window. After growing up in the bakery, Marshall served in both World War

II and Korea, and returned to Mobile with an idea inspired by meeting Sara Lee's father-in-law at a baker's convention in Chicago.

The key to this idea was aluminum foil; it enabled him to package and ship biscuits, pre-baked, to stores "where the people are." Their popularity spread. "Somebody would carry five pans of biscuits up to Mama in Birmingham. That's how I got started."

When Electrik Maid closed its last location in 1965, Marshall focused on the biscuit enterprise, founding Marshall Biscuit Company. Still located in Mobile, and distributing frozen biscuits, the company is no longer owned by family.

But Sam Marshall's recipe still stands; and he remembers the baking life well. "Always at the holidays, when it's time for others to play, it's your time to work."

2 P.M.

A Mobile County courtroom, where men often hang their heads awaiting verdicts, seems an unlikely place to muse on bread.

But in his office behind the courtroom, District Judge Dominick Matranga, 60, is philosophical. "In law school we were told that the law is a jealous mistress, making great demands on your time. The same is true of baking."

His father, Dominick John Matranga, emigrated from Piana dei Grece, Italy—a Greek section of Sicily—to New Orleans where he worked for a German baker who sent him on to Mobile. In Mobile, Dominick John was hired as the first baker for the Malbis Bakery on Broad Street. The Sicilian newcomer started his own shop, New York Bakery, on Dauphin.

"There was the yeasty, clean smell of the bakery that made you feel good," Judge Matranga recalls of New York Bakery from his boyhood. It was a place, he also remembers, where his father labored.

"He'd work 10, 15, 20 hours a day. He'd sometimes fall asleep on the sacks of flour.

"Baking's very hard work because you're dealing with a living organism. Yeast. Once you start that bread, your time is scheduled by the bread rising and proofing. You can't just let it sit there. It's almost like being a farmer. Cows start producing milk whether you like it or not."

With its rye and pumpernickel, New York Bakery was one of several downtown bakeries—among them Star Bakery, Peoples Bakery, Yuille Bakery—that catered to ethnic tastes of nearby residents who attended the synagogue, or Greek Orthodox Church, or Cathedral, or Episcopal Church, all within a few blocks. It spawned other bakeries, too, like Craig's Bakery on Davis Avenue, run by Esse Craig, nicknamed Preacher.

Matranga baked challah—Jewish twist bread—for the Eastern European immigrants in the neighborhood, among them my grandfather. At home, my grandfather would have begun the family meal with the Hebrew blessing which thanks God for "bringing forth bread from the earth."

"Daddy said bread was God's food," Judge Matranga recalls, looking out his office window over the town where not one bakery is in sight. "You can't throw bread away, he told us. If you don't eat it, you give it to the birds."

3 P.M.

In the lobby of Smith's Bakery off Interstate 65—now part of CooperSmith, a corporate enterprise with bakeries throughout the South—there is a penny scale salvaged from the former bakery on Dauphin Street. Not only do I weigh more now; the smiling ladies behind the dessert case are gone. A receptionist, behind glass, receives visitors here.

Tall and genial, Michael Smith Johnson, 61, invites me in. On the wall is a bronze plaque with the initials GS—Gordon Smith—the decal that used to be on the side of company trucks. Gordon Smith, Johnson's grandfather, came to Mobile in 1899 to be a baker for grocer R. O. Harris, quickly launching out on his own.

Johnson talks of the old rivalry between Smith Bakery and Malbis. The Greek immigrant family, after ventures with a canning plant, a

resin-products plant and an ice plant, established the bakery in 1927.
Smith's met the challenge: Photographs of the 1930s show a squad-
ron of trucks with drivers wearing S-monogrammed sweaters and
snappy bow ties.

Johnson tells me how, during the early years, bread men deposited
Smith's loaves at dawn in cypress boxes hung alongside grocery doors;
how, before refrigeration, families consumed a loaf a day; how, he
believes, the in-house bakeries of grocery store chains are the real
storefront bakeries of today.

Explaining how the demand for sliced, long-lasting sandwich bread
changed the industry, he lets me scan a print-out of continuous mix
recipes with far more ingredients than dough, yeast and salt. Customers do not want loaves of dense, crusty bread like his grandfather
might have made, he tells me.

"Watch Mrs. Consumer in the grocery store shopping for bread.
She'll squeeze every loaf to make sure it's soft. It's like squeezing a
goosehorn."

When we put on regulation hair nets and enter the high-speed
plant that processes 10,000 pounds of dough an hour, I feel like a
schoolboy on a field trip, although school groups are no longer invited
because of insurance concerns. Since it is late in the afternoon, the
plant is hauntingly quiet, the bread trucks, spanking clean, resting at
loading docks.

Thousands of bagged bakery items sit on shelves awaiting shipment. The bread names suggest comfort and joy. Brightly printed, on
see-through wrappers, are the words "natural," "country," "traditional," "family."

I ask about the role of bakers here, where human hands seem to
play little part in bread-making.

"My Granddad was a real baker," he answers. "These guys are tech-
nicians more than bakers."

4:30 P.M.

From my office I talk by phone to Johnson's cousin, Donnie Smith,
who no longer works in the business. He is at home, baking bread

Fresh bread right to your door! In the 1930s, this Smith's Bakery truck made deliveries to its customers. On the door is "GS," the initials of Gordon Smith, who founded the bakery in 1900. Of the old family bakeries—among them Pollman's, founded in 1918, and Malbis, in 1927—only Pollman's still exists as a family-owned, walk-in store. Malbis Bakery is long closed, and Smith's was folded into CooperSmith, a corporate enterprise with high-volume bread making and distribution to grocery shelves throughout the South. (S. Black McNeely Collection, University of South Alabama Archives)

by hand. As we talk about his grandfather, Gordon Smith, and the bread he baked, Donnie offers me a gift.

"I want you to taste my bread," he says. "Next time you're in my neighborhood, drive by and I'll give you a loaf. If I'm not home I'll leave it on the porch."

I thank him.

"I think you'll like it," he adds.

I don't get a chance to go by on my way home, but I'm imagining what it'll taste like. As the night settles down over Government Street, and the bakers are collapsing into tired heaps, I can even see it, in a cypress bread box, crusty, thick, just waiting.

Pictures of Overbey

December 1925: Nine young men stride down Dauphin Street tossing a basketball. They turn in the doorway next to the Empire Movie Theater, going upstairs past the aroma of Kenney Coffee Co. and into the Overbey Studio, where a slender man with black mustache welcomes them.

They change into their basketball uniforms, including shirts that read "HAC"—Hebrew Athletic Club. The photographer situates them in a group, ducks under the cloak of his studio camera, slides in a glass plate negative and clicks the shutter. The young men go their separate ways; their image remains.

This basketball team photograph, 70 years later, is one I treasure. Sitting in front, clutching the ball, is my father, Charles, 16 years old. On the back row, just home from college in dress clothes, is his brother, Louie. Some of the other men I've also known.

But there is another man in the photograph you cannot see: the one behind the lens. In the corner of the photograph's mat, in elegant script, is his name: Overbey.

Erik Overbey gives lie to the notion that you have to be born in Mobile to understand Mobile. In 1901 he came, at age 19, all the way from Solvorn, Norway—"a town deep in a fjord," says his daughter Cecilia Zingelmann—to provide a record of how we lived, worked, dined, played and prayed.

"Many of us will remember Erik going about the city encumbered by his great box, a black apron and his tripod," reads the Memorial Resolution for Overbey composed by the Rotary Club after his passing in 1977 at age 95.

My father remembers Overbey in his studio as cordial but quiet, not the kind of photographer who'd entertain children to get them to smile.

Most importantly, perhaps, he was consistent, and he was industrious. In the course of 50 years Overbey clicked the shutter more than 90,000 times, and each impression, in the everyday alchemy of photography, turned a face, or street corner or building cornice into an heirloom, even an icon.

Today, within sight of one-hour photo labs and convenience stores selling sure-shot cameras, Overbey's patiently executed 8-by-10s can be found on the walls of local restaurants, offices and corridors of the airport. In our image-happy time, when people shoot miles of shaky home video and disposable cameras go into the garbage like soda cans, Overbey's art remains.

"He may not have set out to be an artist," speculates George Ewert, director of the Museum of the City of Mobile, "but through dint of hard work, always on commission, Overbey was inadvertently so."

Overbey worked six and a half days a week to make a living as a commercial photographer. Shot by shot, day by day, he also happened to chronicle our time.

• • •

Overbey's daughter, Cecilia Zingelmann, 69, lives in Virginia and keeps a photograph of her father with a painting behind him. The painting is of Overbey's Norwegian village. It hung in their Selma Street home when Cecilia and her two brothers, Erik and Charles, were growing up. Being Norwegian, in fact, got Overbey to Mobile: He'd apprenticed for a tailor in Bergen as a youth, and traveled to Mobile to assist a Dauphin Street tailor named Tvedt. When he left the tailor shop it was to learn the photography trade from another Scandinavian, Johnson. Overbey soon had his own studio, taking over the negatives left by an earlier Mobile photographer, W. A. Reed.

Daily, Mrs. Zingelmann recalls, her father rose early, stoked the fire in the stove, read two Norwegian newspapers, and drove down-town in an auto he shared with a Waterman Steamship executive.

He'd work all day Saturday and frequently return to print copies of negatives for half of Sunday. His family was active in the Lutheran Church.

Of course, there were other photographers in town, one of them named Boyle, whose business was situated near that of the tailor, Fry. A storefront ad read: "Fry the Tailor and Boyle the Photographer." But Overbey got the lion's share of business.

Before World War I, Overbey shot 11,000 glass plate portraits of Mobilians, according to Elisa Baldwin, archivist of the Overbey collection now housed by the University of South Alabama. Between the wars he shot 6,000 nitrate portraits. These are only a portion of the larger number of images he was commissioned to make of building construction, business storefronts, social clubs or athletic teams.

The archives, located in the basement of the old Providence Hospital building now owned by USA, has an index to these portraits, and reprints, for nominal cost, are available. Baldwin describes the emotional response of people browsing through archive records who discover a portrait was made of a grandparent. "It can be touching to see their reactions."

Overbey made all these, it seems, without ado or fuss. Erik Per Overbey, Overbey's son, a Californian now in his late 70s, says his father was "a hard-working but laconic" man. Though a dapper dresser—Overbey once purchased a suit of clothes from my grandfather at the fashionable Toggery, across from Bienville Square—the photographer was not inclined to fancy ways.

"He wore no rings or jewelry of any kind," Erik Per Overbey recalls. "Only a simple tie clasp."

Although Overbey philosophized little about his craft, Erik says his father intended to make subjects "look natural." Erik, a longtime aficionado of movie star photos, contrasts his father's style to that of the English photographer Cecil Beaton, who photographed Gloria Swanson seductive in a hat veil.

Whether he was shooting workmen crawling up the insides of the Bankhead Tunnel like human flies, or the high ceilings and palm fronds of the Battle House Trellis Room, Overbey constructed his photos like Scandinavian furniture: simple, functional and clean.

• • •

Along the stairs leading to the Mobile Municipal Archives on Church Street are Erik Overbey photographs. One shows the Dauphin Street block where the Overbey Studio was; the French grille balcony over-

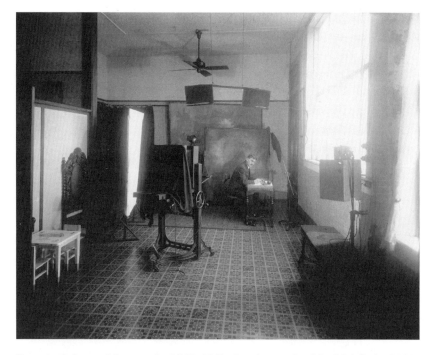

Born in Solvorn, Norway, in 1882, Erik Overbey arrived in Mobile in 1901, apprenticing to a Norwegian tailor. He soon became a photographer, and over the next half century, captured more than 90,000 images, from studio portraits to street-corner goings-on, becoming the premier chronicler of early twentieth century Mobile. Here he muses at his Dauphin Street studio. (Erik Overbey Collection, University of South Alabama Archives)

looks a street filled with shoppers and store awnings rolled down against afternoon sunshine.

Jay Higginbotham, archives director, has written several books on Mobile history, with a focus on the city during the 1700s. Higginbotham speaks to me with scholarly grasp of Overbey's work and its place in Mobile history. The photographs seem to have deep personal meaning for him too, evidenced by Overbey's pictures on his own office wall.

He gestures to them, each showing a grand old building now torn down, in most cases to make room for parking lots. One that holds special resonance is the Downtown Central Baptist Church, where his uncle was pastor. "Now it's gone. There should be a piece of tape on every building downtown saying you can't destroy it."

What if Overbey had thrown away his collection of photographs? "It would have been a tragedy," Higginbotham says. "So much would have been lost."

The Bienville Hotel, the Customs House, the church—in talking with Higginbotham about these places resonant of history, one begins to realize the poignancy these after-images hold. As their subjects disappear, the photographs themselves become the objects we prize.

"These photos," he says, "are all that remains."

• • •

On the new campus of Bishop State Community College on Martin Luther King, Jr., Avenue, in the building that once housed Central High, David Thomas, director of the Museum and Research Center, leads the way down a long corridor to the auditorium. Thomas, a member of the Mobile County Public School Commission, curated the show "Davis Avenue Revisited." Images of African-American Mobile line the walls.

Photographs of the Booker T. movie house, of Jim's pool hall, of the distinguished members of the Utopia Social Club—one by one he pulls them from the top of a stack of photographs used for the show. Eighty of these are by Overbey. One is of Dr. Benjamin F. Baker, founder of Central High—the grandfather of Thomas' wife.

At a time when Mobile was divided strictly along color lines, and when the Blue Light Studio on Davis Avenue covered photography of black Mobile, Overbey still seemed ubiquitous. "He would walk down the Avenue taking pictures," Thomas says. One of Thomas' favorite Overbey photographs hangs in the vestibule of the Big Zion AME Church, Thomas' family church. It shows the Big Zion congregation on Palm Sunday.

Thomas obtained many of these pictures from the University of South Alabama archives. But there were others he discovered in people's homes. Hearing about a portrait tucked away over a bureau or desk, Thomas would visit families and find the images. "Years had passed since some of these people had stopped to even notice these pictures. When I'd express interest in these portraits, they'd take another look. You could see the joy in their faces."

Thomas believes Overbey was "visionary" in his instinct about what pictures to take. "This is history you don't find in the textbooks."

• • •

When Margaret Gwin was growing up, the Overbey Studio was her second home. Her mother, Francis White, started working for Overbey in 1933, and Margaret would visit her mother frequently at the studio.

Margaret remembers her mother developing and painting the pictures, adding tinctures of color to make the portraits lifelike. One of her fondest recollections of Overbey is during Mardi Gras, when she would watch the parades from his second-floor balcony. He handed her a little glass of grape juice. It was blackberry wine.

The journalist Virginia Greer visited with Margaret's mother in 1963, after Overbey had retired. Mrs. White had taken over the studio and was in possession of thousands of negatives, among them glass plates. Virginia Greer reported:

"If you could see these stacks of shelves to the ceiling with nothing but glass plates! The panoramic shots were jutting out from shelves, and you could see the tattered edges of the brown manila envelopes they were slid into. Mrs. White was trying to inventory it, and to see a sweet resting place for others. It was an impossible task for someone to do. To look at that wisp of a woman high on a ladder surrounded by these babies of Mr. Overbey—that's what he called them, his 'babies'—it was one of the tenderest, most expanding stories I ever got to do."

Mrs. White, clearly overwhelmed, sold the Overbey collection. Dallas Balliao, director of the Mobile Library, says the library purchased the collection in two parts, in 1964 and 1974, for a total of less than $10,000.

Unable to effectively maintain the collection—some glass plates were broken and a famous one of Woodrow Wilson in the Lyric Theater disappeared—the library donated it to USA in 1978. Dr. Michael Thomason, director of the USA archives, and his staff receive high marks from other historians for their handling of the collection.

• • •

Etta Campbell, 31, has been working at Wendy's fast-food restaurants since she was 17. At the Wendy's on Government Street near Broad—once the site of a grand home—Etta is a sandwich-maker and management trainee. She noticed the Overbey photographs on the wall when she was polishing the rail. "They're eye-catching." She points to Overbey's interior of a 1940s restaurant, The Juicy Pig.

"It shows how neat and clean and organized it used to be. They didn't have fast food. Maybe you had to cut the potatoes by hand just like, when I started working at Wendy's, you had to devein the chicken. Now it's done for you."

In her career, Etta intends to "go all the way" with Wendy's, and says the Overbey photographs of yesteryear's restaurants would serve as a model for young people in the business. Facing the Overbey photographs is a poster of "Dave," Wendy's founder. "You can see," she explains, "that he likes it to be very clean and organized, too."

Given a slow moment before the Saturday dinner-hour rush, other Wendy's employees join us to study the Overbeys. "These pictures show you how old-fashioned is always in style," Etta continues. She gestures to her colleague Evelyn's hairstyle, which she describes as French roll with pin curls. "Old is coming back, like the 1930s and '40s."

Another worker, Mariea, who just turned 17, studies another Overbey interior. "Is this a Wendy's?" she asks.

"No," I say, reading the caption. "It's the Trellis Room of the Battle House."

She smiles and stares at me.

"The Battle House Hotel," I explain.

As I hear a man's voice ordering french fries over the drive-in loud-speaker, I make it clear for her: "Well, the hotel's boarded up and run-down now but, look, right here, you can see the picture."

Bienville Square Bus Stop

❖

"The square is a great resort for the nursery maids of the city, who 'dump' their young charges on the verdant grass and watch their happy rompings with delight. Last evening we observed a bright galaxy of the juveniles in the square, and to watch their gambols as they flitted hither and thither, would have done good to the hearts of our old bachelor friends, and made them resolve to change their condition on the shortest possible notice."

"Bienville Square," Mobile Daily Advertiser, April 14, 1866

On a bright afternoon in Bienville Square oaks throw long shadows across the iron fountain with its vanished ghosts of goldfish; a preacher calls out to wayward souls who lounge heedlessly on benches; a businessman in bright yellow tie briskly clips by, cellular phone to his ear, pigeons behind him strutting for crumbs.

Fountain, preacher, pigeon, pedestrian—no matter how many times I pass Bienville Square, I see variations on this picture. Much has changed from the era depicted by the author of the 1866 reflection—the year that Bienville Square was officially named for Mobile's founder, Jean-Baptiste Le Moyne, Sieur de Bienville. Even the wording of that pastorale—nannies "dumping" an infant in a park, or "juveniles in the square"—would suggest, in today's edgy world, a bleaker tale.

But there is a timeless quality to the square. It is still the true heart, however battered, of our downtown.

It has been so since our town's beginning.

In a 1989 issue of the Journal of Alabama Archaeology, Diane E.

Silvia wrote of excavations at Bienville Square in 1985 that turned up artifacts from "every period of Mobile's colonial history from the early 18th century through the early 19th century."

That issue of the journal said that the square was utilized right at the start, 1711, when the French moved downriver from the first settlement at 27 Mile Bluff. We were "the onion fields" back then, and the square was for "people in the pay of the king" and, intriguingly, "several women."

The area was soon parceled out in land grants; "a hospital was located near the southwest corner"; on part of the land, an entrepreneur "operated one of several skin houses"—places to process and store animal hides.

"By 1830," the journal said, "the land had been transferred to the City of Mobile by the American government . . . The first City Hall was constructed of wood in the center of the square in 1836."

Before long that building was moved, but Mobilians found a homier use for the square.

A Press Register reporter, in 1947, quoted a book called "Ghosts of Old Mobile," by May Randlette Beck: "Complaints were made that people were hanging their clothes out to dry in the Square after the family wash had been duly laundered. To complete the just causes for complaint, horses and cows were put into the Square to graze. Even hogs . . . were rooting up everything in sight."

One day, Mrs. Beck's story continued, a group of residents, aggravated at the presence of a livery stable, petitioned the owner to move it. He refused. A crowd assembled "and moved it for him, demolishing the stables and removing the horses."

There was even a deer in Bienville Square—an iron deer. In 1890, the same year as the fountain was placed at the heart of the square, the iron deer was moved—to Mobile's Washington Square.

• • •

The Cawthon Hotel, the Bienville Hotel—earlier in our century, they were lodgings that faced onto the square. The Masonic Lodge, Kress' store—these names of bygone places still grace the fronts of buildings. Gayfers—the sign, however faint, continues to trace a battered marquee.

What brings them together, out of the past, is the view they shared out their windows—Bienville Square.

On the walkways of the square I come across a plaque with names of Mobilian of the Year, and in these surnames, too, there are stories. Roberts, Albright, Pillans, Delchamps, Holberg, Langan, Hearin, Toolen, Radcliff, Zoghby, Mitchell—the distinguished names go on, these are just a few.

I have passed the square's stone cross countless times, but only now pause to read the inscription. It was dedicated to Bienville by the Colonial Dames of Alabama in 1906 with its romantic notion that, "He who founds himself a City builds himself a live-long Monument."

I trust that Bienville himself is looking down, pleased at the "Monument" he's built.

After all, as city archivist Jay Higginbotham wrote of Bienville in his history, "Mobile, City by the Bay": After a 1736 defeat by the Chickasaw Indians, "Disgustedly, he drifted back to Mobile. It was the beginning of the end for the fifty-six-year-old commander. In 1743, he resigned from office and returned to Paris where he spent the rest of his life advocating support for the colony. He died in 1767, unsung and forgotten."

• • •

As the Bienville Square afternoon deepens, the shadows grow longer. Some men and women come from the AmSouth building. One is eating a bag of popcorn. A piece of it falls to the ground and squirrels pounce to it, squabbling.

At the bus stop facing the square there are other folks waiting, shopping bags in hand, for a ride home. The noise of an engine rises—a man stands to look—but it is only a truck. He sits back down.

The passengers wait, gazing out at the fountain where sculpted masques are skeeting water; at the band shell where a tape of Mardi

Lee Hoffman frequently records Mobile life, transmuting it with the eye of the artist. In this black-and-white reproduction of his watercolor, "Bienville Bus Stop"—which inspired the author, no relation, to write on the locale—Lee Hoffman, like a Southern Edward Hopper, captures the tranquility and melancholy of a downtown scene. (Courtesy of Lee Hoffman and Gallery 54)

Gras music plays lightly; at a string of carnival beads stuck up in an oak tree; at a couple of sailors prowling for action; at the monument to Bienville, who is hardly forgotten.

Then the bus appears and the passengers clamber aboard and the bus stop and the walkways, for a long moment, are empty. Bienville Square, once again, is the province of silent benches, strutting pigeons, leaning oaks.

PART II

ON THE DOCK OF THE BAY

❖

Without its waterfront Mobile would be a different kind of place. Like other coastal towns—Charleston, Savannah, Tampa, Biloxi, Galveston—its history and character have been fashioned in large part because it looks out to a sea. Mobile River, Mobile Bay, the Gulf of Mexico—these names are inseparable from that of the city. The foods we eat, the breezes we enjoy, the shady romance of characters who appear from ships and roam our streets before heading on—they come about because water laps at our shores.

In 1971 President Richard Nixon came to Mobile with Alabama Governor George Wallace and they pronounced the opening of the Tennessee-Tombigbee Waterway, a river system that was to have rivaled the Mississippi River as a north-south conduit for traffic. The port, some residents believed, would explode with commerce and Mobile would become as large as Houston by the 21st century. I remember the bright, spring afternoon that Nixon "cut the ribbon" for that project. (I can still see the secret service men on the tops of the grain storage tanks, scouting the crowd with binoculars.) When Nixon walked through the crowd, he paused where I stood as an usher with another cadet from my high school—Mobile's University Military School—and shook our hands. "What outfit you boys with?" he asked. "Military school, sir!" (The boy's military school is now non-military and coed.)

Mobile never became another Houston. Nevertheless, the Alabama State Docks continue to thrive, one of the top 20 ports in the nation.

But the water brings much else, too—water sports, fish, lightning storms, hurricanes. Beauty and mystery.

Reading the Lights

❖

Sometimes at night I walk out of my cottage deep beneath the oaks on Mobile Bay and head down the path to the water's edge. Having been a city dweller for many years I've never been one to study constellations, but residing now on the Alabama coast with the southern sky spread above me, I've been peeking into a book by H. A. Rey—not his whimsical "Curious George," but his gently instructive "The Stars." His connect-the-dot drawings, Castor and Pollux hand-in-hand, enliven the heavens I can see from this spot.

Where I face south, toward the mouth of the bay, Scorpius unfurls off the end of our pier; Antares flickers red at its heart. The North Star holds firm behind me, a reminder of New York, my previous home.

If I stroll up the boardwalk to the tip of Point Clear, I come to the Grand Hotel, a 150-year-old resort villa of green wooden cottages tucked in along paths, hotel rooms in two long, red-roofed wings of the main lodge, and immense picture windows opening on the water. From the hotel's band shell, echoing at least for me of last Saturday night's swing band, I look up the bay to where the Big Dipper seems to pour out on the Port of Mobile. At this distance, the lights of the Alabama State Docks' coal chutes, loading ramps, whirlybird cranes, and barges seem festive—a vision that belies the hard, round-the-clock labor that goes on there.

There are other constellations I'm learning to read—the string of lights on Fairhope Pier on my side of the bay, the pinpoints of Dog River bridge on the other. Turning south again, I see the flicker of a radio tower at Dauphin Island, our coastal barrier island. In the Gulf of Mexico beyond are natural gas rigs bright as tiny casinos, their payoffs and risks just as high. Like Antares a red light flickers, answered by a flash of green. Two by two the lights mark the channel from the Port of Mobile to the wooden platform lighthouse of Middle Bay Light to the clanging sea buoy far out in the gulf, where big ships anchor.

I grew up near this bay in the city of Mobile in the 1950s and '60s. Every summer my family would pack up the car, pass through the Bankhead Tunnel at the foot of Government Street downtown, and cross the causeway to our Eastern Shore—Daphne, Montrose, Fairhope, Point Clear, Mullet Point.

Although it has long been superseded by a stretch of elevated I-10, the causeway is a road I still prefer. Tin shed fishing camps with "Bait" signs scrawled on front, seafood shacks on stilts, men standing patiently by the seawalls holding cane poles over the water—its scenery has not changed much in the four decades I've been traversing it.

The bay houses we rented for a few weeks each summer varied from simple bungalows, far down the shore to grand affairs with sleeping porches, plank floors and 10-foot ceilings at Point Clear. Each house had its own pier. I remember pulling up crab traps with my sister, trawling for shrimp with my father, doing cannonballs off the end of the pier with my friends. Sometimes we kids slept out at the pier's end, listening to the swirl and splash of fish feeding all night long, waiting for a jubilee—a rare phenomenon of this estuary where crabs, shrimp, or flounder swim groggily near the shore for a few hours. One summer I learned how to cast a mullet net from a caretaker who lived across the road and used to appear at sunrise on our waterside, hurling circles of net onto the lurking and leaping fish.

I took in the rhythms of the bay: its mirror calm at sunrise; its humid mid-morning when shrimp boats seemed motionless on the horizon; its lunchtime when families gathered to eat crab claws and seafood gumbo on the big, screen porches of raised cottages; its late afternoons when cumulus clouds, on four o'clock cue, closed out the sun and sent gulls hurtling before them. Lightning that cracked at the windows, then sunsets that bathed the porches—I remember those, too.

Then I went to college and headed north and stayed away for a long time except for visits home. The bay, for me, became a vast well of memory from which I'd draw recollections for my friends in New York. But until 1996, when I took a writing job in Mobile and returned with my wife and daughter to rent year-round on the bay, I did not realize how little I knew about other lives unfolding here. The bay was no longer just a setting for hammock swings against painterly sunsets; it became a place of daily commerce, and back-bending toil, and traumatic history. Like H. A. Rey's tales of stellar twins and scorpions animating the skies, the stories I've been told by bar pilots, fishermen, dockworkers, and those with blood-ties to the water, make the bay come alive too.

On Fairhope Pier

In the opening lines of "Moby Dick," Herman Melville's Ishmael confesses his love for the sea, and how going there soothes his turbulent soul. "If they but knew it," says Ishmael, making his way to the New Bedford, Mass., harbor, "almost all men in their degree, sometime or other, cherish very nearly the same feelings toward the ocean with me."

As I head down to the Fairhope Pier at 5:30 on an August morning, I recall that 19th-century sea-voyager's words. All around me on the walk, as the woods turn pale blue from dawn light, are men and women heading toward the sea: silver-haired retirees in loose, pastel shorts and cushy athletic shoes; slender young athletes, pumping their elbows; fishermen, poles over their shoulders, buckets in hand.

There are no whales to be found out here, but one youth has been out all night with his father fishing for shark, way out at the end of the pier where the concrete floor is dark with the blood of catfish and cavalla and the railings are stained from a million croakers cut for bait. Nearby, another man is fishing for flounder—walking patiently along the railing, working his stealthy hook along the bay floor. Another man, cap pulled low, stands quietly in one place, flicking his grub worm near the channel to lure speckled trout.

As the sun strikes through the bluff pines, another morning begins on the Fairhope Pier. Ishmael himself could easily be here, leaning against the railing, peering out at the shrimp boats and swooping pelicans, feeling restored by the sea.

For a hundred years "Fair Hopers"—as the original band of single-tax colony idealists from Iowa called themselves—have been heading out to this pier. Originally the "Colony Wharf" was a wood structure with tracks enabling first a horse-drawn trolley and then a "People's Railroad" to travel to the end to meet the commerce boats from Mobile.

From its earliest days, it jutted out from a shoreline designated as public space by the colonists. During the Depression, when the colony deeded the land over to the city of Fairhope, the agreement was that this stretch of land—embracing an area from the current duck pond to the Orange Street pier walkway—be maintained as parks.

In a village that once extolled cooperative ventures, but where residents now jawbone about how much money can be made buying and selling houses, the pier remains, blessedly, a public space for everyone, whether barefoot or wearing Cole Hahn shoes. On a lively Friday night, when the Pat Boone–handsome rookie cop on duty visits with old-timers and families, black and white, who stroll babies and photograph sunsets, the pier suggests the essence of community.

• • •

This sense of community, according to Sam Dyson, born in Fairhope in 1908, is what helped rebuild the pier after the 1916 hurricane. The former bank chairman remembers how, when he was a boy on his daily paper route, that storm came up all of a sudden the 5th of July and, within one afternoon of howling winds and tempestuous rains, tore the boards off the Fairhope wharf, while completely destroying Battles Wharf, Zundel's, and two other piers at Point Clear. The camaraderie of the Single Tax Colony—fueled by funds from the owner of Fels-Naptha Soap ("For that clean Naptha odor")—restored the Fairhope wharf to good condition.

Mr. Dyson's wife of 62 years, Helen Dyson, a former schoolteacher at the Organic School, recalls a Fairhope where visitors who stayed at the Colony Hotel up the hill went down to the wharf for recreation. Later in the evening they'd attend theatrical events at the Organic School, a progressive institution of its day founded by Marietta Johnson and dedicated to principles of hands-on learning.

Among the well-known visitors who stayed at the hotel, the Dysons remember, was Clarence Darrow, who achieved fame in the Scopes Monkey Trial for defending a Tennessee schoolteacher who taught evolution. I imagine Darrow walking the Fairhope Pier today, confounded that the same issues he scrapped about in court 70 years ago persist still in Alabama.

In those pre-Causeway days, Fairhope was a far-off, exotic locale, according to other elders I've talked to, known for its artists and free-thinkers, a few "kooks" and even some nudists, one of whom mowed his lawn wearing only his convictions.

In 1922, when the Casino—not the gambling kind—was built at the entrance to the pier, replacing the earlier Pavilion, the pier took on new life as a place of romance and dancing, with bands like the New Orleans Five Jazz Babies rollicking in the balmy air. Evelyn Turner, nee Berglin, whose father A. O. Berglin ran the popular Fairhope Ice and Creamery and served as town mayor, smiles when she thinks back to her ingenue years, the 1930s, when she wore silk dresses to dance with seer-suckered gentlemen on the Casino's second floor. The musicians came on the Bay Queen, played Saturday night and Sunday afternoon.

Outside, the boys, in swimming trunks, lined up to hurtle down long slides into the water; the girls, in modest bathing garb, often watched under parasols. Inside, revelers ordered Cokes by saying, "Give me a dope," young men without dates formed "stag lines," and "cutting in" meant a young woman was popular. When the tempo changed to waltz, couples swirled.

At one time there was even a bowling alley where pin boys reset the game after every roll. Years later, after the live bands were gone and World War II was over, a jukebox played 1940s songs and nickel slot machines rang. Leo Jernigan, a dentist who grew up in Fairhope in the '50s, remembers outdoor movies. Chairs were set up on the grass near the seawall while the projector flickered Bogart and Bacall onto a screen by the bluff.

Oliver Delchamps Jr., who traveled the Causeway back then, even remembers a woman nicknamed "Casino Jean," who stirred young bachelors' hearts.

Eventually the Casino was torn down, and in 1968 the new concrete pier was opened, the wooden wharf and night music only a memory.

• • •

"Don't hang my name on nothin' you write," says the man fishing for speckled trout, throwing his line into the water at the crack of dawn. "Just say you were talking to some old feller who doesn't have good sense." He makes a supple jerk of the wrist; other men stand alongside him, catching nothing. A moment later he has calmly hauled in two speckled trout, one hooked to each of the lures.

"I'm only an amateur," he demurs. "He's the pro." He nods to one of his companions sitting on an overturned bucket. The man, whose line hangs slack, laughs.

Old Feller has passed enough years to remember walking under the Casino, gigging flounders, but claims, deadpan, to be only 39. While some men out here fish for flounder on a hook, Old Feller says that he does not have the patience to flounder fish that way. "You got to wait 20 seconds while they play with the bait. I get nervous and pull. Specks don't do that to you."

He hooks another one. "White trout pull to the bottom, specks come to the top. Red fish"—he motions to the Bay—"they go out yonder."

Like many of the fishermen out here in the early morning, Old Feller has spent his working years doing something else, and now, in retirement, is just too restless to sit at home. "If you just go home and set, then you keep setting. I know four people who went in to set and now they're in the cemetery.

"I used to know everybody," he complains, "but now everybody knows me." He liked it better the old way, when there were fewer people in town and paved roads were dirt ones. The fishing was better, too. The chemical plants have sent their sludge into the waters, he mourns, which destroys the plant-life, which means fewer shrimp and minnows, and fewer fish.

One of his buddies, Ed Novak, is a kindly, retired auto mechanic who lost his vocal cords from an operation. He rests against a piling, working his pole, and intones through a voice box that the specks are slow this morning. Cranford Langley, camouflage hat mashed low against the sharp sun, seems happy just to be here, even if his line has yet to grow taut. A retired electrician, Cranford collapsed ill not long ago while driving away from the pier and too long passed before he could return on his own. "How I missed it when I was sick," he admits. "My family brought me down to the pier just to visit, but I didn't like it. I wanted to fish."

• • •

Walkers stream through the morning, like theater director John Heald, a native Englishman, who loops the quarter-mile pier six times often rehearsing theatrical lines; or Charlotte Flynn, a retired legal secretary from Columbus, Ga., who keeps a Walkman clamped to her head, tuned to Chet Atkins. After she quit smoking Ms. Flynn put on 30 pounds and, determined to exercise herself slim, started walking on U.S. 98. When a bicyclist slammed into her, breaking her ribs, she decided the pier was not only more scenic, but safer, too.

If men like Cranford Langley are morning fishermen, another group emerges at night, like Charlie, a retired Coast Guard officer, called by many "The Flounder King," who can read the complex surface of the water for fish like a doctor scans an x-ray. He and his angling "student," bushy-bearded, suspendered Bobby Love—who claims proud resemblance to rotund Nashville comedian Johnny Russell—roam the pier beating all competition for flounder. They give their haul to neighbors who may be ill, or shut-in.

These small acts of kindness run through the loose-knit community of the pier. The most legendary pier regular of all is Ludy "Captain" Anderson, who began coming to the pier in 1968, just after retiring from civil service, and came down daily except Sundays and during hunting season. Captain is now housebound with arthritis. Every day at 3 in the afternoon he yearns to come to his old haunt, a place where, he explains, "I'd sometimes be teaching twenty or more young people to fish along with me."

In the 1890s, single-tax colony idealists from Iowa—"Fair Hopers"—settled on the eastern shore of Mobile Bay and constructed their Colony Wharf, where ferries brought passengers and commerce, neighbors visited, and dances took place at the Casino, a social hall later built near the entrance. Deeded over to the City of Fairhope during the Great Depression, the wooden pier—replaced with a concrete structure in 1968—endures as a kind of town square, a meeting place for folks from all walks of life. Here, boys reenact the timeless ritual of net fishing, hurling for mullet. (G. M. Andrews, Mobile Register)

For Captain, who'd give his fish to his eight children, countless grandchildren, pigs and dogs, any fish would do. "The only kind of fish that ain't good to eat is the one you don't got," he says. "I can catch anything. I could catch a catfish up in that parking lot if you put a little water there."

On a recent night, Captain's friend Charlie Snead, butcher at the Winn-Dixie, drove to Captain's home and brought him to the pier where he was besieged with old friends, among them one strapping youth who'd learned to fish at Cap's knee. No matter that where Captain and Charlie grew up in north Alabama, black and white may not have regularly socialized together. They met here on the pier, and, as with many regulars, the love of outdoors, and fishing, and lively banter matters most of all.

• • •

In the evening, walking with my wife and daughter on the pier, it does not take long to get to know the regulars. One of them, Roger, with a white, Kenny Rogers beard, toils all day in a sand and clay pit and says that he's a "greenhorn" because he's only been coming here, nightly, for six or seven years.

"I'm a people watcher," he explains. "After working all day, I'm too lazy to fish. I come park my basket on a bench and watch people go by."

Another, Rochelle, says she doesn't care for TV and started coming to the pier when her daughter was 5 years old. That daughter is now 21. "When my girls were little, we'd come here and fish all night, watch the sun come up, then go to Hardee's and have breakfast, go home, fall asleep, get up and come back to fish."

Rochelle speaks wistfully of the cycle of years at the Fairhope Pier. She remembers a retired couple who'd take a spirited, nightly walk. For a long while she didn't see them. After a winter passed, the man returned, pacing slowly, alone.

We ask questions of all the fishermen, and, patient with visitors, they generously answer. A welder with the city of Fairhope, who comes down with an arsenal of rods and reels, tells me he spends half his time fishing, and half his time talking with tourists. "They ask me all kinds of questions," he says. "My favorite is what kind of bait I put in my mullet net. Sometimes I put them on."

As we greet other families dressed in shorts and T-shirts, I think of those stories of days gone by recounted by Sam and Helen Dyson and Evelyn Turner, the era when men strolled here with hats and neckties, women in fancy dresses, and ferry boats plied the waters. Near us one elderly couple, regulars for the sunset, take their places on a bench. I hope the next summer will find them here together again.

The night wears on and my family heads in. I am determined to be the last one on the pier. At 1 in the morning, though, others linger. Against the railing a young couple lean fervently against each other. Farther out, a lanky youth is sprawled on a bench under a sleeping bag while his brothers hurl mullet nets into pools of light.

Across Mobile Bay the channel markers are blinking; in the marina, halyards clank. Before long blue light will rise in the woods and silver-haired walkers will swing their arms vigorously, calling "good morning" to each other as they head toward the Fairhope Pier. The fishermen, as sure as sunrise, will already be there, casting their lines.

Coming to Port

❖

A Night With a Bar Pilot

Deep night, Gulf of Mexico, the Sand Island lighthouse is a dark obelisk against the charcoal sky. Gas rigs shine like empty resort hotels. Near the sea buoy off Dixey Bar glow the bow lights of ships from Greece, Korea, Japan, waiting their turns to come to port. The sea buoy sends out a Morse code signal to their radars, dash-dash, for "M," signifying Mobile.

At 2 a.m. in the rolling Gulf waters eight miles off Dauphin Island, a 47-foot pilot launch, the Alabama, rides the swells toward a 476-foot cargo vessel, the Princess Margherita, looming like a ghost ship. Stepping onto the deck of the launch, Capt. G. Wildon Mareno, tall and lean, zips up his flotation jacket, snugs tight his Mobile Bar Pilots cap, and prepares to grab hold of the rope ladder being let 30 feet down the side of the Margherita.

The ladder dangles short. "Lower it more!" he shouts through cupped hands. The vessels are now moving parallel at seven knots, about eight miles per hour. "Lower the ladder!" No one appears.

Several times this same week Mareno has performed the feat of transferring from pilot launch to ocean vessel while both are under way, climbing every manner of ladder to oil tankers, cruise ships, container ships, wood chippers, cargo vessels, taking charge of their navigation. Through the sand bars of the Gulf—hence the term "bar pilot"—he commandeers them for three and a half hours into the Port of Mobile.

Mareno knows these waters like the Mobile streets where he grew up. He and 10 other bar pilots are responsible, by law, for navigating every foreign-registered ship entering or leaving Mobile, indeed any large ship whose captain does not have a pilot's license. He figures they do 2,400 pilot jobs a year.

Since the time he was a teen-ager, he was learning this profession from his father, George Wildon, and grandfather, Alexander, both bar pilots. With his eyes closed he can map the channel: 400 feet wide and 45 feet deep up the middle of the Bay, with variations near Dixey Bar on one end and the Mobile harbor on the other.

But he never knows, exactly, what to expect.

At midnight, the Clipper Atlantic, loaded with Alabama lumber for the Caribbean, makes its way from the Alabama Sate Docks. The ship has a Russian captain, but it will be navigated through the channel—400 feet wide and 45 feet deep up the middle of Mobile Bay—by a bar pilot, licensed to take the helm through local waters, as members of the Mobile Bar Pilots Association have done since the group's founding in 1865. To the ship's port side is the tug Ervin S. Cooper, assisting in maneuvering out from the docks. Moored, off starboard, is the Visayas Victory, brought to port earlier in the day. (Kiichiro Sato, Mobile Register)

Wildon Mareno, a third-generation Mobile bar pilot, looks to the radar as he navigates a ship through the often tricky, sometimes fog-swept Mobile channel. Both his grandfather, Alexander, and father, George Wildon, were pilots during the era when men lived for weeks aboard a schooner in the Gulf, awaiting incoming ships. After Wildon worked as a captain for Texaco Co. for twenty years—rising to master captain on the Texaco Georgia—he returned to take up the Mareno legacy. Working in rotation, the Mobile bar pilots do about 2,400 pilot jobs a year. (Kiichiro Sato, Mobile Register)

As the Alabama roller coasters next to the Princess Margherita stretching the distance of one and a half football fields, there are dark, young faces peering over the gunnel. Uncertain voices—not quite Spanish, nor Portuguese—chatter loudly. The ship is registered in Cyprus, but the crewmen are speaking a dialect of the Philippines.

The ladder drops lower but is crooked, like a contraption from Swiss Family Robinson. Mareno gestures to the man above to even it on the right.

Two years ago, on an icy December night, a fellow pilot was climbing a rope ladder and fell. He crashed to the deck of the Alabama, breaking bones, smashing his hip. Pilots still speak with a shudder of that night. Of the 1,200 bar pilots working American harbors, often in darkness, rain and wind, at least one a year, Mareno says, takes a disastrous fall.

The ladder is straightened and he reaches up and grips the ropes with his gloved hands, stepping off the launch and onto the first rung. He steps again. The Alabama is dropping away.

There is no way back for this 54-year-old husband and father of three daughters, this veteran of sea waters from Alaska to Mobile. While his middle-aged friends are back home snug in their beds dreaming of youth and ocean adventures, he is here clinging to coils of hemp, scaling his way over steel and rust.

At the top rung he latches onto a metal hook ladder and swings his feet up onto the deck. Around him move bleary-eyed crewmen in the last phase of their midnight to 4 a.m. shift. His own workday is just beginning.

• • •

The Gulf night is filled with sounds: the clanging of bell buoys, the moaning of whistle buoys. The gas rigs make ghost sounds, too. On the VHF radio, voices crackle: Channel 16 for calling and emergency, Channel 13 for ships leaving and entering port. Bar pilots talk to launch operators, tug captains contact dispatchers, an ongoing web of men working to move ships. Vietnamese voices break in, shrimpers telling each other of their catch.

The captain of the Princess Margherita, Roy, is a slight, mustachioed 49-year-old from Manila. For more than a year on this voyage he has been plying ocean waters, making port in Rio de Janeiro, along the coast of Chile, in Houston, and harbors in between. As is the practice at port, he relinquishes the helm to the bar pilot—although, as captain, he still exercises ultimate authority. Roy explains, in broken English, that the gyrocompass has a two-degree westerly error. An error is not unusual; a pilot compensates in plotting the course.

Mareno calls out compass points to the quartermaster, who handles the wheel: "Zero two one!"

"Zero two one!" repeats the quartermaster. The direction heads them up the middle of the Dixey Bar channel.

The illuminated dials of the navigational instruments are the only glow in the darkness.

Mareno checks the speed—too slow. The powerful currents may set the ship toward the sand bar. "Twelve knots," he says. "Twelve knots!" His voice is getting edgy.

The rpms increase. Mareno watches the glow of the instruments. He is beginning to pace.

"Zero one three," Mareno directs as the ship moves toward the mouth of Mobile Bay.

"Zero one three," the quartermaster echoes. Past Fort Morgan, up the channel, the direction tends more to the north.

Captain Roy disappears into the chart room, looking over the gift the bar pilot has brought him—the local newspaper.

Some sea captains hungrily turn to the financial pages, others to world news. Searching the Mobile Register, Captain Roy dispenses with stories of political wrangles and shootings and school board squabbles. In delight, he finds a Circuit City pullout. He spreads out advertisements for VCRs, videocams, CD players, boom-boxes. He asks how far it is from the Port of Mobile to the shopping malls.

At the controls, Mareno has quickly realized a mistake. The gyro is not two degrees off, but three. Not a westerly error, but easterly. Captain Roy, a graduate of a Manila maritime school, can surely plot a course, but has chosen the wrong words in English. The ship would have headed in the direction of the Grand Hotel swimming pool.

But Mareno keeps the course true. He leans forward and peers at the red and green channel markers winking in the mist.

Is that fog rolling in?

• • •

Out of nowhere it comes, filling the night bay like a pale breath, sweeping over the bow of the ship. Whereas squalls show up on radar screens, fog does not: it slides across the water, silent, covering the lights of shrimp boats and barges and gas rigs. It touches the bows of the ships, conceals them like cloaks.

At the Alabama State Docks at 3 a.m., tugboat Capt. Mike Yarbrough, of Crescent Towing, receives an update from his dispatcher that the Princess Margherita will be making port in two and a half hours. All night Yarbrough's tug has been chugging out to meet ships as they enter port. Also named Alabama, it works in tandem with the tugs Ervin S. Cooper and Mardi Gras, nosing up to the ships and nudging them into berths.

Yarbrough receives a call from Mareno, asking about conditions at the Docks. He tells the bar pilot that the fog has rolled in and there is limited visibility. The McDuffie coal terminal, Bender Shipbuilding, Alabama Marine—they are glimmers of light through the mist. There is a racket of power hammers and of coal rattling down chutes. They are invisible to the eye.

Ships do not commonly start out in fog. Thousands of dollars a year, Mareno explains, are lost as ships back up when visibility drops to zero. Cargo waits on shore; stevedores fall idle. If fog comes in once the ships are under way, though, they continue.

Mareno slows to seven knots and sends a man to the bow with a walkie-talkie to report what he can see. The ship's radar will show Mareno a lot about objects in the water, but nothing tells the truth like the human eye.

He steps from the bridge onto the wing and presses the foghorn. A blast like a train whistle resounds. He blows it again. Far away another answers.

In Mobile Bay there are push boats, pleasure boats, shrimp boats, not all of them reachable by radio. Not all of them keeping steady courses. Were Mareno to discover an unidentified boat crossing his radar he could blast his foghorn. If he had to stop his ship, reversing engines, it could take a mile to come to full halt.

Now he hears a radio report that a fueling barge broke loose from a push boat during an earlier storm and is adrift. Where? A ship could ram it in the fog, tearing it open, spilling its fuel. Voices fly on the VHF radio. The tug Ervin S. Cooper, under Capt. Joe Tucker, has been contacted to find it and is scouring the Bay.

Mareno receives a call to "Portable Seven," the code name he uses when piloting. Like players on a ball team, the bar pilots have numbers they use—his father also was "Portable Seven."

The call is from "Portable Nine," Capt. Hank Brady, who is navigating a 405-foot cargo ship out from port. The captains stay in close contact as they near each other, the foghorns bounding back and forth.

Mareno's ship, 72 feet at the beam, weighs nearly 10,000 tons. Brady's craft, 62 feet wide, weighs close to 6,500 tons. The channel, 400 feet wide, does not leave much room for error when ships pass each other. In the night. In the fog.

If a pilot were to steer too close to the channel's edge, the water pressure would build against the hull, pushing the bow out across the middle of the channel, pulling the stern in to the channel's side wall. What if another ship were bearing down from the opposite direction?

Mareno, his focus intense, his manner cool, asks that the word "collision" not even be uttered. He looks as though he could burn a hole in the fog with his concentration.

He blasts the horn and talks to "Portable Nine" and out of nowhere a few lights show to his port side and the other ship suddenly rises up like a mountain cliff.

As quickly it is sliding by, enveloped in the sea-level clouds, in the night, gone.

The Port of Mobile lies ahead.

• • •

Visible on the radar is a band of deep color, moving from Dog River out over Gaillard Island, on toward Middle Bay Light—an electronic picture of rain. The real rain comes sweeping through the fog. It splatters the ship's deck, driving indoors the Philippine deckhands on the 4 a.m. shift. One young man wears a souvenir T-shirt: "New Orleans French Quarter." Traveling the world for the first time, he stands at a porthole looking out at the harbor glimmering in the fog. Mobile—a place so far from home.

After McGill High School and Texas A & M University, where he gained a degree in marine transportation, Wildon Mareno intended to become a Mobile bar pilot right away. Although his parents had three other sons, all younger, by tradition only one could be heir to the calling.

Mareno took a leave from college to apprentice with his father, in the last year that the Mobile bar pilots bunked out on the Gulf. Until 1965, the pilots lived aboard a 100-foot sailing schooner anchored near Dixey Bar, waiting for incoming ships. They worked two weeks on and one week off.

Today, they change watch every week, live at home, and bunk at Dauphin Island when schedules catch them there. When on watch, they catnap between trips at odd hours, slip into their flotation vests at the ring of the phone.

The traditions hearken back to the founding of the Mobile Bar Pilots Association in 1865. Today, it is a small business regulated by the state. The pilots are like members of a law firm, putting their revenues into a common pot, then dividing them after paying launch operators, dispatchers, and covering overhead.

But charting the same course as his father proved hard. When Mareno finished learning to be a pilot, there were no positions open for him in Mobile. Where there had once been need for 18 pilots, there was suddenly only need for a dozen. Ship traffic had slacked off, he says, and ships three times larger than in his father's day carried more bulk on fewer runs. He could have become a bar pilot elsewhere, but his heart lay here.

He joined the Texaco Co., working for 20 years on oil tankers, becoming master captain of the Texaco Georgia. He came to port all through the Mediterranean; traveled in the Pacific, weathering the hellish storms of Alaska on the Texaco Florida. He once navigated out of Puget Sound into a tumultuous blow that, he says, was like falling from a bathtub into a gale. As captain, he was in charge of the morphine and penicillin, his duty being to administer medicines to his crew when they fell ill. He recalls, in a storm, talking by radio to a doctor, seeking advice on a crew member who was sick as a dog.

He was gone so long at a stretch from Mobile that he remembers once giving his daughters good-bye hugs just before they got out of St. Ignatius School for summer, and not seeing them again until they were enrolled that fall.

When he was 45, a position finally opened with the Mobile Bar

Pilots. He prized the years he spent on those tankers, but he was ready to navigate home.

• • •

When the port is covered in fog, the sun does not rise from the horizon but sends out a milky glow, like a moon. Close to the water's edge, the downtown buildings suggest themselves: Government Plaza, like the side of a craggy ship, First National Bank, like the Sand Island lighthouse, pale against a paler sky. The rain and wind have churned the fog, and the sun grows stronger. The city emerges.

From the tugboat Alabama, Yarbrough is keeping close contact with the Margherita. Yarbrough takes the tug into the middle of the harbor and tests the current. Not with radar or depth-finders, but the old-fashioned way—by idling the boat and seeing how fast the river pushes it along. In the winter, the river swells and the current rushes faster. He reports his findings to Mareno. All normal.

The Alabama's deckhands ready the line that will be attached to the Margherita. Once they make it fast, they will duck back into the cabin. If the heavy rope snaps, it could pop back at them like a whip.

On the Margherita, Captain Roy has come onto the wing. Soon enough he will be meeting with the ship agent, agricultural inspectors, Customs and stevedores. In the meantime, he keeps the electronics ads under his arm. They are coming to port only long enough to on-load steel coils. Shore leave may be brief.

Mareno is slowing, blasting his foghorn again. Another horn blasts back, but not a ship. It is the whistle of the CSX railroad rumbling through the tunnel under the Mobile Convention Center. Word comes on the radio that the lost fueling barge, far out in the Gulf, has been found.

Cautious in the thinning fog of the harbor, Mareno requests a second tug to assist in the docking; the Mardi Gras makes its way to join the Alabama. Heeding his directions, the tugs position themselves fore and aft, starboard and port. Lines are hurled and made fast. The big ship and the small tugs are tethered.

At what feels like a crab's pace, the Margherita moves upriver to the docking slip, North C.

Ninety degrees—that's the angle of the required turn. Simple as an airline pilot's touching down the wheels of a jet; effortless as an Olympic diver's going for the gold.

With help of the tugs Mareno accomplishes it gracefully, pivoting the big ship as though held in his hand. It lands with a soft thunk against the dock.

"Uneventful," he says, relaxing. "Just what we want."

Bearing the Load

On a cold, November afternoon at the Alabama State Docks, cargo workers with the International Longshoremen's Association (ILA) button up their old Army jackets and snug on muffler caps under their hardhats. Breath steaming the air, they take up their places on forklifts, flatbed trucks, loading ramps, cranes and in the vast holds of the cargo ship Star Evanger. Although brawny and strong-armed, next to the 700-foot ship they look like toy figures in a Lego display.

"Over this way, over here!" shouts a foreman, John Waller, 57, who has climbed high on the Evanger. He is nicknamed "Hook" for his reputed ability, in bygone days, to grab cargo with his hands off rail cars that ran along the piers. He has a wide mustache on his dark, weathered face, and does not care much for talk. As foreman, he has selected his workers at the ILA hiring hall, pacing a ramp and choosing his gang like a coach fielding a baseball team, giving preference to seniority; at the Docks he makes sure they keep pace.

The bales of wood pulp swing out over the hold as the gantry crane lifts them. A bale is composed of crude paper belted in stacks; dozens of bales are wired together to make up a load.

Hook looks up at the "winch operator" high in the crane, Isaac

"Ike" Williams, then 50 feet down into the hold where other men are stationed.

Hook nods, signaling for the load to be lowered. Ike works the crane hydraulics. The wood pulp hovers—30 tons suspended from steel cables—and descends. When it reaches bottom, the men unlatch it and signal Ike to take the crane up again.

Over the next two days, as contracted by Stevedoring Services of America, the longshoremen will continue this process. Their objective: transfer 19,000 tons of pulp to the Star Evanger.

When the hatches are clamped shut to seal the cargo, they will not be reopened until the ship has made its way through the Panama Canal and arrived, 22 days later, at its destination: Japan.

Alabama River Pulp, Ekman, Georgia-Pacific, Weyerhaeuser—their pulp will be unloaded in Osaka, Yokohama and other ports.

The men's objective, as well, is to stay out of harm's way. At $16.50 per hour for cargo loading, a dollar more for the foreman, the ILA workers may seem well paid; indeed, they are said to make more than their non-union counterparts on the Docks.

But longshore work is catch as catch can, the men lingering at the hiring hall playing checkers, or drifting by the corner of Congress and Washington streets peering through the caged window at the blackboard with its updates on incoming ships. When the work finally comes, it can be perilous.

Henry Brantley, 61, who started working in 1955, has been a regular member of Hook's gang for several years. He says he wouldn't want any of his five children to follow his footsteps, because it's "too dangerous." Five years ago, he saw a man get killed when the wire holding a heavy load broke.

Dressed in camouflage jacket, with Red Man chewing tobacco stuffed in his shirt pocket, Brantley holds up his right hand. He lost the middle finger in a cargo accident nearly 20 years ago. He nods to a foot: once crushed when a piece of iron rolled over it.

Brantley now works hooking up the loads to the crane.

John Purifoy, 64, started working as a longshoreman in 1952, left for many years to work for Brown & Brown, a company that made cotton bale coverings, then returned as a longshoreman in 1988. He holds up his right hand, too: a vicious "S" scar curves across the life-line of his palm. It shows where a hook sank in when a load of paper broke from a crane.

"They said I'd never use my hand again. They offered me a penny ante job, security guard. It's silly to sit around watching somebody's money with a pistol. I'm not a lazy person."

He drives a flatbed truck for Hook's crew today. He uses both hands.

As the men toil, the Star Evanger begins to sit lower in the water. Soon it is one inch deeper—the result of 142 tons of load.

• • •

On their noon break, as seagulls scavenge for food scraps, some men linger on the pier, eating lunch. One of them, Wendell Nicholson, 55, sizable and friendly, hunts for discarded soda cans. He flattens them out to take home and store in old oil drums. When the price for aluminum goes up, he'll cart them to the recycling plant.

Nicholson has never been injured at the Docks, but he did get shot in the leg during his first month of infantry duty in Vietnam. He was a soldier in the Army's First Division on a night "when all hell broke loose."

Nicholson says he's from "the country," from Wilcox County. Like many in the union, he has relatives who did this work before him, in his case, two uncles.

In 1960, when Nicholson began at the Docks, the work was back-breaking. Two men at a time would haul 140-pound sacks of fertil-izer, or 100-pound sacks of corn and rice. They'd trudge to the side of the ship and hurl the sacks upwards to be stacked 12 high.

The forklift, Nicholson says, does the labor that a man's back used to do.

Even when cargo was managed by hand, though, work at the Docks, to Nicholson, was preferable to farm work back home. Up there you'd get two dollars a day chopping cotton. Down here you could make that in an hour.

"My uncles came back from Mobile and told us about it. To us it was a little piece of heaven."

• • •

Rolf Garvens, 49, a native of Hamburg, Germany, is a docks super-intendent with Stevedoring Services of America, formerly Ryan-Walsh. SSA has contracts to load many of the Star ships, a Norwegian line, that come to Mobile. Cooper/T. Smith, another stevedoring company, also has contracts for some Star ships.

The stevedores orchestrate the movement of cargo onto the ships, and are responsible for the job. They own the forklifts, the trucks and supplies. They hire the longshoremen who do the actual moving.

Tall and watchful, Garvens paces the pier, walkie-talkie in hand, keeping an eye on the workers, staying in touch with the chief officer on board the Star Evanger, Emmanuel "Sonny" Dapilloza, a native of the Philippines. Going back and forth among various locations is Mickey Matthews, the port captain who works for Star's office in Mobile; Matthews oversees this entire loading operation, and will give the final go-ahead to close the hatches and schedule a bar pilot to guide the Evanger back out to sea.

Garvens learned the maritime trade in Hamburg and Bremen-Haven, and has worked all over the world. In Gonzales, La., he saw a longshoreman get decapitated by a steel beam. In Brazil, he watched rain forests get hacked down. He speaks angrily of those who wrecked some of those forests.

Ironically, the wood pulp industry of America's South sits at the center of a raging controversy between industrialists and environmentalists. Garvens says he believes the wood pulp will be replenished as quickly as it's cut. He says that in Germany, environmentalists have slowed progress. He makes these comments casually, while keeping his gaze trained on the cargo.

After all, the men on the pier are not here to debate the future of Alabama's forests—they are here to get a job done.

Suddenly, there is a commotion near the ship. Apparently, while the crane was positioning a load in the cargo hold, a connecting wire broke. Two bales of wood pulp are brought back out, dangling like gargantuan dice.

They are set back down on the pier. No one is hurt.

• • •

Only a pelting rain halts the longshoremen for a while—the wood pulp is moisture-sensitive. The men change shifts; new men come on, toil for hours, go home. Hook has visited the hiring hall to "shape up" a new gang, taking on several of his regulars. They return to finish up.

Ike Williams, 45, is back in his perch, high up in the cab of the gantry crane. He also serves as Hook's assistant foreman. When Hook retires, Ike may get the foreman's job, depending on what the stevedores and the union decide. If he is chosen, he will continue a father-son longshoreman tradition. Isaac Williams Sr. was a foreman, too.

Last May, when Ike had gone to the ILA hiring center one morning but no cargo jobs were posted on the blackboard, he headed on to B.C. Rain High School, to take some money to his stepson. At the time, Kendrick Cleveland, a senior and basketball star, had a rich future ahead—graduation upcoming, and offers for basketball scholarships.

When Ike got to the school, though, he noticed police. A teacher told him a student had been shot, but they were not yet releasing the name. He pressed her for information.

"She asked me, 'What's your son's name?' I told her, 'Kendrick Cleveland.' 'Come with me,' she said."

Kendrick Cleveland had been shot six times, allegedly by another student in a teen-age revenge drama. Kendrick survived the shooting, but was badly wounded. "He has no feeling in his foot," Ike says, a catch in his voice.

For three months afterward, Ike was too distraught to come down to the ILA hiring hall.

As he operates the gantry crane now, watching the thousands of pounds of cargo being raised or lowered by the touch of his hands on the controls, the wages he makes are critical. He also has the chance to worry about something other than what happened to Kendrick.

"When I get to working," he says, "it helps me get my mind off it."

• • •

"Hey," a longshoreman from another crew calls to Hook and his gang, "y'all gonna sink that ship before you finish loading it."

The Star Evanger sits more than 10 feet deeper in the water than when it arrived in Mobile. If it were much lower, figures chief officer Sonny, it would have to contend with the channel depth of the Panama Canal.

Port captain Mickey Matthews oversees the final locking-in of the ship's enormous steel hatches. The Star Evanger's sea-going captain returns from a sojourn in town and takes command.

Hook, Ike, and the other longshoremen are finished. It is only 4 in the afternoon. There will be another "shape up" for labor crews at the ILA hiring hall at 5 p.m. The blackboard is chalked up with the names of ships due in tonight.

Gathering up their hard hats and lunch pails, the men are headed there already.

Shore Leave

At midnight on Dauphin Street, sailors lean into telephone cubicles punching long-distance codes. 63—the Philippines. 62—Indonesia. Voices rise in a dialect of home. Someone has answered. The sailor tells of this new place he has landed. Mobile.

One tells of a city where the downtown, at night, is nearly empty. To buy the athletic shoes he has promised as a gift from America, he must wait until the morning, when a bus can take him to a place called "the mall."

Another tells of the pier where the ship is moored—the Alabama State Docks—and how when he faces the east to pray to Allah, he looks out at a body of water called Mobile Bay.

Another says there is a Catholic Maritime Club on this street where a statue of the Virgin wears a crown of seven stars, one for each sea, and there is foosball and hot coffee; and at another seaman's club nearby, sponsored by Baptists, there is a gym for basketball.

Other men pass and beckon. A generation earlier, sailors went to downtown haunts like the Princess House Lounge, Club Royal, the 55 Club—all-American hangouts for both sailors and denizens of the downtown Mobile night. These men are headed to Jessica's Lounge on Dauphin, run by a native of Manila; later they will move on to Anita's Diner on Conti, where another Philippine woman is cooking up chicken adobo, a garlicky Philippine dish, and hot Indonesian shrimp.

On Conception Street, on the door of a general-mercantile store there is even a sign in Tagalog, the Philippine national language. It begins: "Kabayan. Bili No Kayo."

"My friends. Nice Store. Cheap Goods. Enjoy yourselves."

• • •

Sailors in port. They are as old a tradition, in cities like Mobile, as the ships themselves. For many years, when cargo vessels flew American flags, they were manned by U.S. Merchant Marines. Among those coming to port, as well, were sailors from Scandinavia and the Mediterranean. The Norwegian Seaman's Mission, in Mobile, was a safe harbor for legions of seafarers.

Most cargo vessels today have foreign registration, and seamen hail from countries where the wages are low, the jobs hard to come by, and American dollars go far.

When Mobile's Catholic Maritime Club was founded on St. Patrick's Day, 1942, it was host, with country-club elegance, to scores of American sailors and merchant seamen. Originally across from the Cathedral, it now occupies a quiet hall on Dauphin Street with faded pool tables, antique phone booths and a guest register signed, in a recent week, by a ship's carpenter from Nicaragua, a fitter from Ecuador, a waiter from Croatia, and a kitchen worker from India.

Rune Nordtveit, a 25-year-old deckhand on the Star Evanger, says he was surprised to find himself the only Norwegian deckhand among a crew of Filipinos.

Russian sailors are finding positions, too. Russian crewmen from the Clipper Atlantic, registered in Cyprus, clutch paper bags filled with household amenities as they cross Water Street and make their way to board the cargo ship for the next port.

Word on the waterfront is that even lower-priced competition is coming from the Burmese.

Joseph Connick, a retired Mobile police sergeant who is director of the Catholic Maritime Club, explains that not every sailor's life is a page out of Jack London. Lousy food, poor sanitation, long hours with no overtime—he has heard all these complaints from men who step in his door. One man came in and reported that he'd been on a ship for five months without pay.

Even with pay as low as $300 to $400 a month, though, few seamen might complain. What is poverty level in America can be prize wages abroad.

Pedro is a sailor from Montenegro, a small remnant of Yugoslavia. On a drizzly afternoon on Dauphin, he pauses at Jessica's Lounge before heading back to his cargo ship, the Zeta, registered in Malta. Forty-one years old, but looking not a day under 60, he drags on an unfiltered cigarette and speaks wearily of the life in his home. Two hundred dollars a month—that's all he could hope to make there if he could find a job at all.

Married, with two children, he has been at sea for many months. He wears a checked shirt he bought in Cape Town, South Africa. Within the month he will land in Valencia, Spain, and Alexandria, Egypt.

His walk up and down Dauphin was uneventful, he says, but he does not seem to mind.

"In my country, oh"—he waves his cigarette in the air—"the
Muslims in Bosnia-Herzegovina, the Catholics in Croatia, the Serbi-
ans . . . " He shakes his head.

He glances at the clock: He is due back on board in 10 minutes.
It is time to leave this peaceful Mobile.

• • •

Tommy is 24 years old and has long black hair that he keeps rolled
into a knot and hidden under a cap. While in Mobile he has been to
the mall and bought an Oakland Raiders football helmet. He has
never seen the team, but likes the picture of the buccaneer. Although
no one plays American football in his native Indonesia, he plans to
wear the helmet when he rides his motorcycle back home in Bogor,
West Java.

Tommy is in Mobile because the cruise ship on which he's employed is in dry dock at Bender Shipbuilding & Repair. For two
weeks, Tommy and hundreds of other crew have several hours a day
for shore leave. When a cruise ship is in dry dock at Bender or across
the river at Atlantic Marine, crew are typically still aboard.

At the International Seamen's Center on Texas Street, Tommy
plays basketball with other kitchen workers from the ship. Indone-
sians vs. Filipinos. A lot of the players wear Air Jordans or Jumpman
Pros—Michael Jordan shoes they saw advertised on CNN and bought
in Balboa, Mexico.

Tommy admits that the Filipinos are better basketball players. The
premiere sports of his homeland are badminton and table tennis. He
says that the cultures are different in another way—the Filipino
women take jobs on ships. "Not Indonesian women," he says with a
sense of pride.

He is approached by the Rev. Aias DeSouza, a Baptist minister
born and raised in Brazil, who came to Mobile in 1979 to direct the
International Seamen's Center on Texas Street. A neatly dressed, ebul-
lient man, DeSouza is constant energy, welcoming sailors, offering

them Bibles, hurrying to the phone where he listens to the woes of a seaman who needs help in returning to Asia for a funeral.

DeSouza asks Tommy if he is a Christian. Tommy says that he's Muslim.

DeSouza finds a Bible written in Indonesian and asks Tommy to read aloud a verse from John. "I want to hear what it sounds like in Indonesian," he says.

After Tommy reads, DeSouza tries to make him a gift of the Bible. Tommy politely declines, but then the men begin to talk about life and death and the passage of this world for the next. Finally, Tommy accepts. The pastor claps his hands with delight.

Later, DeSouza gathers the seamen for a prayer service and invites them to read aloud in different languages from the Gospels. He gives a talk similar to the one he gave Tommy.

He says that in every country men find women beautiful for different reasons. In Indonesia it may be the complexion of the skin; in Brazil it is the shapeliness of a woman's legs. But what happens when people grow old and beauty fades, he asks?

He likens the wearing down of the body to the wearing down of a ship. Ships need repairing; humans, too. The seamen nod.

When the prayer meeting is over, he invites them to the Christmas party that will take place soon. By then, though, these men will be scattered, back at sea.

• • •

As midnight passes and the early hours of the morning begin, the sailors are the only movement in the blocks around Bienville Square.

As might be expected, some women appear, including a sturdy bleach-blonde in hot pants who ambles down Conception Street. In this regard, the seamen say ports in Mexico are much better. Forty dollars, for a date in Mobile, is a big chunk of a monthly salary. Besides, in Mexico, "las chicas" are said to come right down to some ships.

In Jessica's Lounge the karaoke is on and the Filipinos pass the microphone, singing along to Barry Manilow–style love ballads. The pictures on the screen are romantic—beach fronts, young couples hand in hand. One sailor, setting down a beer bottle to pick up the microphone, gets teary as he croons.

Several of the men wear T-shirts that say, "Mobile, Alabama."

Hurricane Chronicles

Hurricane People

July 21, 1997

For two days at our home on Mobile Bay we have watched Hurricane Danny's winds thrashing the oak trees, pounding the wharves, turning walls into instruments that whistle and moan. Power gone, we eat sandwiches by candlelight, play board games and listen to our transistor radio, that lowliest of technological devices.

My wife and I, both born here, are hurricane people. We are reminded of this when storms like Danny begin as counterclockwise swirls in the overheated Gulf of Mexico and soon rage outside our taped-up windows. To people elsewhere, the words "tropical depression" might conjure a melancholy youth in a Caribbean bar. They set us in search of flashlights, ice coolers, six-packs and emergency phone numbers.

Our phone still works, and friends from Denver to Maine call us. Watching the Weather Channel, they know more about the location of the storm than we do.

We were living in Brooklyn during the Blizzard of '96. The snow kept us indoors, closed stores, changed Atlantic Avenue into a lane of cross-country skiers. Our neighbors in Mobile shudder at the thought of a New York blizzard; New Yorkers shrug. In Brooklyn, you could captivate a dinner party with tales of Mobile hurricanes. People here say hurricanes are just part of who we are.

It's still light outside. I hop into the car and navigate to the grocery store, which has a generator. People have plowed through as much water to get there as Admiral Farragut in the Battle of Mobile Bay. Many are filling their carts. But most look like they've braved the storm because they're tired of looking at their four walls. They have come out, like me, to talk.

Frederic, Elena, Erin, Opal, Camille—these names bind us together. One man tells of a red oak that crashed into his den during Frederic, another of walking through the rubble of a fancy hotel after Camille. One ancient mariner goes back to the hurricane of 1926 that wrecked Miami and then Pensacola, before falling to pieces in Mobile. Somebody says his grandmother told him that the hurricane of 1916 lifted river boats onto the flooded streets of downtown Mobile.

Back home, my wife and daughter are lighting the storm candles. Night comes down with a roar. I settle down on the couch next to them, hearing, already, the stories this hurricane will tell.

Old Hurricane Stories

July 18, 1997

Bayview is a wreck . . . The roof of the pavilion's lying a distance away. The waterfront is piled with pleasure boats. One tug up on the land. . . . I'm glad and thankful for our lives. . . . Mrs. N was all to pieces. Says she won't stay here till the next one ten years hence.
>   Letter to Dorothy Burrows from her mother, Pensacola,
>   Sept. 22, 1926, University of West Florida special collections

The 1926 blow started in St. Kitts, West Indies, plowed into downtown Miami where it destroyed hotels, flooded homes, and left two hundred and forty-three dead in its wake. It moved out over the Gulf, and made landfall again at Pensacola, its winds exceeding 100 mph in Mobile just after noon, Monday, Sept. 20.

Meteorologists say that if the '26 storm had occurred today, tracing a greatly populated coastline, it would be one of the deadliest and costliest in our history.

"Florida's Homeless Is Over 30,000," stated a headline in the Mobile Register of Sept. 21, 1926. "Heavy Death List."

As Register reporters fanned out over the Gulf Coast, filing on-site accounts of the destruction, Associated Press wires brought the news of Miami's agony. One report told of Miami looting in the aftermath of the storm, with men wearing pistols in order to protect their property. Three men were said to be roaming the beaches, stealing the rings off dead people's hands, shooting off the fingers if necessary. A mob chased the men, shot and burned them.

Another Register headline about the Miami situation said: "Storm Rumor Monger Is Sentenced to 90-day Hard Labor Term."

"There are thousands who have lost all and are destitute and who must have financial aid in order to get back upon a self-supporting basis," said Miami Mayor E. C. Romfh in his "Official Storm Statement" of Sept. 24, 1926.

The Register reported: "Martial law in Miami, and their safety was reported to Norman Reiss, of the Reiss Mercantile Company by his sister, Rita Reiss, who was in Miami during the hurricane which reaped a heavy toll of lives Saturday."

In a letter from Miami to E. B. Gaston, editor of the Fairhope Courier newspaper, Tom Bowen wrote: "What a sight! Houses turned over, roofs off, big apartment buildings with the sides blown in and furniture showing."

He added, "I received my Courier and was glad to get it. After all, there is no place like home."

• • •

Our people have suffered in a financial way from the effects of the same hurricane that swept over your section of Florida and we are only today recovering from the storm. Nevertheless we are all cheerful and confi-

*dent of the future and have therefore determined to solicit funds . . . to
aid your destitute and needy who we feel are much more unfortunate
than we.*
From Mobile Mayor Harry Hartwell to Miami Mayor E. C. Romfh

'06. '16. '26. As though Mobile were trapped in a numerological
warp, every time a year with a "6" came around, a hurricane hit. No
wonder the woman wrote in the Pensacola letter, "Mrs. N . . . says
she won't stay here till the next one ten years hence."

"We were waiting for one in '36," says Jack Stapleton, 88. Talks
with older Mobile-area residents like him bring to mind not only the
hurricane of '26, but the earlier ones.

On July 4, 1916, Mobile celebrated not only Independence Day,
but also Hurricane Preparedness Day. On July 5, in a surprise attack
from directly south, a Category 3 hurricane arrived in Mobile Bay.
Stapleton remembers being in Fairhope visiting his grandparents. His
father came across the Bay to get him by tug. He watched his father
splash through flooded streets.

The '26 storm blew the roof off Fairhope Coal and Supply Co.,
owned by Stapleton's father. He remembers the way the strong wind
"peeled back" the tin roof.

Sam Brown, 89, was a sophomore at the University of Alabama in
September 1926, and took the train home the 13 hours from Tuscaloosa to Mobile, helping his father sweep out the water and debris
from Brown & Brown. The family's business, which provided coverings for cotton bales, was situated at the Mobile harbor. In the 1916
storm, the building had caught fire and nearly burned down. When
Milton Brown, his father, rebuilt it, he made sure to create several
steps up to the ground floor, in case of flooding.

Cleaning up after the storm was a dirty business. In 1926, Brown
says, the city still emptied sewage into the Mobile River, and that
was flooded, too.

Brown, who recently wrote a history of his family's business, recalls how warning flags, for storms, used to be draped from the National Weather Service offices atop the First National Bank building.

When the storm of 1926 approached, the traditional flags for hurricane emergency were unfurled—deep red, with black squares inside.

In 1917, Mary Buhring's family moved from Coden to downtown Mobile and in 1926 were living on Washington Avenue when the hurricane knocked down the steeple of St. John's Episcopal Church nearby.

Buhring, 94, grew up in Coden and was only 3 years old when the '06 storm played havoc with that settlement. Homes were destroyed, people drowned. She remembers the immense waves.

"My daddy could tell when a hurricane was coming by looking at the weather," she says. "I predicted the one of 1926. I could tell by the way the wind was."

Buhring was not at home during the hurricane, though. She and friends had set out by car to Biloxi shortly before the winds rose, but ended up having to turn back, seeking refuge at her grandmother's house in Bayou la Batre.

• • •

In Bienville Square fallen limbs of great oaks were sawed into convenient lengths and carted away. All over the city the same scene was repeated.

Mobile Press Register

Only 5 years old in 1926, Gloria Yost, of the Demeranville family, grew up in a big house on Dauphin Street near Fulton Street, and remembers the night of the storm. Gloria and her sisters, who usually slept upstairs, for safety spent that night on the kitchen floor. A tree came through the dining room.

On the latticework back porch, where a banana hook held ripening fruits, her parents kept an ice box. She recalls how her mother put extra ice in that box to last out the storm, and insisted the children drink only the water kept in big jugs.

But mostly, in a scene precious to many from a Mobile childhood, she remembers playing in flooded streets. After the storm had passed,

but the rains continued, she and her brothers went to play in the big
ditch down by the railroad tracks.

"For five to seven days," she recalls, "it rained."

But even though the rain flooded Mobile streets, there was no
flooding from conditions far deadlier—storm surge.

The tide was low when the hurricane landed, and the north wind
drove the water out of the Bay. One young Mobile banker recounts
stories his grandmother told him about being at Point Clear in 1926

Children of the coastal South grow up with the late summer threat of hurricanes. These storms bring varying combinations of howling winds, surging
tides, and heavy rain, and they often leave behind broken trees, smashed
houses, and—as in this photograph from the hurricane of 1926—flooded
streets. Early hurricanes were named by their dates—1906, 1916, 1926—
and now, like unruly giants, by names like Camille, Frederic, Danny, and
Georges. Residents of the Gulf Coast, on all-too-familiar terms with these
giants, become tale-tellers of storms—Hurricane People. (Erik Overbey Collection, University of South Alabama Archives)

when the long sand bar from the Grand Hotel out to Point Clear Beacon emerged, high and dry. When the winds subsided, people strolled out to the beacon.

"The greatest damage to Mobile in past hurricanes has been caused by high water," reported the Mobile Register of Sept. 22, 1926, "but this condition only exists when southeast winds prevail, the storm winds of Monday from the north reversing the conditions and causing the lowest tides in the history of Mobile river and bay."

• • •

How About Your Storm Harvested Pecans?
  Headline of a column in the Fairhope Courier, Oct. 7, 1926

Metzger Brothers had a sale on Dobbs hats, the Crown Theater was promoting "Zangar the fortune-teller" to read people's futures between movies, and the town awaited the Jack Dempsey–Gene Tunney heavyweight boxing match—but everything ground to a halt.

For two days, power was out. The street cars did not run. Electric lights and telephones stopped working. At Monroe Park, strong winds wrecked the grandstand, home to the Mobile Bears baseball team.

Up in Camden, the pecan crop was damaged. In Jackson, cotton was stripped and corn knocked down. In Georgiana, water rose over the roads and the L & N railroad tracks fell silent. Days passed before trains could chug south.

On Mobile Bay, workers on the tugboat Echo saw thousands of dead mullet and redfish. The fish, they said, died when winds blew the water out of the Bay.

But Mobile escaped the overwhelming damage seen in Miami, Pensacola, and other coastal cities. Having dropped from Category 4 to 3, and soon moving inland, the hurricane fell apart.

A feud erupted between The Birmingham News and the people of Mobile. The Birmingham paper contended that the Alabama State Docks project in Mobile had suffered $200,000 worth of damage. Mayor Hartwell said these accounts were shamefully exaggerated.

A billboard, half-submerged by waters from the Hurricane of 1926, promotes
Studebaker, while automobiles capsize on flooded streets. Although the Hurricane of 1926 did not leave behind as much devastation in the Mobile area
as some other storms—the Hurricane of 1906 was responsible for the deaths
of hundreds—meteorologists believe that the storm, wrecking parts of Miami and churning into the Gulf Coast, took a path that would have made it
one of the most catastrophic in U.S. history by today's standards. (Erik Overbey Collection, University of South Alabama Archives)

J. L. Bedsole, president of the Chamber of Commerce, emphasized
"the need to discourage and stop if we can the disposition of anyone
to give out erroneous reports as to exaggerated damages."

By Thursday night, Sept. 23, as accounts of the destruction in
Pensacola were still rolling in—the wreckage of planes at the Naval
Air Station, the washing up of the steamer Cardonia onto the beach
—Mobilians were resuming their normal activities.

Five thousand boxing fans, in fact, crowded outside the Mobile Register and News-Item offices to hear the results of the Jack

Dempsey–Gene Tunney match in Philadelphia. As sports reporters received the blow-by-blow details by telegraph, they ran to the doors and reported the fight by megaphone.

"So great was the throng," the newspaper reported, "the Register employed two callers, one at each end of the building, to assure that everyone within hearing distance should get full benefit of the returns."

• • •

Since 1953 tropical storms and hurricanes have been given names. . . . If a hurricane becomes strong and causes significant damage, the name is retired from the list. Andrew, Audrey, Betsy, Camille, Frederic, Hugo and Opal are examples of names that have been retired.

Alabama Hurricane Awareness Week publication

Like a huge brain, the National Weather Service's Doppler radar rests on a high tower near Mobile Regional Airport, receiving impulses from the sky. In a way unimaginable in 1926, the radar reports on thunderstorms sweeping toward Destin, or high winds at Pass Christian.

If the barometer plummets, and counterclockwise winds begin to swirl, the National Hurricane Center in Miami takes charge, issuing its warnings. While thinking back to Frederic or Camille—or keeping a wary eye on Danny—we haul in the lawn furniture, gas up the car, dig out the transistor radio and flashlights.

Before weather satellites searched the skies, we were far more vulnerable to the elements. Hurricane forecasts were limited, even though, in 1926, Mobile meteorologist Albert Ashenberger watched every down-tick of the barometer.

Citizens in those days were skeptical, in general, of weather forecasting. It was hard enough predicting the daily conditions. "When we saw Ashenberger in his bathing suit on the Fairhope Pier," quips Jack Stapleton, "then we knew it was going to be a sunny day."

Gary Beeler, warning coordination meteorologist at the National

Weather Service in Mobile, says the best way you could tell if a hurricane was coming in 1926 was to go down to the beach and look at the water—or get reports from ships that had witnessed it.

As Beeler stands before the bank of computers at the National Weather Service, tracking the tropical disturbance that will become Danny, he admits, "A hurricane is like a giant gorilla. It goes where it wants to go."

When a storm bore down on Galveston, Texas, in 1900, Beeler says, the weatherman ran through town, beseeching people to evacuate. Eight thousand died in that storm.

• • •

Ana, Bill, Claudette, Danny, Erika, Fabian, Grace, Henri, Isabel, Juan, Kate, Larry, Mindy, Nicholas, Odette . . .
                  Names for 1997 Storms, National Weather Service

"I'm a hurricane nut," admits Keith Blackwell, assistant professor of meteorology at University of South Alabama, who talks of hurricanes past as though reminiscing about difficult friends.

He speaks about the storm path of 1926 as though it occurred yesterday; he says its path, coming from the southeast, was akin to the path of Hurricane Elena in 1985 and Erin in 1995. The storm path of 1916, barreling in from the south, was like Frederic's in 1979.

A storm coming in from the southwest, he contends, is one of the most hazardous for Mobile.

Frederic, he says, was an asymmetrical storm, with thunderstorms to the north and west of the eye. Camille, a symmetrical storm, was "well-formed, picturesque, pretty from a satellite—but terrible underneath. The 1926 hurricane," he conjectures, "was symmetrical, too."

At USA's Coastal Weather Research Center, he fields calls from numerous clients—power companies, chemical companies, nurseries —inquiring about Danny. On Wednesday afternoon, July 16, the storm is still small and is drifting northward, toward Louisiana. Blackwell, though, offers various charts—computer printouts of weather systems from Arkansas to Florida—and determines that the storm may build and hit us dead on.

Blackwell's fascination with hurricanes came from his grandfather, Gordon Blackwell Sr., who worked near the Mobile docks and told him stories about the hurricanes of 1926 and 1916. In the earlier storm, his grandfather had chased barrels upriver when rushing waters bore them away.

By the time Camille lashed into the Mississippi coast in 1969, Blackwell was a teen-ager. Seeing the devastation that Camille wrought, he decided to spend his life studying hurricanes.

"People in Mobile in the early part of the century had respect for hurricanes," he says. "They weren't complacent. After 1926 we went 50 years without a major storm. People got complacent again.

"But in 1926, when a brisk, northeast wind started late in summer, and it was warm and humid, people began to relate it to a hurricane."

On a television situated among the computers, a local weather lady is explaining why Danny probably will not affect Mobile at all. "No, no," Blackwell protests, talking back to the screen.

Waiting for Georges

September 26, 1998

Before dawn a crescent moon rode the stars above Mobile Bay and a breeze blew off the shore. Where I walked down to a dock and looked out over calm waters, the year could have been 1906, '16, or '26, but it was nearly the end of the century and broadcast waves, silent as the moon, suffused the air.

Back inside those waves turned into noisy pictures on my TV—

flattened houses, flooded streets, people speaking Spanish in the Dominican Republic, and sobbing. The set of pictures changed to palm trees bent double, people speaking English before blasted bungalows in the Florida Keys.

Our Saturday sun eventually came up beneath a dome of blue but pictures of what the storm had left behind south of us, and what it promises for us, or our neighbors, repeatedly filled our eyes.

In the realm of politics we hotly debate how much we need to know about the intimate lives of public figures. In the realm of weather, a phenomenon that can roil us even more than politics, we need to know everything about characters like Frederic, Opal, Danny and Earl. How big their girth, how fast their gait, how hard their blow—their vital signs are our business, above all which way they plan to go.

This information about Georges set us to crisscrossing our windows with tape, like the three women at Delish's Dessert in midtown Mobile making creative zigzags on the window, peeping out at the heavy traffic at the ABC liquor store across the street.

Throughout town we boarded up our windows—the empty storefronts of Dauphin Street, long boarded up anyway, suddenly did not look forlorn. They appeared to be readied for the storm.

Those of us who usually wait until our gas tanks are on "E" before filling them were compelled to take our places in growing lines. At the Shell station at Ann and Government, I chatted with the station owner and a young attorney about how Internet sites affect our perceptions of advancing weather, and the anxiety that comes from those perceptions—lofty chitchat for guys pumping gas.

We acquired ever more batteries. By Saturday's end I had so many still unopened, in every combination of the alphabet, that their expiration date, March 2002, might arrive before our multiple flashlights run down. While buying batteries I bumped into the butcher from our grocery store. All day long he'd been selling huge quantities of meat—principally ham and other cured meats, he told me—but what he himself needed was a certain sized battery. The store had only three; he was off to find one more.

The butcher, the baker, and the candlestick maker—we turned to all of them the last few days and they turned to each other. We lined up for the lumber man, dairy man and ice man, too. Then we raced back to our TVs to see if Georges was bearing down.

There is a familiar drill, a high-stakes rehearsal, in preparing for a storm. If Georges makes landfall here, the ritual will be played out fully. In front of Fairhope Hardware, owner Bill Baldwin explained to me that after customers buy the necessary goods in this "preparation phase" they will return, during the "sustaining phase," for kerosene and Coleman fuels. During the "clean-up phase" the brisk trade will be in chain saws.

For those from elsewhere, though, an approaching hurricane brings troubling uncertainty. Gena McKay, a nurse who moved here from Chicago, is deeply anxious about Georges, having weathered countless medical dramas but no hurricanes in her Illinois past. How do I tape my windows, she asked?

For all of us it can bring dread.

Of all the natural disasters a hurricane is the slowest to arrive. Earthquakes, volcanoes, tsunamis, tornadoes, ice storms all catch us, more or less, by surprise. I cannot imagine the composure that San Franciscans feel while living on the San Andreas fault; some of them, I know, cannot imagine living on a coast where catastrophe takes days to arrive. At a San Francisco science museum I once visited an exhibition where we stood in a dark room and felt the floor shake and heard crashes over our head. I came out of that simulated earthquake realizing that I preferred the drawn-out menace of sea-monsters like Georges. A woman at the exhibition told me she could more easily cope with her grim hometown threat—the ground splitting beneath her feet.

I vote for turbulent winds.

Yesterday we watched Georges just off the Keys, this morning plowing through the Gulf, by nightfall who knows where? Like an object sighted by telescope hurtling down to earth from the sky, we know it will eventually hit. If we pray that it will not be us, does that mean we wish it on our neighbors?

A World of Water

September 29, 1998

The Eskimo culture has dozens of words to describe snow. On the Gulf Coast, now being pummeled by Georges, we need as many ways to talk about water.

There is the water of Mobile Bay not far from my door. By yesterday it had turned ferocious as the Atlantic Ocean in a squall, ripping the piers of Eastern Shore homes, chewing the Grand Hotel's wharf, creeping into its rooms.

There was the water that surged from the Bay to pound the yards. It formed lakes. The debris—leaves and sticks, a board with nails—seemed as treacherous as snakes.

There was the water that formed a spot on the ceiling, beading, spreading, dripping, banging a pail. It was the sound of coins that will be spent, *ching-ching,* on repairs.

There was the water that kept us indoors all day long so that when we drew back the curtains there were curtains of rain, and when our power went out and we cracked the windows for fresh air, rain spritzed our faces.

We have seen all those forms of water through our counties—water propelled by wind that ruined crops, flooded streets, ripped off roofs, clogged sewers.

It was water that fell on our heads or stung our faces like BBs, water that, on the Mississippi coast, did what no wild fluctuation of the stock market or crisis in Washington could ever do—shut down casinos. Water on Dauphin Island that reminded us that barrier islands are slivers of dune between a mainland and the deep blue sea.

The water from Georges kept us tuned to our TVs and our transistor radios, and when we got tired of hearing what we knew already—that the hurricane was beating down on us—it became part of the talk we carried on with family and friends. One of my oldest childhood friends is William Oppenheimer. I will think of him always, now, as the first person to phone me from far away—from inland, west Mobile—as soon as Hurricane Danny, and now Hurricane Georges, began to chew up our shore.

If we began this hurricane by going out in droves to grocery stores, hardware stores and video stores, we continued it by retreating indoors to make use of what we'd hoarded. We pulled out the Scrabble, the chess, the card games, the flashlights and rehashed old storms. We added a new name to our shared history, too. Like Camille, Opal, and Erin, Georges is not a usual Gulf Coast name. If we were assaulted by Ashley, Charles or Caroline—or even plain George—we'd be teasing plenty of our friends who have those old Mobile names. I'd suspect there will soon be a few Georgeses among us, though—a day or two old.

September 28, when Georges visited us, was my daughter's 11th birthday. She will remember it always, I suspect, by the school that was closed, the yard that was flooded, the electricity that was gone. Since all her friends were stranded in their own homes elsewhere, we went on a family adventure to our very own Splash Mountain to celebrate—the edge of Mobile Bay.

I grasped her hand so she would not be knocked off her feet. We sloshed to the Bay and saw the wreckage of piers, a sailboat thrown near a tree, benches overturned and the ocean in the place where Mobile Bay used to be.

Back inside she began to open her presents, the storm's mid-day gloom brightened by two table candles and the only baked goods we had that were festive—a few muffins.

While she was opening her presents the electricity, to her thrill, surged on reviving the TV, the videotape player and the freezer where the ice cream had been melting.

Our house suddenly lit up like her cake. But those candles soon went out. The power went back down.

The world outside our windows was lost to water.

Jubilee!

On Mobile Bay there is a phenomenon we call a "jubilee." Beyond all the definitions in my dictionary linking the word to religious celebrations, or the singing of spirituals, to Mobilians "jubilee" speaks of fish.

There are different theories why our particular sort of jubilee occurs. Just ask an old-timer the reason and you'll be regaled with any number of theories. One may be that the fresh water and salt water are in a constantly shifting balance in Mobile Bay, and during a jubilee the fish press up to the shore hungering for oxygen. Another is that other forms of sealife—algae, plankton—affect the water, making the fish surrender themselves at the shore.

We're not sure when jubilees will occur, but there are theories on that, too. There are signs, the old-timers and jubilee-watchers say. Just be patient.

2:30 A.M., Saturday morning. We are jolted out of sleep by a pounding at the door.

There is no storm looming in the Gulf tonight. What is it this time? A fire? My wife hurries out, seeing her brother Matt, a doctor. Is somebody hurt?

I hear the door opening and Nancy talking to Matt and suddenly relaying to the household in a shout: "It's a jubilee!"

No matter that we're half-awake, we fumble around for our old clothes and sneakers, repeating the magic word. Where is the wash bucket? The crab net?

In our guest room Kumiko Uchida, 13, an exchange student from

Ichihara, Japan, a Mobile sister-city, is perplexed when we rouse her. She speaks little English.

"Kumiko," my daughter Meredith tells her. "Fishing."

"Fishing," Kumiko answers politely, "OK." She glances at her clock. Yet another unusual American custom?

Fully awake now we head outside. The night is crystal clear, the stars just beyond the oak trees. An offshore breeze, after brutal July heat, is cool.

Matt had predicted this occurrence, he tells us, and stayed up watching the waters. Hot weather, heavy rains, offshore breeze, super calm, incoming tide—those are signs, he explains. Others tell us they were waiting, too. A mini-jubilee the day before put everyone in the mood.

"Jubilee!" a voice peals.

Propane lanterns dance along the shore. Flashlight beams move across pilings. In the early darkness, with the parade of lights and the commotion of fish, the jubilee seems like a dream.

In the shallows flounders drift woozily. Grandaddy flounders, middle-sized flounders, baby flounders—they are underfoot like slippery tiles.

In some jubilees only crabs come to the shoreline; in others, shrimp. By tonight fresh flounder will be the entree.

The young girls in our group turn to little warriors. Kumiko takes the gig, lifts it high and plunges it deeply. She brings up a huge flounder, its white undersides shining in the glow of a propane lantern. Frances jabs the point into the shallows. The water churns, sign of a strike.

Meredith tries to grab one; she lays her hands on the sluggish fish before it scoots away.

The Bay's bounty comes as mixed blessings. Through the water weave thousands of eels. They slither by our ankles, bump into our shoes. One woman rams her gig down and pulls up not a flounder, but a stingray.

Near us a man poles along in a skiff, stopping to spear flounder and tossing them to the bottom of his boat. Rather than gig only large ones he sticks anything he can find. Another man leans from a pier and shakes his head, saying it's not right to take the babies. The man poles on, slashing at the water.

Parties are starting near the shore. Burton Clark, a Mobile Realtor, had invited his three sisters to come visit at his wife's family house on the Bay this weekend. In an odd kind of family reunion they stand high on a pier, catching up on old times while people below impale fish at 4 a.m.

Arthur Davis, who drove over from Magnolia Springs after sensing the right conditions, hopes to make some extra money selling his catch—more than 100 flounder he tugs on a line. His weapon—"the Cadillac of gigs," he says—is a homemade 5-foot stainless steel rod with stringer attached. In one motion he pierces the fish and strings it on the line.

As word goes out through the towns about the jubilee—a plentiful one, folks proclaim, that is stretching from the Grand Hotel down past Zundel's Wharf—more people arrive, some not nearly as well-equipped as Davis.

Some improvise. A man carries a three-pronged hayfork for a gig. Time and again he brings up two flounders at once. A woman has a bamboo rod she has whittled to a fine point. Behind them, two wash-tubs ride the shallows, tugged along by a string.

It does not take long for my family and friends to reach our limit—our buckets are soon full. Throughout Ichihara, Japan, when Kumiko returns to her family, this night of pre-dawn fish-gigging in Mobile Bay will become part of their sister-city lore. We will search the Japanese-English dictionary to explain this custom is not a weekly one.

On the beach just past Zundel's Wharf I come across two jubilee philosophers sitting on a log.

They have an ice chest heaped with flounder.

The younger man tells me his name is Tut. "Just Tut," he says, "like King Tut."

He meditates a moment on how to prepare flounder, an issue

uppermost on the minds of us fortunate enough to have family or friends who pounded on our door yelling, "Jubilee!"

He suggests that the best way to fix flounder is to make a diamond-cut on the back, slather it in seasoning and garlic butter, and run it under the broiler.

As light breaks through the sky, and countless gulls sweep down to take their turn at the jubilee, too, Tut gathers up his haul and says it's time to go home—and begin breakfast.

PART III

THROUGH THE COUNTRYSIDE

❖

I grew up on a lawn, not on the land. The midtown street of my childhood, Williams Court, is a leafy, out-of-the-way block, a haven for kids on bikes and families on porches and neighbors visiting casually through the summertime dusk—and far from fields of cotton, cattle, and cane. I approach the countryside like a tourist, driving down rural highways—thus, it made sense I'd write about Old Highway 90.

What I can tell about the land out my car window is this—people are developing more of it, farming less of it. The signs are the give-away: "For Sale. Will Divide. Residential or Commercial." As one cotton farmer explained it to me recently: Why should a young person who's heir to a farm wish to take on a chancy, round-the-clock, year-round enterprise, when he can sell that land to a real estate developer and take hard cash?

The sheer livability of south Alabama—Baldwin County is grow-ing by leaps and bounds—means more people want to move there to build rather than plow. The development of once-small towns like Foley, Ala., into busy crossroads with movie complexes and outlet stores, or once far-flung neighborhoods like Tillman's Corner in Mo-bile into self-contained commercial centers, means that residents can make a living oblivious to the harvest.

But the land continues on, ultimately oblivious to man. From a story about the return of cotton to south Alabama, to a portrait of a village in Choctaw County where cane syrup–making is still an art, to a watercolor of pecan orchards—both quiet and noisy—I discov-ered that, for many, the land still rules.

Old Highway 90

An interstate is an endless stretch of asphalt, but a highway is a long string of lives.

For many years I have driven the Gulf Coast like most Americans: pushing 70 along I-10, watching the fast-food franchises and service station signs repetitively slide by.

But another highway shadows this one, a local road that was once the central artery of traffic—born of the era when fancy motels offered tourist cottages and gas station attendants would never have suggested "pump it yourself."

That road is U.S. Highway 90, still two lanes in places, running past ranch houses, antebellum homes, trailer parks, junked cars, farm stands, convenience stores, cows, horses and speedways. It is known in various places as Mobile Highway, Old Spanish Trail, the Causeway, Government Street, Halls Mill Road, Blue Star and Jeff Davis highways.

It offers a driver the rare hill, yet oaks as gnarled as time. Never far from the water—at least as the sea gull flies—it has seen blistering heat and hurricane winds. It has watched families benignly rolling along in station wagons and lone men guzzling beer and wrapping their cars around telephone poles. It has carried hunters and fishermen and gamblers and romantic couples, licit and otherwise.

The Interstate may have left behind the starlight motels and diners, but it has left, in its wake, communities not unlike small river towns—each a distinctive community unto itself but linked to all the others.

• • •

It may appear, in places, to be a lonesome, country road—as it surely does here in south Mobile County between Irvington and Grand Bay—but U.S. Highway 90 was once as busy as its modern, Interstate parallel, I-10. By driving Highway 90 across Alabama today—from the Florida to the Mississippi line—one can catch glimpses of its past and hear stories of its heyday. Tales unfold of a mostly vanished roadside culture, from general stores along its rural stretches, to racy motels on the outskirts of town, to its lethal hazards like Dead Man's Curve. (G. M. Andrews, Mobile Register)

One of the quietest stretches of 90 begins as Mobile Highway, which is not in Alabama at all but in the last miles of Florida. Just beyond a yard of rusting tractors and boats, the two-lane blacktop passes over the River Styx to Seminole, Ala.

Greeted first by the highway sign that tells me Fob James is governor and next by a poster of screen star Jeff Bridges in front of the Seminole Video Store, I make my way to Mitchell's Mercantile—a general store started in 1929 that sold men's work clothes but now is a small grocery that seems to function as town square.

Carolyn Mitchell, who manages the store for her son Eddie—the principal of Daphne Middle School—seems to know every person who comes in the store. When the town once had its own post office, Mrs. Mitchell was its postmaster; now it is a rural route.

Before Interstate 10 was completed from Spanish Fort to Pensacola in the 1970s, Seminole bustled with traffic. Mrs. Mitchell gestures across the quiet road to the site of a former truck stop: "I've seen times you couldn't put a tractor trailer there," she recalls.

"It used to be so busy here you could hardly get across the road. When Eddie played football for Robertsdale High and would come home late, I'd be worried he'd be in an accident. I wouldn't sleep until he came home."

A lean man in a blue work shirt enters.

"How much I owe you this week?" he asks, fretting, "I know it's going to be high."

Mrs. Mitchell punches at the cash register keys.

"Slow down, girl," he mutters.

When she tells him the amount, he peels several bills from his roll of hard-earned dollars.

"You know who you can give credit to around here," she tells me.

One customer, J. R. Gulledge, who indeed looks a little like Jeff Bridges with florid arm tattoos, drives his 18-wheeler from Marianna, Fla., to Mobile hauling equipment to farms cultivating corn, cotton and soybeans. With his mother's having driven a school bus on this highway when he was a boy, it's as though the road just stayed part of him.

"I'd rather drive Highway 90 than the Interstate," he explains. "I see something different every day. I might see a deer. Or five deer."

After hearing about other stretches of the highway between here and Robertsdale—about a man who tends goats, about another who deals buggies and other antiques—I leave and drive by those goats and buggies, by quarter-horse farms, soybean crops and driveway signs printed with Scriptures.

At the end of this bucolic road, where 90 is swallowed up by Alabama Highway 59 and its cavalcade of beach-goers, I stop at the BP station and ask a young woman behind the counter for directions.

"Am I in Loxley?"

"No," she corrects me. "This is Robertsdale. Loxley's just a little, small town."

By Burris' fruit market, by fried chicken franchises and the Loxley town hall, I hunt for Highway 90 again, finding where it splits off from 59, reassuming its rural identity. I pass an automobile graveyard. Looking out at rusting and dated Chevies and Olds, I suspect many of them once crowded this road.

• • •

At the junction of 27 is Malbis, a community founded by Jason Malbis, a Greek immigrant, in 1906. The private village is still populated principally by family members, as I am told by Gertrude Malbis, who gives tours of the magnificent Greek Orthodox church that stands a few hundred yards from Highway 90.

If this Byzantine chapel seems to stand outside of time in its pristine beauty, the Malbis motel, back on the highway, seems of another era, too—a highway billboard promotes "Color TV," with a sign for "Satellite TV" added later. Maxine Hicks, who works at the motel desk, used to waitress at the complex's restaurant in the early 1960s and remembers how Mobilians "used to ride over on 90 just to eat the gumbo."

She also recalls when George Wallace stayed at the motel, and one Easter Sunday, long ago, "when the air conditioning went out in the restaurant but we stayed too busy to stop even a minute. We worked ourselves to death."

The restaurant is no longer open for dinner.

Driving on, I am stirred by the sight of Mobile Bay, stretched out, glittering. The way for one to catch its atmosphere, though, is not while speeding along the elevated Interstate 10 Bayway but from poking along the local Causeway, cold drink from Argiro's package store at hand, car windows open.

"There's nothing like the Causeway," says Evelyn Johnston, owner of the Blue Gill Restaurant, which was part of a fishing camp when she opened it with her husband, Wallace, in 1957. "You get it in your blood."

Judging by the customers who greet her—some have booths named in their honor—this stretch of road, like the one at Seminole, is virtually a village unto itself. "The customers are my family," explains Mrs. Johnston, who counts politicians among them. "We welcome both parties alike," she teases a visitor, "Republicans pay cash."

The story of the Blue Gill, like other restaurants that flourish here, is one also of survival—or renewal. Mrs. Johnston thinks back to the days before Hurricane Frederic when far more restaurants—Silver King, Sea Ranch, Ben's, Palmer's—stood along the road. She returned after the storm in 1979 to find the Blue Gill structurally intact. "I knew I was so lucky."

I drive on past the U.S.S. Alabama, which will always put me in mind of our grammar school fund-raising drive to contribute to its arrival, and pass through Bankhead Tunnel, which reminds me of the guards who used to pace its internal ramps. I'd feel sorry for them, breathing our fumes as my family sped to vacation homes.

• • •

The next morning, I pick up Highway 90 at the Loop—not the four-laned road of car dealerships and shopping centers that opened in the early 1950s, but Old Highway 90, Halls Mill Road.

"Get your hiney to the Tiny Diny on Highway Ninety." It is an old slogan, I am told, from the days when the Tiny Diny sat across the street from its present location and curb hops serviced the drivers wheeling up in their convertibles.

I hear this, and a great deal more Highway 90 lore, while breakfasting at the Tiny Diny, surrounded by what the Rev. Thomas Weise, a Mobile Catholic priest, calls "the truth table." "If you sit at this table," he jokes, passing by, "you have to tell the truth."

Every morning, at this table, congregate men who swap stories and regale a visitor with their own embroidered truths. Among them is Bill Darnell, who now works as a constable but who once, as a show promoter, booked Elvis Presley for a concert at Blakeley Island.

These regulars tell me of a time when Old Highway 90 was vibrant with motels—Canary Cottages, Stars and Stripes, Maryann's Tourist Court—and late-night social spots such as the Club Manor and Copa.

Another motel, said to be busy with amorous goings-on, "got so hot it used to catch sparks," recounts one man at the table.

Darnell tells about tragedy on the highway, too: about Dead Man's Curve, close to Grand Bay, not straightened out until the late 1940s and where so many drivers made their last mile. While once riding a Harley-Davidson motorcycle there, Darnell watched a friend, on another motorcycle, lose his life: "He hit something on the road—and went flying."

I drive on past the Farmer's Market and to Tillman's Corner, once literally just a corner, I learn, with a store owned by a Mr. Tillman, but now a bustling thoroughfare close to where I-10 cuts across the local highway. At Theodore, set back in a field of grass and trees, is one of the few residences left along this part of Highway 90, crowded with used car lots and super stores: the home of 92-year-old Henry Edgar Bolton and his wife, Constance.

Bolton was born close to Highway 90, on the other side of the L & N tracks, and remembers clearly when the highway was a dirt road traversed by horses and wagons. His father helped build the Baptist church in 1896, now called the Little White Church, that's been moved to Bellingrath Road. Mrs. Bolton, a Wisconsin native, came to Irvington with her family, farther up the road on 90, when she was only 4. Her father had responded to advertisements to come south to work in the satsuma-growing business.

As the Boltons recount freezes that ruined crops, wind storms that hurt farming, they also remember riding on Highway 90 and smelling the sweet satsuma blossoms. While they speak positively of developments on the highway—"Any improvement will change a way of life," Mr. Bolton says—the commercial buildup is daunting. "Sometimes you can't get out of the driveway," Mrs. Bolton warns.

When I head out of their drive, in fact, I wait long moments before a break in traffic allows me to enter the flow of the highway.

• • •

Within 10 minutes I am back where 90 becomes empty again, driving the road by St. Elmo, Irvington and Grand Bay, making my way to the Mississippi state line. Years have passed since I have taken this road, and as I watch the L & N tracks on the left—the old highway paralleled its tracks to the Mississippi coast—I could be driving back in time. Only the Irvington Speedway and a few people at Palmer's gas station in T-shirts with the names of Mississippi gambling casinos bring me back to the present.

At Freeland's Produce in Grand Bay, Hiram Freeland recalls how, when this highway was the main route to Biloxi and New Orleans, there were seven gas stations nearby. There's not nearly as much traffic as then, but light industry in the area and local customers—"people come here to buy peanuts before going to the speedway"—keep stores busy. He remembers, from when he was a boy, how the bag of mail was delivered by the L & N train and how his uncle, the post-master, used to stand by the tracks and hand the sack of out-going mail up to the express train. A hand reached down and snatched it up as the train hurtled by.

As Freeland shows a customer from Pascagoula varieties of water-melons he grows and sells—among them, "All Sweet," "Jubilee," "Black Diamond" and "Sugar Baby"—I say good-bye and drive to Mississippi. Before long, I see roadside bars and I am reminded of times, as a teen-ager, when I drove with other boys to this state line to obtain beer. As I turn back to the Alabama line, I say a hopeless prayer that no teen-agers will ever again be as foolish as were we.

Just before Grand Bay, with the skies beginning to send down a deluge, I turn off to explore an arc of old roadway that runs through the woods and realize this was Dead Man's Curve. With thunder rolling around me and my windshield beginning to mist, I come out the other end of the curve, onto Highway 90 again, relieved to find four lanes, good markers and clear road signs leading home.

King Cotton's New Face

When Alabama skies are autumn blue and fields are fluffed with cotton, there is music in the air. It is not the exaltation of "Dixie" with its nostalgia for "the land of cotton," nor the work songs of a day when rag-headed workers bent under broiling sun.

The music of today's cotton fields comes from the radio of Teal Corte III, who drives a picker in Baldwin County, listening to the Sports Babe on talk radio; from the Walkman of a module operator nicknamed Stick, who has rap music pouring into his head; from Nida Nettles' hydraulics booth at the Loxley gin, where, through the din, rock music blares.

Forty years ago, most of the cotton left Baldwin and Mobile counties, and with it the back-breaking, gospel-singing lore of field hands and overseers riding herd. "Go around and ask about picking cotton by hand and some people'll cuss you out," jokes Stick, whose mother, clearly without romance, picked from sunup 'til dusk in the 1940s.

In the 1950s laborers wanted year-round employment in the city, grains were easier and more productive to grow, and mechanization meant big overhead costs that family farms could not handle.

But since the late '80s in Mobile County, and the early '90s in Baldwin County, cotton has been making a return. With the defeat of the boll weevil, genetic engineering of plants, and the decline of grain prices during the 1980s, cotton has become attractive again.

Not only the field music has changed. In big operations like Corte Land and Cattle, in Baldwin County, and Driskell Cotton Farms in Mobile County, computer screens flicker with the changing prices of crops on the Chicago Commodities Exchange, and the farmers' fickle companion, the weather, is monitored 24 hours a day through satel-

Teal Corte stands tall amid the cotton on Baldwin County land that has been
in his family for a hundred years. Parked behind him is a vehicle he commandeers—a cotton picker valued at about $150,000 that moves through
the bright fields at nearly 4 mph, swiftly completing the task that laborers
did by hand. When the picker is filled, Teal will dump the cotton into a
module at the edge of the field; when the module is stuffed, it will be hauled
to the gin, the nearest being Alabama Gin in Loxley. (Bill Starling, Mobile
Register)

lite data transmissions. "The weather screen," says Arthur Corte, "is our second Bible."

In fall, when huge pickers rake through thousands of acres of flowering bolls, cotton farming entails a high-wire act of labor, mechanization, and faith. That churches are situated across the road from fields throughout this area suggests the fortitude still required to tend cotton, even as the beat of the music has changed.

• • •

The story of cotton, like much farming here, is one of families. For the Cortes and Bertollas, an extended farming clan in Baldwin County, it begins in the Italian Alps, at the end of the 19th century.

Leaving a small patch of land on a rugged hillside, Alessandro Bertolla traveled to America and made his way to Minnesota. His sister married another Italian immigrant, Angelo Corte. Seizing on opportunities to travel south and buy land being advertised along the railroad line, the families traveled to Baldwin County. "What my grandfather did inspires me," says Arthur Corte.

"This county was being colonized by land developers," explains Andy Bertolla, who farms cotton and runs Bertolla Farm Supply. "They were trying to sell land, which in those days meant plots of eighty acres, not a half acre in Lake Forest."

Baldwin County may now be largely flat, treeless fields, but a hundred years ago it was covered with timber. Bertolla describes how his forebears—after timber companies took their due—helped clear the land, dragging up tree stumps with mule teams. Years later, the first iron-wheeled tractors got stuck in mud. When rubber tires came, he explains, farmers were skeptical: how could you keep them filled with air? they wondered.

In the early days there was cotton, but mostly, for the Bertollas and Cortes, there was produce: Irish potatoes and corn and sweet potatoes and later soybeans. The railroad sent this produce north. Bertolla's office in Robertsdale today is an old packing shed long owned by the family.

To look at an agricultural map of south Alabama is to gaze at a family tree: interlocking sections of land are owned by brothers and cousins. Wives sometimes handle the flow of paperwork, like Francie Herndon Bertolla, savvy in the world of faxes and computers; sons and daughters learn from the fields up. At Corte Land and Cattle, Arthur works with his cousin, and other cousins run another Corte farm.

Common knowledge has it that the family farm is dead in America, but Bertolla says that's not true at all: The family farm is alive and well, it's just got to be bigger to survive.

• • •

Harold Foster is a cotton scout.

"What I do," explains the soft-spoken Mississippi Delta native, "is babysit the cotton." Wading hip-high through a field of leafy plants (a field is defoliated only 10 to 12 days before picking), Foster explains how if cotton is left to grow wild it will tower over your head. He uses terms like "growth regulators" and "genetic engineering" to explain innovations in plant design.

Foster has been breathing and living cotton since he was one of eleven children of a farm mechanic on the Mississippi Delta in the 1940s, and came home after school to carry a sack through the fields.

"When you pick it by hand," he says, "you have to be careful how you grab the cotton locks. It can cut you up."

Foster remembers when the first, one-row cotton picker came out. Now machine pickers eat through four rows at a time.

In his 55 years Foster has seen it all: boll weevil, boll worm, drought, flood, bad soil. To hear Foster and cotton farmers tell it, the saga of cotton growers is not unlike the trek of the Israelites from Egypt to Canaan. Gin blow-outs, hurricanes, bugs—at every point along the way a different setback awaits.

To old-timers it seems a miracle that this season's variety—Nucotton 33, engineered by Monsanto and Deltapine—stops boll worms after one bite. Cotton's ancient nemesis, the boll weevil, is fought by the government's eradication program which places traps in the fields. If boll weevils appear, it's time to take protective action.

The average American throwing on a cotton shirt in the morning has little notion of what this saga entails.

As a cotton guru, Foster can help farmers do what's best for their crop. With the constant marketing of cotton varieties and chemicals, the consultant can help balance the farmer's needs.

Foster touches the cotton plants and the open bolls, turns them, goes home and comes back in the afternoon, then the next morning. He watches the skies for rain and checks the soil for dampness and when it's time he is the one to say, "OK, go ahead, let the picking begin."

• • •

Through the hot, bright cotton fields of Corte Land and Cattle, Teal Corte, 30, drives a picker. High up in the air-conditioned cab, watching the digital speedometer reach 3.7 mph, he pilots the $150,000 piece of machinery down the rows. A windmill stands dormant at the field's edge; it used to draw water for cattle that once grazed here. On other Corte acres, where soybeans or potatoes grew, cotton has taken its place.

This land, Teal explains, has been in the family for a hundred years, otherwise there'd be little way for a farmer to obtain it today. He'll spend his life here most likely. He came up through the family business, although he did leave for a while, back in the '80s, "when produce was down and there wasn't much happening on the farm." He went to Sun Valley where friends he made kidded him about being "like Jethro from The Beverly Hillbillies."

When Teal's cotton picker fills he drives it to a "module," which looks like a big trough. The back of the picker groans to one side, spilling its contents. An avalanche of cotton cascades into the trough; when filled, it will be hauled to the gin.

Working the gears of one module, standing all day in the broiling sun, is Randy Hastings. He wears a T-shirt that says "Bourgeois Pigs."

"People ask me what that means and I say I have no idea," Randy says, "but I bought it at a rodeo out West. When I'm not out here working in the cotton fields I like to team rope for fun."

As if the long, Dixie day does not already provide enough wear on his body, he adds: "That's what I'd be doing right now if I wasn't standing here. Roping."

• • •

It is early in the morning in Grand Bay when Darrell Driskell and his brother Dillard lean against the hood of a maroon pickup truck and talk about cotton farming with a visitor. They can trace their lineage back to South Carolina, and from there, to England. Their late father, J. A. Driskell, came here with his grandfather as a boy. They began farming in Mobile County.

No matter that it's thousands of miles from Grand Bay to Beijing or Moscow. "It used to be you worried what your neighbor was farming," says Darrell. "Then you worried about what they were growing in the next state—that was your competition. Now you got to compete with the whole world."

The rain is beginning to spatter on the hood of the truck and they cast a worried eye up at the heavens. The bolls are opening and the season is beginning and racing dark clouds do not bode well.

"Being a farmer is like being a doctor," says Darrell. "You're always on call, and under a lot of stress."

Dillard adds: "But doctors don't have the money-stress like farmers do."

They head into the farm office where the weather screen on his computer shows an alarming red dot moving toward them quickly. The wind begins to bang on the cotton picker outside. Lightning cracks the skies.

They grow quiet, listening to the howling, knowing what it means to be at the mercy of the elements. These weeks the cotton, painting the Alabama countryside with a bright brush, is vulnerable: too much water will ruin it. High wind will knock it loose as a prize fighter's teeth.

The lights flicker; go off. The computer screen dies. In the other room is the sound of the fax machine clicking off, on; off again.

"Sixty-five-mile-an-hour winds," Darrell says, and Dillard nods. "Close to a tornado."

Moments later the sky is black but the winds have quieted. Without leaving his chair Darrell figures that the passing storm affected 100 acres, and cost $20 to $30 an acre. High rollers at Biloxi casinos have nothing on these men. It takes a lot of time to grow equity in cotton, but it can plummet in a bad afternoon. Nobody makes "a joke about hurricanes" around here.

"But there's nothing we can do about the weather," Darrell says stoically. "Whatever the good Lord sends, we just deal with it."

• • •

Nothing signals the return of cotton to south Alabama so much as the presence of two recently built cotton gins, Producers' Gin in Theodore and Alabama Gin in Loxley. Farmers no longer have to haul their seed cotton to Atmore or McCullough.

The Loxley gin manager, Mark Nettles, learned cotton in Louisiana, and presides over an operation of high-tech vacuums and heaters and balers that look like a nuclear reactor. Instead of splitting atoms the gin accomplishes what, for generations, seemed just as confounding: separating the seed from the lint. As seeds are rapidly sawed out of the lint they rain like hail into one trough; down a nearby chute comes an avalanche of cleaned cotton. Moments later, out of high-pressure chambers, appear neat, tightly packed bales. It is a magic show unimaginable fifty years ago.

Nettles, like others in the business, was glad to see the appearance of wrinkle-free cotton shirts, and the public mania for polyester wane slightly. "Nothing worse than wearing polyester on a hot day," says one gin worker. After all, every purchase of cotton napkins, tablecloths, or dresses makes the work these men do a little more in demand.

Despite the intense pressure of his job, Nettles did find time to court a bride: Nida, who walked into the gin where he worked in

Louisiana looking for a job. She was wearing red cowboy boots at the time, and it's said he took one look and said, "She's the one."

While Nettles roams the gin floor today, making sure the high-speed operation goes smoothly, Nida sits high up in the hydraulics booth. She can be there as much as 84 hours a week, working two joy sticks "like a big Nintendo game," as she puts it, that operate giant sucker hoses. The hoses draw the cotton into the processes of the gin.

Slender, 35, Redbook Magazine splayed open on the floor, music pumping, Nida would dazzle the ghost of Eli Whitney. Some folks tell her it's odd to find a woman high up in the hydraulics cab. She tells them, "It's 1996. Grow up!"

Besides, she's been waiting all year for these six weeks of cotton harvest. "When the cotton is being picked and you smell it in the air," she says, "I get it. Cotton fever. I can't wait 'til ginning season starts."

The Miller's Tale

If you ever pass through tiny Needham, Ala., a couple hours north of Mobile in Choctaw County, you probably won't notice what Clyde Dykes, a local carpenter, calls "our museum"—the sugar cane mill in the town park.

Hardly as dramatic as the statue of Vulcan in Birmingham, or the Boll Weevil Monument in Enterprise, the mill looks like nothing more than a few gears from an old industrial plant. Set down on a barren strip of dirt, where the AT & N Railroad used to run (even the tracks were stripped out after teens began to drive trucks over the crossties), the mill comes no higher than your chest, and the pile of crushed cane around it, ratty and brown, speaks little of lore.

But pull up in front of Needham Cash Grocery, directly across from the only other store, Gibson's Grocery, and ask for Columbus Manley. He'll be pouring coffee for the deer hunters who visit his lunch counter in December like camouflaged commandos.

"I had five sisters and three brothers and didn't any of them catch a name like I had," he says.

In 1919, when his mother was expecting, a farmer said he'd buy her baby a suit of clothes if she'd let him name the child. "That's how I got Columbus."

At 77, Columbus has been a logger, sawmill operator, grocer, and, in 1980, presided over the incorporation of the town and became its first mayor, serving eight years.

For his triumphs in office—among them building a $10,000 town hall with citizens pitching in labor—Needham honored him with his own "Columbus Day."

As if he had not contributed enough, at Needham's recent town fair Columbus cranked up the sugar cane mill for the first time in years. Just like his father taught him in the 1920s, he fed cane stalks through the press, funneled the extract to a pan over an outdoor furnace, separated the skimmings from the juice, tested the thickness with a paddle, and poured the syrup into buckets. He sold every last, sluggish drop.

"You never seen people so crazy for syrup," says his wife, Eathel, whose name is often mistaken as "Ethel."

Despite the rage for his old-time syrup, Columbus knew he could not play favorites—especially since he's related to most of the hundred or so citizens in town. "Even my wife's own sisters had to wait in line," he says. "People would be coming up to me and saying, 'Columbus, hold some syrup out for me.' 'I can't do that,' I told them. 'Just like everybody else, you've got to wait your turn.'"

· · ·

In Needham cooking cane syrup is what 83-year-old Lindsey Whittington calls "a tradition, but when you tell it to young people it sounds like a fairy tale." Having grown up when the area was wholly rural, Lindsey remembers decades ago when a Meridian, Miss., entrepreneur developed the town and sold the housing lots for $25 each.

"If I had ten dollars now for every stalk I fed into a cane mill when I was a boy," says Lloyd Turner, 60, "I'd go to town."

"I'm 58 and never seen a crowd like was wanting to watch the syrup-making," says Bernice Clark, a man whose first name rhymes with "furnace" and creates ample confusion when spelled out over the phone.

"Syrup was a staple," adds Manasseh Broadhead, 71, whose name at the grocery counter is "Nas."

Even Needham has another name here—Bogueloosa.

"A long time ago the town was Bogueloosa," says postmaster Arthur Broadhead, 52, Manasseh's half-brother. "When they established a post office they wouldn't let them call it Bogueloosa because of Bogalusa, Louisiana. My Daddy was the postmaster in 1922 and that's what he told me. It didn't seem right to have to change it since there are three other Needhams in the United States."

Lindsey Whittington says that the town took its new name, around 1903, from a Dr. Needham who lived down the Bogueloosa River. "He was a country doctor. He cured you with sody—baking sody."

When the AT & N Railroad, later the Frisco and then Burlington Northern, continued to call the depot Bogueloosa, townspeople split the difference. "If you got off on one side of the train," explains Manasseh, "you were in Bogueloosa, out the other, you were in Needham."

There was never a commercial sugar cane industry in this county, any more than tobacco or rice. "But we grew cane for ourselves, tobacco and rice, too," Lindsey recounts, sitting on a stool at Columbus' counter, wearing the bright orange cap he keeps on during hunting season "so the hunters don't shoot me."

That tradition often became life-supporting during the Depression, still referred to here as "the Panic." During the 1920s, E. J. Jackson Lumber Co. was a vital employer, based in nearby Riderwood, a company town at the time with its own electrical plant, ice plant, and jail. By the time Jackson Lumber "logged out" the area in the late '20s, they closed down and moved on. "It near 'bout killed us," says Lindsey.

• • •

Syrup-making is more than a tradition in Needham—it is a public right. Under the mayoralty of Columbus' nephew, Greg Manley, 39, a pharmacist, the town council decided to seek out a mill for public use and move it to the park, where a grist mill for corn had once stood by the Bogueloosa River.

Columbus was dispatched to find the mill. Rather than hunt for one that relied on mules in the turn-of-the-century fashion, he sought out a later model that could be hooked up to the drive mechanism of a tractor. It seems only fitting that the mill he found—purchased from Buddy Napier in Water Valley—has Columbus printed on its iron front. (It was manufactured in Columbus, Ga.)

To date, only Columbus himself has exercised his civic right to make syrup, but others are already thinking cane.

As Columbus fries an egg and sausage for a regular who just called from two houses down to have his plate ready, Manasseh and Bernice visit at the counter. They agree that sandy soil is ideal for growing cane, that sugar cane in all its varieties—ribbon cane, white cane and blue cane among them—makes far sweeter syrup than sorghum cane.

Someone mentions that Jesse Kelley intends to plant cane. Columbus shakes his head. "Planting's not all there is to it," he warns.

"Jesse grows those butter beans."

"You got to plow it," Columbus says, "hoe it, fertilize it, hoe it again, strip it, break the tops off and cut it down." He adds that when you do fertilize it, it's got to be with cottonseed meal. "No ammonia."

Jesse, 71, enters. Like many older men in Needham, Jesse is retired from work at the James River Corp. paper mill on the Tombigbee River in Butler. He says that, like Columbus, he learned to grind cane from his daddy. During "the Panic" he remembers federal government programs that supplied an ox and horses to help farm, and low-interest loans with the mandate to farm specific allotments of crops, like peanuts and cotton.

"Back in Rehabilitation days," he says, "we'd make up to 350 gallons of syrup a fall. We had old-fashioned blue cane, and tall, red-looking cane, called P.O.J. I don't know what P.O.J. stood for, but we said it was Poor Ol' John, after my Daddy. There was a wooden pole on the mill and the mule used to pull it."

Mary Ann Clark, "not family but related by marriage," takes her place behind the cash register. She raves about Needham's sugar cane syrup, even though she grew up in Quitman, Miss., also known for good cane. "I'm one of five sisters who married Alabama men, and three of us married Needhamites. We just figure these Alabama boys had to come to Mississippi to find the best girls."

Whether Jesse's sugar cane syrup will compete with Columbus' does not concern her; she is far more taken with his ability to play harmonica. "I've asked Jesse to play at my funeral," she says, although a youthful picture of health. "When he plays 'The Sweet By-and-By' that'll make people so sad!"

• • •

The idea to purchase the sugar cane mill and set it in the park—"we could turn that park into our own Dollywood," says postmaster Arthur Broadhead—came from Lindsey Whittington's son, Lindsey Earl Whittington, 58.

No one in America could evidence more love of his hometown than this man. Standing in his yard, pointing to kinfolks' various houses, Lindsey Earl speaks of "Needham's clear air" and artesian well water. "You'll never see a for-sale sign in front of a house here."

In this hamlet of several extended families, all white, and all attending the Assembly of God Church pastored by Brother Tim Cleveland, Lindsey Earl feels he's at the center of the world.

An armchair historian, Lindsey Earl speaks frankly of one regional tradition others only whisper about here—moonshine.

He explains that one way investigators tracked whiskey-making was by monitoring large sales of sugar. Sugar, mixed with corn, begins the fermentation process. Some whiskey-makers got around having to purchase sugar by simply making their own: growing cane, squeezing out the juices, and using it to jump start the sour mash. The syrup skimmings, locally called "drugs," meaning "dregs," will also, if left on their own, ferment into home brew.

At the Choctaw County Historical Museum in Gilbertown— where, along with a 1902 sugar mill and old farm tools, one can view novelties like the county's first personal computer—curator Roland Hutchinson agrees about moonshine. "Folks would sweeten up their liquor with the syrup and save the skimmings, too. Back in the Good Ol' Days. Now you have to go to the state store."

• • •

Driving back roads from Needham to Water Valley, a village not listed on the state map, you can see where white communities stop and black ones begin—age-old patterns little changed, it seems, by the sweep of history. At Banks Grocery in Water Valley, Annie Banks does not know Columbus Manley, but she does know Buddy Napier, calling him "the last syrup-maker around here." As Bobbye Banks fixes hamburgers, Scott Pearson and Keith Ray, students at Alabama State, are home visiting.

"Buddy's syrup was so thick," says Keith, "it was like an insulator. If you'd put it on your leg you wouldn't even feel the wind blowing around it."

Not far away, on land he has long tended for its owner, Buddy, 75, is slopping hogs. As he pours crushed corn and salt into their haphazard pens, the lazy swine root and snuffle. He'll show you another pen, high and enclosed, holding fidgety, wood hogs that bang up against the boards when you approach. "It used to be they wouldn't eat with you watching. Then they got settled. Listen at them crunching."

Behind the hog pens is a red Chevrolet Bel Air, weeds grown around it, backed up to a collapsed shed.

It was at the back of this Bel Air that the sugar mill sat for many years. The car's rear axle was hiked up on blocks, and a belt connected one of the free-spinning tires to the mill wheel. It was the same mill that Columbus Manley would purchase and move to Needham.

"Used to be a lot of syrup made in this county," Buddy says, chewing tobacco. "I tell you one thing, I ate my share of it. I was raised on that, milk and butter."

He pushes through the weeds to the defunct Chevy.

"There was many a person who'd come here for syrup. So many cars would be parked up in here it looked like a big association."

If people brought their own cane Buddy would only charge them for gas to power the Chevy. One man would trade cane for juice. "I loved fooling with cane."

He looks out over the fields of weeds and bushes, saying how it used to be filled with cane as high as your head. "I used to go possum hunting. The dogs would tree the possum, but we'd be sitting down eating cane."

Buddy and countless visitors from around these parts were not the only ones who enjoyed those days of cane milling and syrup cooking.

"Once we had buckets of skimmings out in the field and it set in the sun," he says in his own version of an oft-repeated country tale. "Leave it there awhile and it'll go to working. The hogs got into it and ate it up. The durn hogs were laying out there drunk."

The Music of "Pah-cahns"

You may think that the sound of pecans falling from a tree would be pleasing as rain—that they drop, when their time comes, with a gentle thump. Perhaps you have never witnessed a shake.

At B & B Pecans on Greeno Road in Fairhope, Ala., Clarence Bishop, 67, demonstrates. He backs his International Harvester tractor up to the first tree he ever planted—a beat-up, though still glorious Stewart pecan that he set into the soil on Oct. 1, 1956. On the back of the tractor is an attachment that clamps around the tree.

"Nineteen fifty-six," the longtime pecan grower tells me. "The year I got married and opened B & B." He waves to Highway 98, where sport-utility vehicles zoom by an industrial plant across the road. "I bought my first five acres for $325 an acre, money I'd sent home to Momma from the Korean War." He soon purchased more.

In Korea, he tells me, he saw Marilyn Monroe perform for the troops. "I took a picture of her up close just like you're standing there." He remarks at the high price paid for Monroe's dresses at a New York auction.

If he were to sell the land today where his pecan grove stands, I ask him, would he have enough money, say, to bid on a Marilyn Monroe dress? More than enough, he shyly admits.

But in his work clothes and Barnwell, Ala., hat—"Barnwell's for farmers, shrimpers, and lovers," it reads—he is clearly a man of the land. Harvesting pecans, farming with his brothers, and having served as a Baldwin County commissioner, Bishop sent his three children to college, one of them through medical school.

He stops the tractor as it reaches the tree now. The clamp, cushioned with rubber tires, tightens around the trunk. "Here goes."

At B & B Pecans in Fairhope, Clarence Bishop shows off his autumnal harvest. His first tree, planted on Oct. 1, 1956, was a Stewart pecan, and the tree endures like a weathered patriarch over the grove of Stewarts and other varieties—Desirable, Elliott, Cape Fear, Cheyenne, and Success. A good tree, he figures, will produce about 150 lbs. of unshelled pecans, which produces about 60 lbs. of shelled nut. No matter the stature of pecan trees, though, they are especially vulnerable to high winds, given their shallow root systems. At B & B pecans—as at groves throughout south Alabama—saplings, by their very presence, tell of storms past like Hurricane Danny and Hurricane Georges. (Victor Calhoun, Mobile Register)

With a roar the clamp gyrates and the tree, as though demon-possessed, breaks into heebie-jeebies. It vibrates, it shimmies, it rattles. Nuts pelt the earth.

Standing near the tree, I cover my head, bombarded by a meteor shower of pecans.

Then all's still. Bishop drives the tractor away, shutting off the engine.

In row after row, pecan trees in several variations—Stewart, Desirable, Elliott, Cape Fear, Cheyenne, Success—stand serenely, silently, in the autumn sun.

• • •

Autumn in south Alabama means ripe pecans are falling—unhurriedly, or hastened along. For the most part, Bishop uses a mechanical harvester to suck up pecans during these autumn weeks when trees are maturing, and pecan sheaths are opening, and nuts are kicked up like tiny, hard footballs. A good tree will produce about 150 pounds of unshelled pecans, Bishop says, which produces about 60 pounds of shelled nut.

But he makes use of an old-time implement too.

Under the just-shook tree he holds a stick with a coiled basket at the end and presses it over one pecan, another. He tumps the pecans into a tub and scares up some more.

I know that tool well. My mother's mother, Sadie, had one in her garage on Michigan Avenue in Mobile, and every fall I'd dig it out for her and my Aunt Mildred and we'd go foraging through their back yard, harvesting a solitary tree. One magical autumn weekend years ago, not long after we'd plucked the last fruits from her fig tree and had them chilled in her icebox, her pecan tree offered its bounty. We gathered a whole bucket.

As we sat in the kitchen afterwards, cracking the pecans with a hand-vise, we ate the cold figs and talked about what my grandmother might fix. Easy answer—pecan pie.

By that time, Clarence Bishop had already invested in mechanical pecan-crackers—the same, flywheel-driven machines he still uses these forty years later. Even though he sends his pecans, ultimately, to be shelled at Gulf Pecan at Tillman's Corner in Mobile, he does the first-round cracking himself.

He takes orders to "custom crack" pecans for others—either small commercial growers, or homeowners with a lot of trees in their yard.

"Crack pecans?" asks Perry Outlaw, from Fairhope, lugging some sacks in the door.

"Bring 'em on," Bishop says.

"Not crack cocaine, now," Outlaw teases.

"No-o, none of that here," Bishop says, chuckling at the gag.

Outlaw tells me he has over a hundred trees on his ten acres of property, most of them Elliott pecan trees, which produce a small, round pecan often used in desserts. He mostly gives them as gifts to friends.

As Bishop dumps the pecans into the old-time cracking machine, a noise starts up like a slow jackhammer. Pieces of shell fall out one dispenser. Pecans, half-unshelled, fall out of another.

• • •

Jerry Tew is a local farmer who brings his sacks of pecans to B & B to be cracked. Afterwards, he invites me to view his five hundred pecan trees down the road.

Tew, 64, was an administrator at the Alabama State Docks before moving to Baldwin County. He bought a farm where, with his family, he not only grows pecans, but also cultivates azaleas and adopts abused dogs.

He sounds a little like Bubba, in "Forrest Gump," who listed ways to prepare shrimp. "Well," Tew says of pecans, "You can roast them, make cookies, make pies, make candies."

Or they can be used as a garnish, he says.

If unshelled pecans, once the sunshine has dried them, are allowed to lie too long, he warns, the oil will pool to one side. By refrigerating them, "the oil is suspended. I remember one big cooler at the State Docks filled with pecans."

Tew has some saplings on his property, as do many pecan growers

—a legacy of hurricanes past. Storms yanked up many pecan trees' shallow root systems.

Hurricane Danny and Hurricane Georges—their names, invisibly, are inscribed on the limbs of the young trees.

• • •

Back at B & B I meet two tattooed Scotsmen, Hugh and Milton, who have been in Baldwin County as part of their employment with B. F. Goodrich. They are about to return to Glasgow after several weeks working here, a period when they've also taught local bartenders to mix up a Scottish drink called "Shandy," half lime juice, half beer.

They are curious about the nuts in Clarence Bishop's shop. "I've never seen a pecan," Hugh admits, pronouncing the word, like non-Southerners all over the world—"pee-can."

"Pah-cahn," I correct him.

He tries, and fails, to say it the right way.

Bishop reaches into a bin and pulls up a handful of unshelled nuts. "Take these back with y'all to Scotland," he offers.

"Thank you," Milton says.

"For the pee-cahns," Hugh adds in his Scottish lilt, putting the nuts in his pocket. "For the"—he corrects himself—"pah-cahns."

PART IV

COLORFUL COMPETITIONS

❖

You could fill a book with stories about sports in Mobile. Some, for spectators, are important yearly activities—the Senior Bowl, for example, at Ladd-Peebles Stadium, where the best college seniors from around the nation go head-to-head, North vs. South. Like the Junior Miss Pageant, the Senior Bowl—now joined by the Mobile Alabama Bowl—puts Mobile on the television map. It's always nice to think of a fan in Fargo, N.D., or Tucson, Ariz., leaning back in his recliner, tumbler in one hand, chips in the other, cheering on a competition in south Alabama.

Over the years I've enjoyed taking part in the breadth of sports our coastal town provides—from the Alabama Deep Sea Fishing Rodeo off Dauphin Island, where my father and I, after coming upon a school of Spanish mackerel, promptly blew the sparkplug from our outboard engine and had to be towed in; to golf, where my friend William Oppenheimer and I, way back in our teen-age years, used to whack Titleists down the shimmering fairways until we could barely see through the dusk. I played my share of pick-up football, too, as we turned Pat Semmes' side-yard on Williams Court into a stadium where Pat, the Dumas brothers, and the Beaird brothers hiked, blocked, faked, and threw "bombs" toward the end zone, the street.

Baseball, boxing, and basketball are three sports I've written about here—and since I am not a sports writer by profession, my focus, as always, is on the lives behind them. The basketball is a special brand—wheelchair basketball. And one more "sport" is here, too, an anvil shoot; that article, being one of the most peculiar pieces in this collection, has also been one of the most widely reprinted.

"Baseball in the Blood" combines a 1998 piece on the new Hank

Aaron Stadium with a 1996 look-back at Mobile baseball history. Since that 1996 piece, Herbert Aaron Sr., Hank Aaron's father, passed away. I'm grateful that I was able to capture a few of his colorful stories. We also lost Eddie Stanky. Another person in this story, Palestine Caldwell, made vivid her brother, who's long become myth—Satchel Paige.

Baseball in the Blood

American baseball is as old as an Iowa cornfield, as close to the notion of an American home as any sport we have. Baseball parks, too, create their sense of place, their legends and lore.

For the glum decades when there was no Mobile baseball—before Hank Aaron Stadium opened and the Mobile BayBears, a San Diego Padres double-A farm team, won back our hearts—Hartwell Field lingered as the park of our dreams. Long after it was torn down, South Ann Street near Virginia, for many, still conjured hot summer nights and the cry, "Play ball!"

Just beyond the outfield billboards—Burma Shave, First National Bank, Hammel's—the GM & O passed, railroad cars clanking and thunking through the innings. Nearby were the somber paths of Magnolia Cemetery.

The scoreboard, changed by hand, showed the runs. On clown night, a painted performer with floppy shoes and a red-ball nose danced around the base paths.

Named for Mayor Harry Hartwell, the stadium, through the 1950s, was segregated. Hank Aaron, attending the games, would have been sequestered in stands along the right field line.

"We'd have to sit way off to watch the game," explains Baker Perryman Jr., 81, a retiree from the Brookley Field air base who works part-time selling programs at the entrance to Hank Aaron Stadium. He shades his eyes with the flat of his hand, as though peering into the distance.

Many at Hank Aaron Stadium relish stadium memories. BayBears second baseman Greg LaRocca, a native of small-town New Hampshire, grew up going to Boston to watch the Red Sox play in Fenway

Park; pitcher Cam Smith, from Albany, N.Y., used to go with his parents to Yankee Stadium.

Don Shirey, 67, a retired accountant, stands by the stadium turnstile taking up tickets. As a youth in Pittsburgh he'd go watch the Pirates play at Forbes Field. Tickets were 50 cents.

Bill Shanahan, vice president for the BayBears, fell in love with baseball as a kid, too, spending San Francisco afternoons in Candlestick Park. While watching a Giants warm-up game, he caught a ball that Willie Mays tossed his way. "I still keep it in a plastic bag," he says.

Shanahan says that minor league baseball, as an industry, realized in the 1980s it had to update its image from that of lazy summer nights where the sound effects were crickets and trains.

"We provide an electric atmosphere now." Enormous speakers, computer-driven sound effects, electronic scoreboard, special promotions—the game, Shanahan explains, delivers not only sport, but also great family entertainment.

For those of us who love baseball, and are from Mobile, it's a story, as well, of our communities coming together, after long separation, as one.

• • •

The game of baseball, like a stadium itself, draws us together from all over town.

What two Mobile boyhoods could have been more different, for example, than mine and Cleon Jones'?

White and born in the '50s, I played organized Little League for teams with crisp uniforms and brand new bats. Black and born in the '40s, Jones played sandlot ball in pick-up games with Plateau friends, among them Tommie Agee, often using broken bats held together with nails. Fielding balls late into the front yard dusk with my friend, Bobby Beaird, I let countless ones bound between my legs.

Jones' capacity to field a ball was, undeniably, better: in the 1969 World Series against the Baltimore Orioles, playing left field for the

New York Mets, his old friend Agee in center, he snared the final out, clinching the championship for the "Miracle Mets."

As I meet Jones at Bishop State Community College, where he is the baseball coach, I realize that however much our childhoods varied, we shared, like many kids from Mobile, an early love of baseball.

I remember my 7th birthday party at Hartwell Field in 1960, gobbling hot dogs with buddies, rooting for a Mobile Bears victory over the New Orleans Pelicans. During the seventh-inning stretch my name was called and I went up to the announcer's box to receive a ball signed by the Bears. Exalted, I came back down, my friends eager to touch the magic planet I cradled in my hands.

Jones recalls Hartwell Field as well, the segregated one of his childhood, where black fans sat beyond the right field line. Going there with his friends, he watched as his idol, George "Shotgun" Shuba—who went on to play with the Brooklyn Dodgers—hit a curving foul into those right field stands. Jones reached up and caught it and waited outside the stadium for "Shotgun" to sign it afterward. "My friends and I," he remembers happily, "tossed that ball back and forth the whole seven miles we walked back to Plateau."

• • •

Between the Bears' final season in 1960 and the BayBears' first in 1998, Mobile was the home of minor league pro ball only a scant four summers—the Mobile A's in '66, the Mobile White Sox in '72, the BaySharks in '94 and '95. But baseball has always been in the central nervous system of this town.

"In Mobile, in terms of popularity, football is number one," admits Eddie Stanky, a native Philadelphian who played for the Cubs and Cardinals, married a Mobilian "who made a Southern gentleman out of me," and returned here to serve 15 years as the highly regarded coach of the University of South Alabama baseball team. But, as he emphasizes, the city still thrives with youth leagues, baseball camps, high school ball and college ball; and the University of South Alabama has sent a flow of young players into the majors.

In baseball history Mobile is legendary. Not only can we claim Cleon Jones and Tommie Agee, but also Amos Otis, the entire Mets outfield for a brief time. There are the McGill High graduates, the Bolling brothers: Frank, who played for the Tigers and the Braves; and Milt, who came up with the Red Sox. There is Tommie Aaron, also a Braves player.

Then there is the pantheon—Satchel Paige, Hank Aaron, Billy Williams, and Willie McCovey—four Mobile sons in the Baseball Hall of Fame. When I call Cooperstown, N.Y., for information on them, the researcher is astonished these four hail from the same town. "The Hall of Fame issues no official statements about ball players," he advises me, "but personally, I think it's safe to say, for a city the size of Mobile, it's nothing short of remarkable."

• • •

Why so many extraordinary players?

To one 88-year-old Toulminville gentleman, the explanation is easy: "I guess you could say you go over yonder in that pond and catch fish, and you go right back over here and can't catch none."

That this wry wisdom comes from Herbert Aaron Sr., the father of the greatest home run hitter of all time, makes it also profound. Welcoming me in his Toulminville home—which I reach by way of Henry Aaron Loop and Henry Aaron Park—he shows me the trophy case where many of his son's treasures are kept. Even though the light above the case is broken, visible on one shelf are baseballs, on another, newspaper clippings. "What are those?" I ask, pointing to a long row of drinking mugs.

"Oh," he says casually, peering in, "Henry got those in the All-Star games."

As we scan the case—in one shelf is a gold hammer presented to "Hammering" Hank—Mr. Aaron tells me how, "when Henry was a boy, I couldn't keep a ball out of his hands." Even though he tried. Worried that his son "would get hurt" playing the sport, and angry when he found Henry was sometimes not showing up for classes at Central High, he put him in a private school, Josephine Allen. Before

At his trophy-rich home in the Mobile community of Toulminville, Herbert Aaron relaxes before a photo of two of his sons, Hank and Tommie, suited up for the Atlanta Braves. "When Henry was a boy, I couldn't keep a ball out of his hands," he says of "Hammerin' Hank," whose bat he grips. It was Herbert who threw out the first ball for the Braves-Dodgers game when son Henry hit his 715th home run, breaking Babe Ruth's record—cheered on by most Americans for his triumph, but vilified by some. In the Baseball Hall of Fame in Cooperstown, N.Y., Hank Aaron, as a Brave, takes his place among three other Mobile natives—Satchel Paige, who spent the stellar years of his pitching career in the Negro baseball league; Willie McCovey, of the San Francisco Giants; and Billy Williams, a Chicago Cub. (G. M. Andrews, Mobile Register)

long, after a stint with a local black league, he made it to the majors whose color line had been broken in 1947 by Jackie Robinson.

"Jackie Robinson said he didn't think Henry would make a good player," Mr. Aaron laughs, because he'd field the ball with his knees. I said, 'Would you rather have a man running behind the ball or stopping it with his knees and throwing the runner out?'"

Mr. Aaron is of slight build, but his hands are large, like a baseball player's hands. It was his hand that threw out the first ball for the game between the Braves and the Dodgers when his son smashed his 715th homer, breaking a record long held by Babe Ruth. Hank Aaron received great honors for that record, but also hate mail, some charged with racial invective.

When I talked with Cleon Jones, he told me that shortly before Aaron broke Ruth's record, Aaron had gotten in touch with him in New York and the two men had gone to dinner together. According to Jones, Aaron confessed that the hate mail saddened him, and that he almost felt like quitting. Jones said he told his fellow Mobilian, "Records are meant to be broken. Joe Louis did it. Jackie Robinson did it. You can do it."

The successes of Henry Aaron, like those of Robinson, Roy Campanella, and Don Newcombe, soon came to inspire not only younger black athletes like Cleon Jones, but generations of white ball players as well.

That Aaron honed his early skills on shabby ball fields, oddly, may have strengthened his talent.

"At some of the schools where we learned to play, Williamson, Blount, Mobile County Training School, the fields were in bad conditions," says James Aaron, Henry's youngest brother. "At Central, where my brothers and I played, the field went straight down at the back. Nobody had to teach you how to catch a ball on a bad hop. With the field full of rocks, it always took a bad hop."

• • •

"There's something in the Mobile water. That's what Dizzy Dean used to say." These words are spoken by Gold Glove winner Frank

Bolling who, being white, reflects that while growing up he and Aaron had little chance to know each other. They both went to the big leagues in 1954. In wonderful irony, after a stint with the Detroit Tigers, when Bolling went on to play for the Braves, he and Aaron had lockers side by side.

"Hank Aaron, Billy Williams, Willie McCovey—at home we hadn't crossed paths," Bolling explains, "but in the big leagues we were Mobile guys. We'd see each other on different teams and shout, 'Hi, Mobile! Hey, Mobile!'"

Having come along before organized youth ball, Bolling, a second baseman, learned moves by watching the Mobile Bears' second baseman Stan Wasiak. He studied other Bears, too, among them Cal Abrams who, like "Shotgun" Shuba, went on to the Dodgers.

In talking to Bolling—and to his friend, 1947 Bears' bat boy, Donnie Wagner, now a retired pharmacist—I glean a sense of how wildly popular this team was in its heyday, often drawing more than 8,000 fans on a single night to Hartwell Field at South Ann and Virginia streets. "It was good, family-oriented entertainment," Bolling says.

It was colorful, too. Among the Bears' 1947 Southern League Championship team was handsome, poetry-spouting, 6-foot-5 Chuck Connors, who had only one hapless at-bat with the Dodgers, but found fame as television's "The Rifleman." Connors—who squired at least two Mobile women I know of while in town—starred in numerous Western films, and is said to have lifted Leonid Brezhnev off the ground with a bear hug when President Nixon included him in a White House entourage to welcome the Soviets.

The lively presence of the Mobile Bears, as well as the earlier Shippers—and the Negro League counterparts, the Black Bears and Black Shippers—certainly inspired many a young man to play ball.

Bolling believes there was a pocketbook factor also at work. "For kids who had little, it was the cheap thing to do. All we needed was a ball and bat. It made us earn it a little better."

• • •

Palestine Caldwell has no theories about why Mobile has borne a legion of great baseball players. As the tall, lively woman stands in her Selma Street home, making a few abrupt moves suggesting a pitcher's wind-up, she tells me that is the way she remembers her brother, Leroy "Satchel" Paige. "We come from a family of 11 children and I'm the only one still living," she says. "My Mama, Lulu, washed clothes in a number three tub, and my Daddy, John, cut grass. Mama Mama, my grandmama, was born in slavery."

Although Paige has been portrayed in movies by Lou Gosset Jr. and Billy Dee Williams, neither summoned as clear a picture for me of Paige as Mrs. Caldwell did. "I can still see him as a little boy. He had a sun hat, a ball and bat. Mama said, 'Where you going?' 'I'm going to play ball.'"

The history books have it that Paige got the nickname "Satchel" from carrying bags for travelers at the train station, but Mrs. Caldwell says her brother never worked down at the train. "Mama called him Satchel because he'd carry his baseballs in a little satchel when he went to play."

It was at W. H. Council School that Paige began his career, and one of his friends was Amos Otis Sr., the father of the player who'd go on to field along with Jones and Agee for the Mets. Leon Paige, Satchel's nephew, remembers a little boy who'd follow after his uncle when he'd come home to visit—Willie McCovey, who himself would go on to be a power hitter for the Giants.

Mrs. Caldwell and Paige recount Satchel's stellar career in the Negro League, how he'd pitch every night, have his infield sit down while he struck out the side, and won more than 2,000 games. As they tell me how he'd barnstorm through Mobile, sometimes playing with the Black Shippers, I come to understand how these Mobile players continued to dazzle, and inspire, youngsters on hometown streets. Many of them, as Leon Paige explains, learned to hit by playing "top ball," using a stick and soda bottle tops, or "tie ball," using inch-long sections of a rubber hose as the ball.

Batters who faced Paige, among them white players who played against him in exhibition games, found him unbeatable. Baseball experts consider Satchel Paige to have been one of the greatest pitchers, if not the greatest, of all time.

As Mrs. Caldwell and I head out to her porch, she tells me that this is where Satchel last visited before he passed away in 1982. "Children were coming from up and down the block, black and white, big and little, onto this porch," she says, taking a seat in a chair. "Everybody wanted to meet Satchel Paige."

• • •

In his office at Bishop State, Cleon Jones tells me he believes Mobile has just as much raw baseball talent as it ever did, but that it may never come to the fore. Baseball gloves and shoes are becoming more expensive, there's little organized competition for inner-city kids, and basketball stardom is the new playground dream.

The presence of adults in the community who look out for and guide the boys in their baseball ambitions is especially vital. In south Mobile—Down the Bay—Jones remembers the critical efforts of Jesse Thomas to nurture baseball talents and scout for the pros, hooking up McCovey with the Giants. In Plateau, there were two men in the neighborhood—James Robinson and Clyde Grey—who took it upon themselves to make sure the boys, after school and on weekends, put their energy into constructive activity like baseball. Jones feels indebted to their efforts.

These men, teachers and coaches and scouts and dedicated members of communities from Whistler, where Billy Williams grew up, to Toulminville, home of the Aarons, were the heroes behind the heroes.

They enabled young men to realize amazing dreams, like Cleon Jones' first game in the majors:

"All of a sudden you're in the clubhouse and dressed in the New York Mets uniform and Casey Stengel is in the middle of the floor and going over the opposing team. I couldn't focus on Stengel because I was watching Duke Snider, Gil Hodges, Richie Ashburn. I had baseball cards of these guys.

"Then, it's time to go on field. I'm in awe. Willie Mays played here. Bobby Thomson. I hear somebody call me, 'Jonesey, it's your time to hit.' I've never been the type who gets nervous. I've got Duke Snider and all the others standing around watching me hit.

"It's unreal, but then it's time to play, you throw that out and become one of the guys. It's quite an experience. You don't ever outgrow those memories."

Tommie Littleton: Gentleman Boxer

❖

Cathedral Square in downtown Mobile is a public park now, but until the early 1970s it was lined with buildings. Through the door of one of those buildings, facing Conti Street, you entered Littleton's Gymnasium.

The summer I turned 16, 1969, I went to Littleton's to learn to box. I did so for the same reason I took Latin in high school. Boxing lessons were not intended to make me a pugilist any more than Latin was supposed to make me a classicist, but both disciplines were considered by some, my father among them, to be part of a broader education.

In his heyday, the 1920s, Tommie Littleton—his real name was Sam Impastato—had been a middleweight, a term referring to fighters weighing between 147 and 160 pounds. He was 73 years old when I met him, and was still lean. He was bald-headed, had bushy eyebrows and large ears. Once his dark eyes fixed on you they did not stray—perhaps the instinct of an old boxer ready to duck a punch. His voice was low and raspy.

As Mobile businessman Jack Friedlander recalls, Tommie was reminiscent of the actor Burgess Meredith, who played Rocky Balboa's trainer in the movie "Rocky." The Friedlander family's store, Mobile Rug and Shade, was on Dauphin Street near Littleton's. Jack and his brother, Jerry, both took physical training from Tommie.

Littleton's had become far more than a boxing arena over the years. On the wall were signs: "No Exercise Without Deep Respiration, Circulation, Perspiration." On another: "A Good Digestion, Assimilation, Elimination, Through Corrective Exercise."

Along with the men hitting punching bags were others skipping

In 1900 the Impastato family left Sicily for New Orleans and ran a grocery store that became what is now the popular Napoleon House Bar in the French Quarter. One of the Impastatos, though, had a different career in mind—boxing. When Sam Impastato left home, he changed his name to Tommie Littleton, became a middleweight champion, and made his way to Mobile, where he would draw crowds to the wharves for fights. Here, in the early 1930s, Littleton (1896–1973) hits a punching bag for 24 straight hours in the window of Thoss Sporting Goods on Dauphin Street. In addition to entering the annals of "Ripley's Believe It or Not" as a result of this feat, the champ was able to publicize his boxing and fitness center, Littleton's Gymnasium. (Erik Overbey Collection, University of South Alabama Archives)

rope, or lying on massage tables; women, too, had come to Littleton's. A 1931 Mobile Press Register feature had shown two "modern" women with pixie haircuts, shorts, and boxing gloves, with Littleton behind them helping them practice "boxercise."

As a fitness guru, Littleton "was ahead of his time," says Red Impastato, 66, one of Tommie's sons, a retired nurse anesthetist who lives in Lacomb, La.

Long before Jack LaLanne led floor exercises from the television, or Richard Simmons got Spandex-clad Americans to hyperventilate to disco, Littleton was boxing and exercising and kneading into shape those who entered his gym.

Charles McNeil, now 77, went to Littleton's when he returned from World War II with a severe rash on his legs. McNeil, who owns an insurance agency, had been a pilot in the war and was shot down behind German lines. After coming home safely, he says he developed the rash as a result of "tension" he'd felt as a prisoner of war. No Mobile doctors could cure him.

Tommie Littleton told McNeil to appear at his gym at 5 in the morning. The trainer slathered McNeil's legs in Ben Gay balm, wrapped them in hot towels, made him lie under a heat lamp, then rubbed them with alcohol.

"When he put on the alcohol," says McNeil, remembering the shock, "I wanted to get up off the table and hit him. He pushed me back down." Littleton put him in a "hot box," with only his head showing, then told him to come back twice more that day.

Thanks to the boxer-trainer, McNeil says, the rash was cured.

McNeil says that Littleton not only helped his malady, but also taught him principles of good health. "He taught me how to relax, to take a 'power nap.'" To this day, McNeil reclines in the afternoons, turns on his side, and takes a 10- to 12-minute nap as Littleton showed him. "You close your eyes, let your mind go blank and wipe it clean. It refreshes you."

Just like my father sent me to Littleton's to train and box, McNeil sent his son, Chuck McNeil, when he came of age.

In 1969, when I appeared there, I had my doubts about learning much from a one-time pug about either fitness or boxing. After all, when I heard "boxer" I thought not of a lean septuagenarian but of muscled, colorful Muhammad Ali.

Tommie told me to stand straight, then examined my hands. He pushed some gloves onto my fists, laced them, and had me bang at a punching bag. Tommie had once achieved fame in "Ripley's Believe It Or Not" by hitting a punching bag for 24 straight hours in the window of Thoss Sporting Goods on Dauphin Street. Within five minutes of slapping a bag, my own arms turned to lead.

He had me turn around and stand back-to-back with him and he laced his arms through mine. First he leaned over, giving me a "stretch," until I could feel my body lengthen an inch. I found out that he'd performed the same "stretching" exercise with many others, among them, on a dare, Oliver Wintzell. Wintzell, who owned the restaurant by his name, was a very large man, a Paul Prudhomme of Dauphin Street. Tommie won the dare, picking the hefty restaurateur up on his back.

With his arms still hooked through mine now, Tommie flipped me over his back. I watched the gym turn upside down—punching bags and exercise machines and fitness signs spinning—and landed with a thud on my feet.

• • •

It may seem like a long way from a sweaty gym on Conti Street in Mobile to a breezy cafe on Chartres Street in New Orleans, but Sam Impastato—aka Tommie Littleton—was of both places. In 1900, when Sam was 4 years old, the Impastato family came from Sicily to New Orleans. At the Napoleon House Bar and Cafe in New Orleans today, owner Sal Impastato, 50, Sam's nephew, tells the story of the immigrant generation.

At the turn of the century, the father of the clan, Salvatore Impastato, and his eldest son, Joe, had arrived before the rest of the family. They worked in macaroni factories and in the grocery business. They brought over the others—Salvatore's wife, Fara, and their four other children. Two more children would be born in America. The Impastatos took over the Labourdette Grocery in the French Quarter, across from the St. Louis Hotel. (In later years, the St. Louis would burn to the ground and be replaced with the Royal Orleans.)

In 1916, with Joe in the lead, the Impastatos bought the building and, while it remained a grocery, turned part of it into a social establishment. They lived upstairs.

Inspired by a story of the original Girod Home that had stood at the location—it was to have been a refuge for Napoleon if the French emperor fled to these shores—the Impastatos named it the Napoleon House Bar. Eventually there was a courtyard with a fountain; ceiling fans whisked overhead; classical music played on the turntable and customers could change the records. A cafe was added in 1972. The old upstairs living quarters would one day be turned into banquet rooms named in honor of family members.

Red Impastato, Sam's son, tells the story of how his father became a boxer instead of a cafe worker. In the early days, when Joe ran the business, he lorded over the younger siblings. Sam disliked being told what to do. To bend his will, Joe once tied Sam to a chair and gave him a whipping. Sam, with the help of friends, broke free, took some money from the cash register, and set off for New York. He was 14.

It was on the docks of New York that Sam proved his strength and prowess as a scrapper; and in New York where he first boxed amateur. He met the great prize fighter Jack Dempsey. Later, when Dempsey visited Mobile, he came to Littleton's gym.

Sam did not stay in the north, as Red tells it. Mama called him home. No matter; the spell of boxing had taken hold.

On the New Orleans waterfront there were public matches, and Sam would go see them. He'd developed a reputation already for being a fighter—once, the family lore goes, he subdued a bully named "Rat Pete," who'd been terrorizing other kids. To prove his strength, Sam also dared swim the Mississippi River, setting out from the levee at the French Market and stroking his way through the cross-currents to the parish of Algiers. His nickname on the street became "the giant."

Knowing his parents would disapprove of his becoming a boxer— "They didn't want him to become a punch drunk thug," Red explains —Sam entered exhibition fights borrowing the last name of a well-known New Orleans boxer, Happy Littleton.

Sam's alias was soon discovered. A family friend saw young man Tommie Littleton in the ring. The young welterweight was Sam Impastato!

When the United States entered the First World War, Sam enlisted and saw duty on the Italian front; and he continued to box. On the ship transporting the servicemen overseas, he'd staged an exhibition fight against a military policeman and knocked him out. He soon fought and K.O.'d Italian boxers during his stint on the front.

Sam returned, enrolled in Spring Hill College in Mobile and joined the boxing team, felling the Southern Amateur Champion, Eddie Duffy, of the University of Alabama. As the new champ, Littleton started fighting for money. He knocked out the South's middleweight champion, Red Hill, and claimed that professional title, too.

Littleton began a career in the ring, but then thought to change direction. He stopped boxing in 1923, traveled West, and, according to his son Red, contemplated becoming a Jesuit.

In 1925, Littleton returned to Spring Hill College, but not as a priest. He signed on as Spring Hill's athletic trainer and boxing coach, and he was back in the ring.

• • •

Tommie Littleton was called "the scholar boxer," and "the gentle-man boxer." In the rough-and-tumble world of his sport, Littleton's model was Gene Tunney, the heavyweight champion known for his polish and class. In an album of old fight memorabilia of Littleton's, there are clippings about Tunney.

Littleton's daughter, Farra Ward, the youngest of the four children, looks through this memorabilia with me at her store, Ward's Army-Navy Store, at the Loop. She keeps photos of her father hitting a punching bag, shots of the front of the gym, fading newspaper accounts of countless matches.

She remembers him on his bicycle, riding with her and her brothers clinging on when she was a child. She paints a picture of him cycling through downtown streets as an old man, too. I can also see the boxer, cycling slowly up Conti Street, coming to meet me at the gym.

In the world of boxing today, we hear of million-dollar purses. But boxing was a hard way to support a family in the early days. In Farra's collection of papers there's a boxing contract for a match in

1928, at El Dorado, Ark., between Littleton and Jimmy Bean of Enid, Okla. The advance payment to Littleton was one round-trip bus ticket from Mobile, and he had to deposit a $25 dollar check, which would be forfeited if he failed to show up, or was too heavy on the weigh-in. After the match, he would receive 20 percent of the gross receipt of tickets minus 5 percent to the boxing commission. Presumably, those funds would be divided with other boxers.

No matter his take, Littleton gave a million-dollar show, and boxing writers for the Mobile newspapers loved him. In fights staged by the American Legion in Mobile, Littleton defeated middleweight champion Jimmy Cox: "Cox landed a terrific right to the face in the second round, but the tough Littleton did not wince for a second. Tommie came back and drove Cox to the ropes."

He defeated Judge Horning of Savannah, Ga.: "Littleton came out of his corner in the fifth round and started the fighting from the jump, and, rushing Horning to the ropes, battered him hard and finally broke away from him and landed the knockout."

The most legendary battle of all was between Littleton and pugilist Jimmy Barrett. Littleton was older than Barrett, and the two Mobile fighters were scheduled to fight at the open-air ring that was on Mobile's waterfront, at the foot of Dauphin Street.

My father, who saw that fight in the 1930s, recalls the fervor of the outdoor crowd that pressed around the ring, cheering the boxers on.

John Connick, 80, who served on the Alabama State Boxing Commission, remembers it, too. He says the match was "a puncher against a boxer."

Barrett was the puncher. "Jimmy Barrett could knock a building down if he hit it," Connick says. "But Littleton was clever. He could make you miss him.

"Boxing's like playing checkers," he says, explaining that you coax your opponent to move where he thinks you're going to be, then you move somewhere else. Littleton was a master checker-player that day.

Barrett, as Connick recalls vividly, "never got the chance to hit Littleton. Tommie outboxed him. He'd get inside and uppercut him. He put his head down and walked on in."

· · ·

If I were telling a tall tale, I'd say that, as the summer of 1969 wore on, I became a terrific boxer and soon my friends came to cheer me on. But it was hot, the air was moved only by buzz fans, the gym reeked of sweat and liniment balm, and, newly in possession of a driver's license, I could think of better places to spend sweltering July afternoons.

When I sparred with Tommie, he seemed to have half a dozen boxers' hands reaching out to tap me on the gut or chin; there was no way I could keep up my guard with only two.

Then he began to talk up a practice match between me and another newcomer to his gym: an enormous, pro wrestler who'd lumber around, flexing his muscles in the mirror.

"He's huge!" I said. "He'll kill me."

"He's slow," Tommie rasped. "You can take him."

As the pro wrestler and I worked out together in the upstairs gym, the big lug seemed not only slow, but also sorrowful. He was tired of getting body-slammed, he told me. He was weary of being choked in scissors holds and having his back cracked in full nelsons. He wanted to make money. He wanted to be a boxer.

I looked up at him, nodded and wished him well. I have not been in a pair of boxing gloves since.

Men of Steel: Wheelchair Basketball

❖❖

New Orleans, January 1997

Teammates for unenviable reasons—a car wreck, a motorcycle crash, a hunting accident—the Mobile Patriots whirl down the court with enviable grace. They pass the basketball rapid-fire, chair to chair, driving toward the goal.

Bent on ruining their chances at the New Orleans Invitational are the New York Warriors, sponsored by the Eastern Paralyzed Veterans Association. As Patriot Milton Courington, 45, spins to the outside, sweat streaming around his sport goggles, a red-bearded Warrior is hurtling toward him.

Their chairs clang, lock, but Milton dishes the ball to Phillip Eddins, 32, who gets jammed up between two Warriors, leaving Darren Hallman, 28, free to the outside.

Phillip flips the ball to lean Teddy Alvis, 27, who passes it off to Darren who takes it, black ponytail flying, moving with the speed with which he once ran the football for Theodore High. His hands do the hard work now, pushing the wheels of the chair.

A black-bearded Warrior hurtles into his path.

Darren's shot bounces off the rim and chairs bang; there's a flurry of arms. Teddy pulls in the rebound and whips it back to Darren, who is gliding toward the goal as smoothly as a hockey player.

The shot thumps the backboard and drops in.

• • •

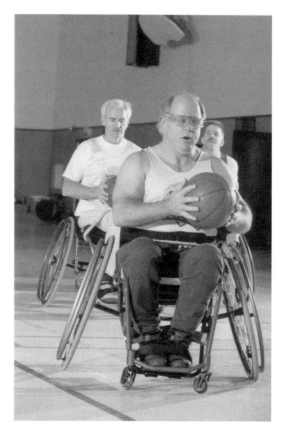

Going through the paces at the Texas Street gym in downtown Mobile, the Mobile Patriots get ready for their trip to the New Orleans Invitational, where they will compete against wheelchair basketball teams from other cities. Leading the charge is Milton Courington, who became paralyzed in a car accident. Following is O. D. Vann, whose spinal cord gave way after he fell from a horse stable he was helping build. At the rear is Phillip Eddins, who lost one of his legs in a motorcycle accident. These men and other teammates may come from different professions and backgrounds, but they are bound together in the disabilities they endure and in the spirit of the game in which they thrive. Cheering them on—her face not visible here but her voice resonating even in the photograph—is coach Stephenie Jeansonne, who stands like a swan above the sweaty, determined men. (G. M. Andrews, Mobile Register)

A white car veering across the road straight at him, Milton Courington wrenched the steering wheel and his pickup flew off the road.

Three days later he woke up in a Meridian, Miss., hospital with a broken spine.

"You never forget the date," Milton says. "It was early Sunday morning, June 16, 1974. He'd probably been out all night drinking."

The driver of the other car had just kept on going.

Milton began the uphill comeback of a man who'd lost use of the lower half of his body. Twenty-three at the time, with only a high school degree, he decided "to get serious about school." He enrolled at the University of South Alabama and pursued a field he'd never paid attention to before—therapeutic recreation.

Twenty years later he is manager of Therapeutic Recreation at the J. L. Bedsole/Rotary Rehabilitation Hospital.

Wheeling down the hospital corridors, looking in on patients, presiding over the crafts room, organizing field trips for those making the arduous re-entry to daily life, Milton is a study in composure—a contrast to his hard-driving basketball self. Thirteen years ago, inspired by stories about teams in other towns, he started the Patriots with funds from the rehab center.

"Sometimes we pick up players through rehab," he says, gliding by the team's trophy display table near the center's elevator door. "We use it as a therapeutic tool to get them involved, to let them know life's not over."

A sport that originated for wounded veterans after World War II, Milton explains, wheelchair basketball has gone on to accommodate players injured for a variety of reasons.

In addition to the people injured in car and motorcycle accidents are an increasing number—not soldiers on foreign battlefields, but civilians on hometown streets—paralyzed by gunshot wounds.

Whatever the cause, patients are sometimes reluctant to sign up for the sport, or any other, believing it's just a matter of time before they're back on their feet.

"Ninety-five percent of people think, 'This is not permanent, I'll beat the odds.' People have to hope, but they also have to realize they may not walk again and to prepare while in rehab. Getting a person involved in basketball can be an important step."

Milton hurls himself into physical activities: scuba diving, weightlifting. Twice a week he works out at ProHealth with teammate O. D. Vann.

"People with disabilities can't afford to be non-active and overweight. We don't need extra problems loaded on."

On Milton's table at work is Sports 'N Spokes magazine, crammed with articles about wheelchair tennis, wheelchair racing, even bungee jumping. He proudly points to a story inside about a Kentucky basketball tournament: "The Patriots, from deep in the heart of Dixie, stole the show in Bluegrass Country."

• • •

It was a hot July day and O. D. Vann was helping build a horse stable in Fairhope. No matter that he was used to scooting up poles as a telephone lineman, and had worked in all kinds of weather. On the barn he got flushed, dizzy and passed out. When he came to on the ground, his legs were paralyzed.

It was 1971 and he had a wife and two young daughters. He enrolled at USA to finish his college degree.

"Coming into life you have no idea what cards you're going to be dealt," he says, silver-haired in business suit, the computers of International Paper, where he is an executive, humming around him. "But you have to learn to play the cards you're dealt."

After his accident, O.D. admits he had a sour attitude. "I had always enjoyed playing tennis and golf—I went out and sold my clubs. . . . There was no one turning point; it just was day to day. Having a network of family and friends helps the most."

Recently, he counseled a young woman paralyzed after trying to kill herself with a gun, showing her photos of his daughters when they'd been small, and then as grown-ups. "I told her I had decided, years ago, I wanted to be part of their lives."

Trying to shore up the young woman's spirit was of no avail.

O.D. speaks remorsefully of others who have lost not only their bodies, but also their spirits. Whenever possible, he brings patients, men and women both, into the circle of wheelchair basketball.

At 51, nicknamed "old man" by his teammates, O.D. holds onto his place as one of the starting five. "I'd love to give up my position to one of the men half my age. But they'll have to beat me out of it!"

• • •

Gary McKinley didn't really care much for hunting. "I'd had enough of guns in Vietnam," he says. "But I wanted a getaway with my son."

For a year in the infantry, Gary had crawled through the jungles of Vietnam, watching buddies die all around. "You just wonder when your time's coming."

He returned home unscathed.

For 15 years Gary rode a fire truck for the city of Mobile, maneuvering his way through burning buildings, bringing children down ladders. He spent time as a fire truck driver. He remained unhurt.

That January morning, 1992, in Clarke County, he was biding time high up on a deer stand. For two hours he'd been completely still, waiting for game. His father was 800 yards away in one direction, his son in the other.

The deer stand collapsed.

"The jar was so hard it knocked my watch off. My legs didn't move. I could feel blood gurgling inside my body. I knew in two seconds I was paralyzed."

The operations, the hospital rooms, the 18-inch rod planted in his spine—Gary tells the story softly, sitting in his wheelchair at the Fire Department's central supply office. His work is now maintaining the gas masks firemen pull over their faces in the pitch of a blaze.

"I've always been told that to everything there's some good, or a reason for it." He shakes his head, looking out the window.

Like O.D., Gary speaks of "the hand I've been dealt" and making the best of it. At 47, he is still getting accustomed to hopping curbs, negotiating doorways, taking spills. "One day in rehab the therapist said, 'Now you're going to learn how to fall out of your chair.' Fall out of the chair! It happens."

He rolls by pictures of fire trucks on the wall, by snapshots of burning buildings and safety manuals. "Life is really weird."

It was O.D. and Milton who brought him into the basketball fold. "I told them I'd never played basketball when I could walk. Why should I play it now?"

They kept after him until he agreed just to come watch a game.

"I've been playing with them ever since."

• • •

Now the Patriots are leading. In white jersey and sneakers, coach Stephenie Jeansonne, a former LSU cheerleader, paces the sidelines shouting advice. Although the Patriots are ahead, the red-bearded Warrior is tough, and black-beard is wheeling speedily around the edge, stealing the ball.

A volunteer, Stephenie runs the team through practices at the Texas Street gym. Standing like a swan above the sweaty, beaming men, she critiques their efforts and tells them, with sweetness and grit, to go out and do it again.

The wheelchairs they play in—brands like Tornado, Hurricane and Quickie—are not workaday chairs, but sleek models with spokes like racing bikes. The wheels are angled out so that players, coming alongside each other, don't rip up each other's hands.

By regulation, every wheelchair basketball team includes some players, like Milton and O.D., who are paraplegics; and some, like Darren, Phillip and Teddy, who are amputees. The men who've lost legs but retain upper body strength are often the top scorers.

High scorer for the Patriots the year before was Phillip, who had his lower leg ripped off in a motorcycle accident. A scrapper on the court, Phillip ends up sprawled on the floor after collisions today more than any other Patriot.

"I get the mop handle award," he says.

When a Warrior missing both legs crashes into Phillip, both men get knocked from their chairs.

"I had to lift my leg out of the way," Phillip wisecracks. "The other guy didn't have a leg so he didn't have anything to worry about."

• • •

Jonathan Brown, an eighth-grader with spina bifida, joined the team because another volunteer coach, Joe Connick, saw him on the beach in a wheelchair.

David Hollyfield, who suffered a spinal injury when a stockroom shelf collapsed on him, signed up after T. J. Wills, a rehab volunteer, spotted him in a checkout line. T.J., a retiree, drives David and other Pensacolans to Mobile practices and games.

This sharing across age groups, across backgrounds and professions, is at the heart of the Patriots.

And some also share stories of drunkards and cowards.

Sammy Duffy would still be working as a deckhand on the Black Warrior River if it weren't for the drunken driver who ran his car off the road in 1989, damaging his spinal cord.

On his Harley one night in 1990, Darren Hallman, a former running back for Theodore High, was pushed off the road by a drunk who kept on going. With his leg severed, he lay in the ditch throwing rocks at cars until one stopped.

• • •

The Patriots vanquish the Warriors, and other teams get ready to take the court.

The red-bearded Warrior turns out to be a schoolteacher from Albany, N.Y., paralyzed from a motorcycle accident. The black-bearded one is a man from Manhattan with a bone disease. He had spent his youth in a body cast dreaming of playing sports.

O.D., Milton, Darren and the other Patriots weave past their opponents' chairs, exchanging powerful handshakes.

The Great Anvil Shoot

On a drizzly afternoon outside Fairhope, Ala., David Blackwell, NASA ground and technical engineer, pours a pound of double-F black gunpowder into a hole, tamps a plug into it, and lugs the 150-pound missile over the opening.

As he strikes a match, his partner, Neal Collier, speeds away in a pickup truck.

With his black beard and NASA cap, Blackwell looks like a high-tech loner, a whiz kid gone mad. He leans over, touches the match to a long fuse—and hauls.

Over the rutted cow pasture, onto the red clay road he runs, joining the ranks of Old Engine Show participants and 10-year-old boys and farmers with cameras.

Smoke billows around the launching pad. A sonic boom rocks the sky. A passing motorist looks out in astonishment, the bucolic hillside echoing with thunder.

Higher and higher the object goes until it looks like a bird, a pinwheel, a scrap of rag. And then it begins to fall—a meteor plummeting back toward the ground.

As it thuds into the bed of the pasture, the flock of little boys hurry out to the landing site to see, leaning over, hands on knees—amazed at the blacksmith's anvil buried deep in God's green earth.

This is an anvil shoot—a couple of men blowing a blacksmith's tool as high as possible into the air.

"It's a guy thing," says Blackwell.

Odd as the sport sounds—and lethal as it could be among bumblers—it is popular among those fond of antique tools, rending noises and gravity-defying acts on Saturday afternoons. The usual venues are old engine shows and blacksmith get-togethers along rural high-ways in the South.

Outside of city limits, says a Baldwin County sheriff, there appears to be nothing illegal about it, although the sport does strike him as "strange."

Champion anvil shooters can launch their cargo at least two foot-ball field lengths into the sky.

As the fuse sizzles down, David Blackwell of NASA (National Anvil Shooters Association) hauls from the launching site of a blacksmith's anvil about to receive the force of a pound of double-F black gunpowder. Blackwell's anvil partner, Neal Collier, traces the "sport" back to the settlers of the old West who blasted anvils to celebrate, explosively, holidays like the Fourth of July. (Collier has a photo of a painting displayed in a Cody, Wyoming, museum, of pioneers heralding an anvil's arc into the sky.) While the non-anvil shoot-ing populace may view this endeavor as inane, or at best bizarre, anvil devo-tees—who engage in interstate matches—pursue it with passion, strategizing over how to send their missile the highest, get it to fall back the closest, and keep it from landing on their heads. (G. M. Andrews, Mobile Register)

"If we shoot our anvils any higher," says Neal Collier, "we'll need aviation approval."

To Collier and Blackwell, shooting anvils is not so much a sport as a passion. They wear belt buckles in the shape of anvils, affix flying anvil hood ornaments to their cars, and wear clothes emblazoned with the insignia of NASA—the National Anvil Shooters Association.

"Our anvils," Collier figures, "have more miles on them than a Greyhound bus."

Part of the challenge, of course, is getting the anvil to fall back to the site whence it is shot. To this end, anvil shooters put their ingenuity into creating launching pads, such as the cast iron base Blackwell made in the Brewton foundry where he works.

All this firepower can take its toll on the life span of an anvil. Having blasted the horn off their old faithful, Collier and Blackwell now use one donated by Richard Goode, a Chickasaw telephone systems analyst who dabbles with radio-control airplanes. He met Collier and Blackwell when he saw their NASA caps and figured they worked out of Houston, not Bogia, Fla., or Flomaton, Ala.

Blackwell believes that "just because anvil shooting is crazy," it originated like stock car racing—in the South. "Everything crazy starts here."

But others take issue with this casual view of history.

Floyd Daniel, 79, a retired furniture company manager from Madison, Ga., widely credited with reviving anvil shoots in the South, speaks of religious origins. Even though conventional stories tell of St. Clement drowning with an anchor around his neck, Daniel believes St. Clement's neck was really strung with an anvil. At blacksmith gatherings a hundred years ago, says Daniel, blacksmiths fired off countless anvils in commemoration of their patron saint.

Collier traces anvil shooting to the settlers of the Old West who, lacking canons, blew up anvils to celebrate holidays. On his personal computer, he keeps a digitized photograph of a painting from Cody, Wyo., which shows pioneers astonished by the smoke and fire of a flying anvil. Bathed in celestial light, the anvil looks as though it's levitating. Might it be something less bizarre, like an alien craft hovering over the prairie?

Mike Stringer of Laurel, Miss., says that anvil shooting has its origins in the Union destruction of the Confederacy.

"The Yankee soldiers, being naturally lazy, didn't want to drag the anvils to the river to get rid of them," Stringer says. "When they tried to blow them up, they discovered the anvils just went up into the air."

As cultural historians, anvil shooters may be squabbling professors. But when it comes to head-to-head or anvil horn-to-horn competition, they get ornery as wrestlers.

"Alabama anvil shooters," says Mike Stringer, "are good folks. But when it comes to anvil shooting, they'll lie to you. What little they know they picked up from us boys over in Mississippi."

Oil company employee and amateur blacksmith Anthony Goodrum of Coden, Ala., explains how his friends, Collier and Blackwell, "packed up their anvil and headed out to whip" Stringer.

"We said we're not going to let any Mississippi rednecks outshoot us," Goodrum says.

Indeed, in competition against a half-dozen other teams at the Laurel invitational, Collier and Blackwell set a new world's record and brought the championship back to the Heart of Dixie. They blasted their anvil an epic 615.47 feet into the air.

"I never found a use for calculus until I started anvil shooting," says Collier, who spends his non anvil-shooting hours designing computers. He claims to have developed software for calculating anvil heights and trajectories.

Stringer laughs ruefully.

"What these guys do is strictly illegal according to NASA and WASS, the World Anvil Shooting Society," he says. "They shoot their anvil from a launching base like a canon. They get height but they don't get accuracy when it comes back down. Besides, I had to loan them my anvil. Theirs was broken. It was my anvil that went 615 feet."

Floyd Daniel grows impatient with this swagger and bluster.

"What those guys are doing is not anvil shooting," he laments. "What they're doing is spectacle. In real anvil shooting, one anvil is placed upside down on top of the other. Back in the early days, they didn't shoot for height. They shot for the blast and the explosion."

Daniel even mails out an essay, "Shooting the Anvil," to curious fans. He concludes: "This is not a how-to-do-it article and the author . . . disclaims all responsibility for any injury sustained or caused by anyone attempting to shoot the anvil."

He points out that two people were, in fact, killed when an anvil—cast iron instead of wrought iron—blew apart in Texas, and that the Artist Blacksmiths Association of North America (ABANA) does not allow anvil shooting at their national conventions.

But none of this dampens the spirits of Collier and Blackwell. As they set up for a second shoot at the Baldwin County Old Engine Show—this one using two pounds of black gunpowder and a hundred pound anvil—Collier says that they have only one final ritual they perform before the fuse is lit.

As he roars away in his truck he explains, "I tell David, don't light your cigarette."

• • •

As Blackwell strikes a match and leans to the fuse, he now looks like a weathered hippie, an innocent refugee from a '60s group like Creedence Clearwater Revival, his favorite band.

Perhaps anvil shooting is just another form of male, middle-age malaise, the same impulse to be wild in one's 40s that drives other men to buy sports cars and cruise around discos. Or perhaps, in a Robert Bly way, it's about men getting in touch with their inner selves, the little boys tucked away inside who like to crack neighbors' eardrums with Black Cats and M-80s.

When Blackwell ignites the fuse this time and the anvil soars with a deafening blast into the afternoon, the covey of little boys is waiting. When it plummets back to the planet, they scurry across the fields to look, and there is even one little girl among them.

As Blackwell, NASA cap tugged low, stoops to dig out the magic anvil, the kids surround him in admiration.

PART V

Tangled Legacies

❖

Look into the stories of families in south Alabama and faces, black and white, usually appear. The ties may be of blood, as in the story of Peter Dais and Peter Alba told here—a piano mover and a Confederate cavalry officer—or of history, as in the descendants of the slaves who came to Alabama on the Clotilda and the descendants of those who brought them here.

Slavery, the Civil War, Reconstruction, Jim Crow, Brown vs. Board of Education, the civil rights movement, the Voting Rights Act, Affirmative Action—the great tidal movements of American history, and issues arising from them, have rolled through the South defining our landscape. Peoples of two different histories and cultures have come together sometimes fitfully, sometimes violently—sometimes with compassion and understanding—to make one culture we share.

Race, as a defining aspect of our town and environs, runs deep beneath many of the stories in this book. Movie theaters, neighborhood drugstores, baseball, profiles of important players on our artistic and civic stages—in pieces earlier and later in this book, relations between black and white leave an impact.

Sociologists, for sure, have tried to measure how far we've come in Mobile. David Johnson, of University of South Alabama, has measured our progress in a series of studies that reveal there is more contact between black and white both in the work place and socially than in the past. But, Johnson concludes, we still have far to go. The members of black-white coalitions like Mobile United, with their origins in the 1960s, and in keeping with the spirit of biracial groups like the Southern Regional Council in Atlanta, continue to monitor the progress we make toward creating one town, not two.

But our "tangled legacies" can also be glimpsed in small dramas, and sharp ironies—the visit home to Mobile of then U.S. Secretary of Labor Alexis Herman, and the remarkable scene where she, a black woman, is heralded by a bevy of Azalea Trail Maids, black and white; and the event in Monroeville, Ala., just north of Mobile, where Harper Lee's "To Kill a Mockingbird" is dramatized by a hometown cast and where a "brown-skin boy from Mobile, Aladambama," Albert Murray, receives the Harper Lee Award as Alabama Writer of the Year.

Peter's Legacies

In his old moving truck, Peter Dais Jr., 74, who is black, creeps along the main road of Magnolia Cemetery, looking for the grave of Capt. Peter F. Alba, a white Confederate cavalry man and king of Mobile's Mardi Gras. Dais comes to a tall obelisk, parks and climbs out. He passes beneath a trellis and stands before the monument to the man he believes was his grandfather.

"It was a hush-hush thing in those days," he says, gazing up at the name, "Peter," above chiseled flowers. Dais received his surname from his grandmother, Rebecca, who worked as a servant for Alba and, the tale goes, bore him two children. Alba also had a child by his wife, Sophie; they are buried alongside him as are others with the Alba name.

Rebecca, however, rests in a grave with no headstone—"with my people," Dais says—in his own family's plot some miles to the south near Alba Club Road, close to Dog River. When his day comes, Dais says that's where he'll rest, too.

Peter Dais Sr. is said to have felt wronged by not being accepted by his father, and, out of indignation, refused property eventually offered him, although this story is unsubstantiated. Peter Jr. says his father never talked openly about Alba, but that the second child, Anna, did. Rebecca revealed the story of her relationship with Peter Alba to some of her seven grandchildren from her deathbed.

In Alba's sizeable will, probated after his death in 1915, "the sage of Coden" makes no mention of Rebecca or her children, leaving only a modest sum to the "Colored Old Folks and Orphans Home."

But Peter Dais Jr. embraces the notion of a grandfather who would

Peter Dais Jr. (left), who moves furniture for a living, also shoulders his family's hidden heritage. His grandfather, he says, was Peter Alba (right), a prominent white Mobilian, and his grandmother, Rebecca, the black servant who worked for him. In the 1910 photograph of Alba, the former Confederate cavalry officer and Mardi Gras king appears wise, influential and debonair. Two generations later, Dais stands before Alba's name etched on a large white monument at Magnolia cemetery. "I'm not trying to claim anything," Dais says of the hush-hush side of his family's ancestry. "Just talking history, that's all." (Photo of Dais Jr., by Bill Starling, *Mobile Register;* portrait of Alba, from the Overbey Collection, University of South Alabama Archives)

not embrace him. "I feel proud of him," he says, looking up at the stone.

He shrugs off the fact that, short of exhuming Alba to test DNA, it is impossible to determine, beyond scientific doubt, if the man was his grandfather. In his heart, and in the pale coloring of his brow, he has no doubt.

After all, he says, what should he hope to gain by believing a lie?

He has been married 54 years and still counting. He has toiled for decades, like his father, as a furniture- and piano-mover. His maternal grandfather, General Gatewood, was a drayman, who hauled with a mule and wagon. He has put four sons through college: a doctor, a teacher, a computer programmer and a postal executive. He is well-respected; even Liberace used him when he played Mobile.

"I'm not trying to claim anything," he says, stepping across the cemetery grass, making his way to his truck.

He glances back at the monument to the long-bearded man known for his love of horses, his lavish villa, his colorful ways. Alba School convenes classes still on land in south Mobile County donated by the captain.

"Just talking history," Dais says, "that's all."

• • •

There are secrets tucked away in the Mobile Public Library's division of Local History and Genealogy.

Peter Dais III, 54, who works as a manager for Mobile's U.S. Postal Service, wants to unlock them. Peter III enters the library, looking for background on the Confederate captain whose first name he feels certain he bears. He finds clippings and research papers on how Alba was the descendant of Spanish royalty. Alba's father was Don Juan de Alva, mayor of Pensacola; his grandfather was Pedro de Alva y Lopez, first viceroy of Spanish Pensacola.

Peter III wants to know, without doubt, his link to these men.

"It's more important to establish a claim to identity than any money that might have been lost," he says, echoing his father. He says he feels like he has been denied part of his heritage, and, "I just want closure. I realize this was a part of Peter Alba's life he hoped would not be made public."

He offers the example of his own wife, who is black, but had a German great-grandfather. "She has his picture and knows his background."

Holly Eckert, historian at the library, guides Peter in his search. In assisting people everyday who are on a quest to discover their backgrounds, Eckert knows the difficulties that arise in proving lineage.

There were no birth certificates in Alabama prior to 1908, she says. And federal census-takers from the North often had trouble understanding Southern accents, recording surnames incorrectly.

Church records of baptisms, if available, might reveal names of parents. But who would rush, in the old South, to offer details about a child born out of wedlock to parents of different races?

"People in general didn't leave a paper trail in those days," Eckert says. Even in the best circumstances, genealogy "is an inexact science," she adds.

But the U.S. Census of 1900, and its index, may hold a key to the story of Peter Alba and Rebecca Dais.

In that census, Peter Alba was listed as residing at Coden, Mobile's turn-of-the-century resort, just east of Bayou la Batre. He had one male servant with him. Rebecca "Days" was listed as a servant living in the household of Sophie "Alma" and grand-daughter Sophia, 9, at 259 N. Joachim St. in downtown Mobile. "Days," no doubt, was a faulty spelling of Dais, "Alma" of Alba. Sophia was there because her own mother and father were dead.

Rebecca was then 35, and listed as having two children, although neither was recorded in the household. Peter Alba, 61, was listed as married, although living with the one servant in Coden.

The Joachim Street address frames the story. In the Mobile City directory of 1900, Peter Alba's address was also given as 259 N. Joachim St.—the same as for Sophie, Sophia, and Rebecca.

Was Peter Alba living a double life, having children by Rebecca unbeknownst to Sophie? Or did Sophie and Rebecca understand the arrangement and dwell peaceably under the same roof?

In 1906, during the aftermath of the Hurricane of '06, a photograph was taken of Peter Alba at his badly damaged Coden villa. A widower by now, he is flanked on one side by an elegant young white woman in a fancy hat, most likely Sophia. On the other is a black woman, also in fancy hat, a little older.

When shown the photograph, Peter Dais Jr. props his glasses on his nose, holds it to the light and nods. "Could be," he says. "Could be."

• • •

Joan Lloyd, 55, is a banker in Long Beach, Calif. As a girl, she used to visit Mobile with her mother, Mary Alba Warren, to see her grandmother, Sophia. On those trips, she'd be taken to Coden and Bayou la Batre, shown the school named for her ancestor, Peter Alba.

Peter Alba became bigger than life in her eyes—a man who imported circus animals from Europe, who had the finest cut diamonds, who commanded a grand villa in Coden. He was a landowner, funeral director and ran a livery business. He had presented a horse to Winnie Davis, Jefferson Davis' daughter, and had exchanged letters with the Confederate president.

By his appearance alone—Dostoevskian beard, rumpled cap—Alba was an intriguing man. A Catholic of Spanish heritage, he was chosen in 1875 as Mobile's Mardi Gras king.

On her trips to Mobile, though, Lloyd experienced a segregated South foreign to her as a Californian. She remembers how, on a bus ride in Mobile with her grandmother when she was 10, she made the mistake of taking a seat in the back of the bus. Sophia "was upset" and lectured her that the back of the bus was "for colored."

Until I contacted her, Lloyd had never heard that Peter Alba might have fathered other children, much less those who would have sat at the back of that bus.

Then she begins to think back on her trips to Mobile, saying it seemed odd how her grandmother "never mentioned a word" about Sophie, Peter Alba's wife. "I never had the chance to find out what happened to her," she says. Sophie remains a shadow in the background.

She contemplates returning to Mobile one day.

"We're a small family. It's good to find new relations. What are we, half third cousins?" She laughs, then says she'd be interested in talking to them by telephone.

• • •

Oliver Washington, 44, is the son of Cleo Dais Washington, 79, the
sister of Peter Jr. He studied horticulture at the University of Florida,
and owns a plant nursery near Bellingrath Gardens. He found out
the story of Peter Alba and Rebecca from his mother, although not
until he was grown.

"I'm not bitter I had a great-grandfather who was white," he says,
chuckling. "Most people look at me and say, 'We knew this!'"

A few years ago, Washington drove to "Coden Days," a celebration
of the community's history. It was held at a Methodist church. He
went to a booth set up with information on Peter Alba and introduced himself as a descendant.

That part of Alba's life is part of the "secret history" of the town,
as one woman, assembling a history of Alba High School, calls it.
"We don't go into that," she says. "We just say Peter Alba donated
the land and leave the rest alone."

On the day Washington told his story at Coden, Velma Rabby
Steele was there. It was the Rabby family who sold to Alba their land
in Coden and Bayou la Batre. There's a Rabby Bridge in the area
today.

In a bygone era, Steele says, if Washington had divulged his story,
"all those older Methodist women would have passed out."

No one passed out at Coden Days.

"People were ashamed of it back then, but things like that took
place," she says. "Afterward, some older people came up to me from
the area and said, yes, it was true. . . . He's a descendant and he
should be proud of it."

He is proud of it, he says. Washington wants to piece together the
"connections" of his family's past. He has even researched the Alba
coat of arms. "If someone wants to look at my color, that's their
problem," he says. "I am who I am."

Search for a Slave Ship

Winter 1998

Deep in the muck under Mobile waters, some say, a slave ship lies.

Intrigued by gloomy tales of its wreckage and murky photographs of its purported remains, searchers have long puttered and prodded near the mouth of Chickasabogue in north Mobile.

Once again a search is under way, this time by underwater archaeologists with magnetometers and sonar scanners. The "Clotilda Project," under the auspices of the Alabama Historical Commission, has focused on the marshlands and bayous of the Mobile River delta sprawling north of the city.

The Clotilda—called Clotilde by some—is said to have arrived in Mobile's harbor in late summer 1859, carrying West Africans bought in the Kingdom of Dahomey, in a strip known then as the "slave coast."

Slavery was still legal in Southern states, but the federal government had outlawed slave importations since 1808. After the financial backer of the expedition, Timothy Meaher, a steamship-maker in Mobile, and William Foster, the sea-going captain who built the Clotilda, saw the ship to port, they dispersed the slaves, then destroyed the evidence, scuttling the Clotilda by setting it afire.

A naval historian in Mobile, Jack Friend, who is a member of the Alabama Historical Commission, believes the Clotilda was a two-masted schooner, 86 feet long, 23 feet wide, with a copper hull. Its 110 slaves would have been crowded, for 72 days at sea, in a dark hold 7 feet high.

The Clotilda, though, as with the controversy over its name, has never offered certainties. Commonly dubbed "the last slave ship" in local annals, its very voyage has been called into doubt by one prominent historian.

But Friend believes the Clotilda will be found—its copper hull dredged up and restored for public view, its grim slave chains and manacles, too.

. . .

Martha West Davis, 75, a retired schoolteacher, has no doubts the Clotilda existed. Her great-grandfather, Cudjo Lewis, whose African name was Kazoola, came on that ship.

As a young girl, she and her twin sister, Mary, visited "Grampa" in north Mobile's Plateau community at the wooden house he'd made himself. They watched how he told time by the sun and made a favorite stew of canned salmon and tomatoes.

"His shoe," Davis remembers, "was almost three times the size of my foot. It was a skin shoe—a sandal. I wore patent leather shoes with buckles, and I'd put my foot into his shoe. I would think it was going to bite me!"

Journalists made pilgrimages to Cudjo's house, listening as he told about his tribe in Togo, a people who sustained themselves by farming, and whose laws included: Tell the truth, do not steal, do not commit adultery—although men were polygamous—and punish murderers with death.

Among those who recorded his tales were Emma Langdon Roche, a schoolteacher whose family owned a Mobile funeral home; and Zora Neale Hurston, who would become one of America's preeminent authors. Erik Overbey, a Mobile photographer who'd immigrated from Norway, took a picture of Cudjo with Martha and Mary at his knees.

Cudjo told how he was captured in Togo, by warriors from neighboring Dahomey, now Benin; how he watched friends and family slaughtered, their heads severed and held aloft; how he had been taken to the port of Whydah, thrown into a slave compound and sold by another African, the prince of Dahomey, to William Foster.

When the Africans arrived in Mobile that Sunday in August 1859, Cudjo and 30 others became the property of Timothy Meaher. The rest became scattered, some to Burns Meaher, Timothy's brother, others to John Dabney, who had a plantation upriver. Some, legend has it, were abandoned in the woods, appearing at local doors looking for food.

Within two years of their arrival, the Civil War began; in another four years it was over. As freed slaves after the war, Cudjo and others from the Clotilda established themselves in Plateau, on land acquired from Timothy Meaher—by purchase from Meaher, in one version of the story; by gift from Meaher, in another.

In the neighborhood that would become known as Africatown, they appointed their own rule-keepers. Christianized, they formed the African Church, later Old Land Mark Baptist—forerunners of Union Baptist Church in Plateau.

At the church, Martha Davis remembers, Cudjo tolled the bell.

At Cudjo's own funeral in 1935, Martha Davis remembers, her mother Angelee rang the bell. She rang it like Cudjo had taught her—one way to signal the death of a child, another for someone old.

Although one newspaper account of the time put Cudjo's age at 96, Davis says he was 115.

• • •

In front of Union Baptist Church today, the likeness of Cudjo Lewis, chiseled from stone, presides over the landscape.

Weed-choked lots, road construction, modest homes—the locale appears, outwardly, unlikely for historic recognition. The community's concerns—how to remain a haven for hard-working, close-knit families, and keep drugs and guns off the street—seem light-years from the story of a slave ship.

But the Clotilda story still counts.

Israel Lewis III, Cudjo's great-great-grandson, takes the story to the city's surliest audience—teen-agers who've broken the law. At a boot camp for juvenile offenders, he holds up a picture of Cudjo and tells them what his forebear endured, how he thrived.

In 1927, at his Africatown home in the Plateau community of Mobile, Cudjo "Kazoola" Lewis embraces his twin, 4-year-old great-granddaughters, Mary (left) and Martha West. Cudjo was born in Togo and captured by warriors in neighboring Dahomey, now Benin; sold by the prince of Dahomey to a white sea captain from Mobile, William Foster, acting on behalf of another Mobilian, Timothy Meaher; and with thirty other slaves, brought to Mobile in 1859 on the Clotilda—believed to be the last slave ship to America. (Erik Overbey Collection, University of South Alabama Archives)

Stories of Cudjo (on facing page with twin granddaughters) endure not only in accounts by writers of the day, among them Zora Neale Hurston, but also in the memory of one of those twin little girls, Martha West Davis, who went on to become a school teacher and is pictured here at age 75 in 1997 with a drawing of "Grampa" on her living room wall. (David Mercer, Mobile Register)

Lewis turns to his African heritage in teaching schoolchildren art, and has written poetry in which he imagines himself, alongside Cudjo, being abducted as a slave.

When his own father, a riverboat pilot, was on his deathbed, he showed the son the "ancestral handshake"—a clasp of forearms that sent a jolt into Israel's body, a force of energy, he believes, linking him closely to Cudjo.

One of the slaves on the Clotilda, along with Cudjo, was Lottie Joseph. Her granddaughter, Mable Dennison, now 77, labored for seven years to write a book about Lottie, and another book about James Dennison, an American slave who married Lottie and was Mable's grandfather.

Part native American, James belonged to Timothy Meaher, and helped him pilot a steamboat that played a role in spiriting the slaves from the Clotilda to a plantation upriver for concealment from federal agents.

Mable Dennison works at the National African-American Archives-Museum in downtown Mobile. She remembers how, in her youth—an era before the term "African-American" became a source of pride—some blacks shied away from their own family histories, ridiculing the children of the Clotilda slaves as "old Africans."

While speaking with quiet sorrow of how her forebears were brought here, she speaks philosophically of those responsible. "The Meahers," she says, "are part of my history, too."

When asked for the Meahers' version of the Clotilda story, a descendant of Timothy Meaher, who would not be identified by name, responded by saying that "now is not a happy time" for a story about the slave trade.

He gave glimpses of "Captain Tim" as a large landowner who was a benefactor of Spring Hill College in Mobile and helped build the pillars on the Cathedral of the Immaculate Conception downtown. Captain Tim was also a savvy businessman. A story has long circulated among some local historians that Meaher set the Clotilda mission in motion because others simply dared him to do so—that he was just taking a bet. This descendant raised doubts about what may well be only a legend.

Might there come a time when discussions, on the record, could take place?

In 20 years, he said.

• • •

Henry C. Williams, a welder and Plateau historian, is not a Clotilda descendant, but he is vocal on issues regarding the ship. He says he created the sculpture of Cudjo Lewis in front of Union Baptist Church, and that he spent time with Cudjo as a child.

One of Williams' complaints is that a historic marker in downtown Mobile needs the spelling of Clotilde corrected to Clotilda. He finds an unlikely ally from a century ago in Capt. William Foster, who wrote an account of his voyage on the "Clotilda."

"Clotilda" is also used by Albert Murray, reared at Magazine Point, near Plateau. In the classic book "South to a Very Old Place," Murray ruminates on home, mentioning the ship.

Williams has another objection—that the Clotilda should not be called a "slave ship" because its cargo "was not actually slaves," since slave imports were then illegal.

In a roundabout way, Williams may have a point. The story of the Amistad, for example, the basis for Steven Spielberg's 1997 movie of that name, revolves around the courtroom question of whether the black people aboard that ship had been abducted from Africa, or whether they'd come from servitude in Cuba.

Mobile never had a case of the magnitude of "Amistad," though the Clotilda did come front and center in local courts.

In 1861, the U.S. government attempted to prosecute Burns Meaher and John Dabney for their roles in the Clotilda venture. The Civil War soon began, and the case was dismissed.

Timothy Meaher went on trial before a jury, but he walked free. Meaher, the builder of steamboats, had also captained them, a fact that served him well in court.

Thirty years later, a correspondent for the St. Louis Globe-Democrat interviewed Meaher and explained the defense strategy: "Capt. Meaher . . . saved his neck through his ability to prove that he had made fifty-two consecutive trips on the (steamboat) Roger B. Taney between Mobile and Montgomery that year, the attorneys thus convincing the jury that he could not have imported the slaves and made these trips also."

Capt. William Foster leaves no doubt in his account of the journey that Cudjo and his brethren were purchased, manacled and brought to Mobile as chattel.

In elegant longhand, Foster tells of harrowing storms and skirmishes with Portuguese ships. He explains how he moored the Clotilda near Petite Bois Island, off the coast of Mississippi, having altered the masts to disguise it as a "common coaster." He then contacted Timothy Meaher to send a steam tug to haul the ship to the Mobile River.

The Clotilda is commonly called, by people in Mobile, "the last slave ship" to America. Although it made its slave expedition in 1859, was it the only slave ship that year to ply the oceans?

In "Battle Cry of Freedom: The Civil War Era," esteemed historian James McPherson writes of slave importation: "Federal law had banned this trade since the end of 1807. Smuggling continued on a small scale after that date; in the 1850s the rising price of slaves produced an increase in this illicit traffic."

One eminent historian, Hugh Thomas, scrambles long-held notions about the Clotilda in his 900-page "The Slave Trade," published in 1997. Thomas dismisses Mobile's slave ship in his brief mention of it, while also seeming to juggle facts: "The case of the Clotilde, under Captain Meagher, alleged to have landed 116 slaves in South Carolina in July 1859, may have been a hoax."

• • •

Jack Friend is fascinated by the Clotilda. A retired businessman who's writing a book on the Battle of Mobile Bay, Friend sometimes lies awake at night imagining what went through Capt. Foster's mind—where he might have navigated the ship before it was burned and sunk.

Friend has been instrumental in raising private funds and securing a state grant for the new search.

In the "Clotilda Project," an underwater archaeology company, Pan American Marine, based in Memphis, Tenn., has been hunting for "anomalies" in the waters.

Friend admits that with all the junk that has sunk over the centuries—from timber buoys to old washing machines—finding the rotted remains of a wooden ship is tricky business.

He will not draw an "X" on the map. Looters, he warns, are notorious in Alabama waters.

To date, he says, two anomalies have been detected.

The ultimate goal, he emphasizes, is to bring up what's left of the ship, see it preserved, maintained and appropriately displayed: "The Clotilda belongs to the people of Alabama."

Where would it be displayed, if found?

He points to the controversy over the sunken Confederate submarine Hunley. After divers found the Hunley off Charleston, S.C., a civic free-for-all broke out among interest groups staking claims to its legacy.

If the Clotilda is found and raised, Friend hopes that Mobilians will be more reasonable.

Alexis Herman Comes Home

August 1997

Pudgy, black-haired, 8 weeks old, Victoria Alexis Castro is waiting for the motorcade to begin. Though no blood relation to Mobile native Alexis Herman, U.S. Secretary of Labor in the Clinton Administration, the baby girl was named in her honor.

"You'd be surprised how many Alexises there are in Mobile," says the baby's grown-up cousin, cradling her.

Nearby, also waiting for Ms. Herman to arrive from the Mobile Convention Center where she earlier addressed the public, is state legislator Vivian Davis Figures, peering through sleek sunglasses. From this point Ms. Herman's car will be joined by those of local officials, and they will wind their way through the communities where the Secretary of Labor spent her childhood.

It's only right, Ms. Figures says, that Ms. Herman is parading through her old neighborhood. "She's a home girl."

Mayor Mike Dow, also waiting, pauses to pose for a photograph with a woman and her two children. City Council candidates mill about, shaking hands, looking available for photographs, too; no one asks.

A retired postal worker, Marshall Wormley, stands with pals in front of the Mardi Gras den, where the Mobile Area Mardi Gras Association—Mobile's black carnival organization—is building its floats.

What do the floats look like?

"I don't know," Wormley says, "but if I did, I wouldn't tell."

It is only fitting that Ms. Herman's motorcade begin in sight of the Mardi Gras den where she once reigned as Queen Alexis, and within a block of Pure Heart of Mary School—historically by fiat, and now by tradition, a black parochial school—where she graduated before going off to Xavier University.

Men linger on porches a half-block away, feet up on railings in the

Mobile born and bred, Alexis Herman, U.S. Secretary of Labor in the cabinet of President Bill Clinton, surveys the downtown scene near the old GM&O Building. The day-long event included a public address by Ms. Herman and a journey, by motorcade and foot, through the neighborhoods of her youth. Along the way she would pass sites of personal meaning, like Pure Heart of Mary School, where she studied as a teen, and the "den" of the Mobile Area Mardi Gras Association, the black carnival association for which she reigned, as Queen Alexis, in 1974, continuing the tradition of her father, Alex Herman, king in 1940. Escorting the Secretary of Labor are, from left, Dr. Yvonne Kennedy, president of Bishop State Community College, state Sen. Vivian Davis Figures, and Mobile Mayor Mike Dow. Behind Mrs. Kennedy is Al Stokes, Dow's executive assistant. (Courtesy of John David Mercer)

bright, late August day; other houses, that once stood here, have been demolished and plots of grass yawn wide.

Renee Little, 43, a social worker, says that Ms. Herman's being from Mobile makes it special. "She knows what it means to come from lower levels. Even though her father was in the carnival association, she knew plenty who weren't. I feel so good for her, but so sad because her parents aren't here."

The motorcade arrives and people crowd around.

Elaina Mosley, an 11th-grader at McGill-Toolen High, says there are too few role models for youths. In the same breath as she talks about Alexis Herman, she reveres Savion Glover, tap dance star of Broadway's hit, "Bring In Da Noise, Bring In Da Funk." She got to dance with Glover at a tap workshop in New Orleans.

"It's ironic," says Sheila Mosley, Elaina's mother, "that a black woman could come through the ranks of Mobile to achieve what she has in her life. You wouldn't think a woman . . . a black woman." She smiles proudly. "And from little ol' country Mobile."

● ● ●

Al is 40, wears a baseball cap backwards and purple jeans with sneakers. He sits on a porch on Dr. Martin Luther King Jr. Avenue with other family members. Among them is Lucy Thomas, who studied to be a beautician down the street. "I used to be scared to be on the Avenue," she says, "but now I sit out here on the porch every night."

Al's not sure, exactly, what Ms. Herman's exact position is in Washington, but he thinks it's great that she hasn't forgotten where she hails from—that she's come home.

"Mobile is a slow thing," he says, shaking his head, contrasting it to Philadelphia, where he spent many years before returning.

"I love Mobile," protests Lucy, who admits if she lived anywhere else she'd be lost and "have to be led around like a puppy dog."

"It's a good feeling to go way up into the White House," Al breaks in, "to be with the president. I never thought a black woman could make it."

When the motorcade reached their house, rather than stop as at some key locations, it just raced by. "The children had bags for candy," Lucy says. "They thought she was going to throw them something, like Mardi Gras."

"She waved at us through the window," Al says.

And if he were in Washington, D.C., and trapped in some dire emergency?

"I believe I could call her," Al says, "and she'd react."

• • •

Everywhere on the parade route, people speak of Alexis Herman as though she has come home to see them, to speak to them, one-on-one.

Some, of course, are related, or knew her from the neighborhood, Down the Bay. Some, like J. D. Whitfield, a retired piano teacher, knew Alex Herman, her daddy, when he was an important figure in Democratic ward politics.

"She calls me on the phone like I'm her daddy," Whitfield says. "She likes seafood, and I'll be going out to get redfish and catfish for her later."

But some feel a connection to her because they, too, are from Mobile; and they grew up in a similar time, a similar place.

Out front of Bishop State Community College on MLK Avenue, several people refer to themselves as "Centralians"—graduates of the former Central High School.

Sharon Scott is beaming. "I'm ecstatic." She got the chance to shake Ms. Herman's hand. "You'd have thought I was 6 years old!"

Along with Ms. Herman, Scott admires Yvonne Kennedy, president of Bishop State, and Vivian Davis Figures, who was elected to the Alabama State Legislature in the slot her husband, Michael Figures, had held before his untimely death. Scott's greatest idol is the late Texas Congresswoman Barbara Jordan.

Near the women, a group of youngsters come running from the playground and begin to quiz each other—a kind of political one-upmanship.

"Do you know who's president?"

"Bill Clinton."

"How many times has he been elected?"

"Twice. Now you tell me, who's vice president?"

"Al Gore," the other exclaims, and grabs him in a headlock, tussling him to the ground.

Alexis Herman's motorcade has roared off, but the boys are still at it—a scrappy civics lesson.

"Did you see she had a Secret Service agent!" says Shakio Populus, a seventh-grader at Dunbar. He hops up on a playground wall.

"I want to be president one day," he concludes.

• • •

At Government Plaza, when the motorcade is over and Alexis Herman moves toward the stage to give final remarks to the crowd, the Bishop State band plays "Amazing Grace."

One of the onlookers, Jill Chow, had been in the court of Queen Alexis of Mardi Gras. Earlier, at the Convention Center, Ms. Chow had taken her 5-week-old daughter to hear Ms. Herman, but now her baby is at home, sleeping soundly. The infant girl's name—Janey Alexis Chow.

As Alexis Herman walks onto the stage, the Azalea Trail Maids, of all backgrounds, in powder blue and lavender and soft yellow antebellum dresses, curtsy to the floor.

Long Lives the Mockingbird

In Monroeville, Ala., where Harper Lee and Truman Capote once raced by Boo Radley's house as children, the 1903 courthouse still rises in the square, its bell tower, now electrified, chiming the hours. After a new courthouse was built in the 1960s, this one was marked for demolition. But citizens who prized the landmark and its role in "To Kill a Mockingbird"—as a fictional setting in Harper Lee's novel and the model for the courtroom in the movie of the same name—managed to preserve it.

The building also serves as a stage. On several weekends every spring, since 1992, Christopher Sergel's adaption of "To Kill a Mockingbird" has unfolded on the courthouse lawn. When I attended one of the performances this 1998 season, the audience included not just local families and tourists but others who had come to town for a symposium on Alabama writing. As real mockingbirds jabbered in pecan trees and recorded ones echoed from loudspeakers, we were all sent back to the summer of 1935:

Atticus Finch ambles home and meets his daughter, Scout, on the porch. He has taken on the impossible task of defending Tom Robinson, poor and black, who is accused of beating and raping Mayella Ewell, poor and white.

"Atticus," Scout asks her father, still stung by the taunts of the other children, "do you defend niggers?"

"Of course I do," he answers. "Don't say 'nigger,' Scout. That's common."

This exchange, taken directly from the novel, made me cringe, just as it did when I first read it in high school 30 years ago. But the fact that I was hearing it in this setting is a measure of just how far my state has come. Here was the era of segregation dramatized by amateur actors from the community, among them an appraiser, a farmer and an air-conditioner salesman. A former police chief, in brown uniform with suspenders, played the role of Sheriff Heck Tate; a county commissioner played Tom Robinson, the defendant unjustly convicted and shot dead, supposedly while trying to escape a prison farm. "It hits down deep," Commissioner Charlie McCorvey Jr. said of his role as a character who could not cast votes, much less campaign for them. "I get emotional."

There were other ironic glimpses of Alabama's history to be seen on this courthouse lawn. Near me in the audience, his hand cupped to his ear to catch the dialogue, was Albert Murray, now in his early 80s, chosen to receive the inaugural Harper Lee Award as Alabama's most distinguished writer. He'd come from New York, where he now lives, for the occasion.

Act I concluded and Sheriff Heck Tate called names from the audience to serve as jurors when the production moved indoors for Act II. My name was among them. By the play's 1930s standards, I was qualified—white and male. The Harper Lee Award winner, "a brown-skin boy" from "Mobile, Aladambama," as Murray musically describes his fictional alter ego, was not.

Albert Murray grew up in Magazine Point, on the Mobile River near downtown Mobile, a setting he evokes with literary jazz riffs in his travelogue, "South to a Very Old Place," and in various novels that begin in fictional Gasoline Point, Ala., during the 1930s— "Train Whistle Guitar," "The Spyglass Tree," "The Seven League Boots." His "brown-skin" narrator, Scooter, shares a host of coming-of-age stories, describing his early schooling, his first love. He pays comparatively little attention to race, a subject obsessively poked and prodded by many white Southern writers.

"Somebody's always asking me, 'How was it growing up in Alabama?'" Murray told me. "They expect me to stretch out this long list of atrocities having to do with race relations, but I'm thinking about the chinaberry tree where I was figuring out how I was going to conquer the world."

Harper Lee grew up in rural Monroeville, two counties away from Mobile—Maycomb in "To Kill a Mockingbird." She hasn't published another book since her novel appeared in 1960, winning a Pulitzer Prize and alienating a town. Her narrator, 8-year-old Scout, takes us gently into a community torn ever more harshly by race. Scout's father, Atticus Finch, is a white Southerner with a conscience, a lawyer with a soul, a widower doing his best to teach his children right and wrong. To most of us, he will forever be the actor who played him in the movies, Gregory Peck.

Murray, who has written about American culture in books like "Stomping the Blues" and "The Hero and the Blues," said his prose draws its sensibility from blues and jazz. Harper Lee's novel, he observed, can be thought of in terms of spirituals or Methodist hymns. Murray believes it is the "Sunday school lesson" of "To Kill a Mockingbird," with its "strong moral statement," that has now inspired the citizens of Monroeville. Murray likens this re-creation of the story to a Passion play: "It becomes a part of the town ritual, like the religious underpinnings of Mardi Gras. With the whole town crowded around the actual courthouse, it's part of a central, civic education—what Monroeville aspires to be." The courthouse, in Murray's view, has become key to the ritual. The Harper Lee Award is even a small replica of the building.

Albert Murray's Magazine Point is gone, replaced by paper mills along the Mobile River; only his stories remain. Much of Harper Lee's Monroeville has been leveled too. At the site of the house where she grew up on South Alabama Avenue with her lawyer father, A. C. Lee, and her sister Alice, who also became a lawyer, there is now an ice cream shop. The woman making root beer floats at Mel's Dairy Dream said she'd never heard of Harper Lee. Next door, where Truman Capote once lived with his cousin Sook Faulk, there is only a rubble-filled lot. The Boo Radley oak has been uprooted.

Most folks in Monroeville share glimpses of Harper Lee—drinking cappuccino at a cafe across from the courthouse, visiting with friends at the local stores. She's not reclusive, they say, just deeply private and defiantly silent on the subject of her novel. One woman told me that at a Christmas party last year an "outsider" foolishly accosted Lee with chatter about "To Kill a Mockingbird." Lee simply walked out.

According to Kathy McCoy, the director of the play, Lee has never attended a production. In another irony, though, this version of "To Kill a Mockingbird"—and the restoration of the courthouse as a museum filled with Harper Lee and Truman Capote memorabilia—helps keep the town alive. Lee's story, which at first seemed embarrassing to much of the town, has proved kinder in the long run than some industry. When Vanity Fair Mills relocated part of its operations offshore, hundreds of jobs went too. When a discount shopping center lost out to new stores in another county, business dwindled. Most of the shops now sit empty, as ghostly as Boo Radley's house once was.

With fiction surviving fact, a deli named Radley's is one of the liveliest places around; the town square is spruced up, thanks to visitors' dollars attracted by the museum; outdoor murals create the illusion of 1935 streets; and a mockingbird looms on the Chamber of Commerce's billboards. Jane Ellen Cason, whose great-grandfather oversaw the design of the courthouse and who works with county eighth-graders studying Lee's novel, told me that people often phone the museum to ask for information on the "re-enactment." A work of the imagination has become a chronicle of history. There's even a virtual destination: www.tokillamockingbird.com.

Inside the courtroom in Act II, the ceiling fan was turning, a fly circled and, just as in yesteryear, the jury was streaming sweat. From the jury box, I had an onstage view of the courtroom's pressed tin ceiling and the upstairs gallery once designated for "colored."

Atticus Finch was played by a minister of a Nazarene church in nearby Excel, Ala. As the other jurors and I listened to his closing argument, it was clear again—as it has been for the millions who've read the novel and seen the film—that left-handed Bob Ewell was the one who battered his daughter Mayella, not Tom Robinson, played year after year by Commissioner McCorvey, his left hand in a sling.

• • •

But as the time warp began to feel real, I looked out at the "town" crowded into the courtroom and sensed the pressure a juror must have felt in 1935—the pressure to vote with the pack, no matter his conscience. Sheriff Heck Tate herded the jury offstage. Hidden from the audience for several minutes, he gave us our instructions: on cue, we would resume our places in the jury box and our foreman would hand him a slip of paper reading "Guilty."

Some of us wondered aloud what it would be like to change the verdict, to alter what Albert Murray calls "the ritual" of this event. The sheriff told us that only once had a jury insisted upon doing just that—in 1996, when this production played in Jerusalem and 12 Israeli men had at first refused to convict Tom Robinson. The sheriff explained to them that they had no choice, that it was crucial to the story.

"No," the Israeli jurors protested backstage.

"I told them," the sheriff said to us, affecting a backwoods growl, "I talked to the authorities here and y'all better do what I say!"

In Jerusalem, with the script on his side, he had prevailed.

Our time to deliberate was soon over. The sheriff nodded toward the doorway. We filed in and faced the accused.

PART VI

Newcomers Among Us

❖

Mexico and Southeast Asia—the locales may be far-flung from each other on the globe, but natives of both cultures have made their way to south Alabama. Mexicans and Mexican-Americans from south Texas toil, on a seasonal basis, in the Baldwin County potato fields. Laotians, Vietnamese, and Cambodians have rooted into Bayou la Batre and other waterfront areas in Mobile County, sustaining themselves with work in shrimping and seafood processing.

Who are these "newcomers" to the coastal South?

In the summer of 1997 I met a Baldwin County farmer who was gracious enough to let me spend time in his fields, and in his work shed, talking with potato pickers he employed. At the same time a Mexican-American family—and the crew boss, who was the family's grandmother—opened up their migrant home to me. A story of one farmer and the migrant family who come to his potato fields is a window into a world little seen, and often little understood. What's more, some passers-through—especially those finding year-round work on turf farms—are deciding to stay.

Summer of 1999, I entered a different but not dissimilar world— that of the Southeast Asian refugees in Mobile County. Hard physical labor, large families, strong religious faith, and a struggle to push the next generation upwards to a better life—these were some of the attributes that the groups shared. Once again I found families willing to open their homes to me in order to share their stories about a new life in America's Deep South.

Stories on the Mexican migrant workers and the Asian fishermen were originally written as long, three-part, summertime chronicles. "Newcomers Among Us" offers large portions of these series as they originally appeared—a peek into the South unfolding with the 21st century.

Las Familias de la Tierra

❖

By the Sweat of Their Brows

Summer 1997

Black hair pinned at the back, clipboard in hand, Martina Ledesma, 50, stands like a rock in the broiling sun. As crew boss at Childress Farms in Baldwin County, she peers through dark sunglasses at the field-workers, among them her grown children. Down endless rows of dirt, the "campesinos," some in baseball caps, a few with shirts pulled up like cowls over their heads, bend and pick potatoes.

"Que calor!" says one. How hot it is! He scrapes at the ground.

"Gracias a Dios que ha terminado la lluvia," says another, thanking God for stopping the rains. At 30 cents for each bucket picked, each bucket weighing 50 pounds, the dollars earned mount slowly. To earn $300 a week, a worker must pick 1,000 buckets, 50,000 pounds.

Having traveled from the hardscrabble life of south Texas to earn, at best, minimum wages for six weeks in south Alabama, few workers complain. Far worse for them is when the rain turns the fields to mud and they must linger about their ramshackle housing, earning nothing at all.

Near Martina is Fernando Uresti of Donna, Texas, a man of large girth who wears a back-support belt as he stoops and huffs. When his foot recently became infected from a bug bite, he lost three days of work. Alongside him is his married daughter, Erika, hands raking at the dirt. Next month they will go to Georgia to pick tobacco; the

Bending into the dirt of a Baldwin County field, huffing and sweating in the 90 degree heat, Fernando Uresti of Donna, Texas, plucks up red potatoes, hustling to fill another fifty pound bucket—thirty cents more in his pocket. For many of the migrant workers who sweep into south Alabama in June, the toil is a family endeavor. Behind Fernando is his daughter, Erika, whose husband is picking in another field. Although potato crops are dwindling in Baldwin County, the migrant workers still appear in force every June, speaking blends of English and Spanish, some in their third and fourth generation of workers. After setting up their homes in crude migrant camps for a few weeks, they head on in the "stream" of crops that take some to Sand Mountain, north of Birmingham, to pick more potatoes, and others, like the Uresti family, to Georgia to help with the tobacco harvest. (Kiichiro Sato, Mobile Register)

Ledesmas, and most others, will head to north Alabama to pick more potatoes.

The sun grows hotter and Martina touches the ring on her hand: San Benito High School in south Texas, 1995. It belonged to her son, Elijio, whose name is inscribed. On Good Friday, Elijio was killed in a hit-and-run on a Colorado highway. He had just received certification from the U.S. Department of Labor to become, like Martina, a Farm Labor Contractor—a crew boss.

As is often a tradition, Elijio would have assumed the powerful role once held by his father Jose. In the tough world of migrant farm work, women crew bosses are rare. Martina became one only after Jose collapsed in an onion field in Colorado. With her nine children still young, and the family deeply in debt, she had to figure out a way to provide.

By becoming a crew boss, Martina has the chance to earn far more than pickers. Farm owner Floyd Childress says he pays the crew boss in the field 70 cents for each bucket filled and delivered to the shed.

Childress says that of that 70 cents, 30 cents normally goes to the worker who picks the bucket, and 10 cents to the man who loads the bucket on a flatbed truck and drives it to the shed. From the 30 cents remaining, the crew boss pays for the flatbed trucks, gas, repairs and other expenses. Whatever remains is the crew boss's profit.

Childress says these numbers are his best guess, since the crew boss, as labor contractor, handles payments to the pickers. Although Martina can be talkative when she gets to know someone, when the subject turns to money, she grows mum.

As crew boss, Martina is responsible for hiring the laborers, getting them to the fields by sunup, making sure they work hard until evening. They take a break at the hottest time of day, from 11 a.m. to 3 p.m.

In the potato fields, she clusters a family together, allotting them an area to pick. Family members who pick quickly make up for those who cannot. Both in the field and at the camp, Martina must also keep the peace.

One worker describes the Saturday afternoon ritual in which

Martina, having cashed the week's wages from Childress, gives each
family its due.

With pride, Martina says that on two of the best recent days, her
crew picked up to 8,000 buckets.

Pam Childress, Floyd's wife, makes out the payments. In 1996,
she says, Childress Farms paid about $43,000 to Martina, the field
crew boss, who distributed it among the workers.

How much the workers ultimately earn depends on the number sharing in the total payment. This year, Fernando Uresti says
with discouragement, he'll perhaps make only $2,000. One worker,
though, who hustles in the dirt, tells Floyd Childress that he can
make as much as $90 in a day, picking 300 buckets by himself.

During the part of the year they're back in Texas, the migrant
workers pick local crops, or take minimum-wage jobs at the car wash,
Wal-Mart, or the Fruit of the Loom plant. Or wait out long, dreary
days unemployed.

Hundreds of buckets are loaded onto the truck now that rattles
by. When the truck reaches the shed, another crew boss, Felipe, a
Mexican-American from Bainbridge, Ga., commands his own workers, who wash, grade and bag the potatoes. Shed workers, says Childress, make a straight $5 an hour. The shed crew boss is paid a bonus
for each worker employed.

It's lunchtime. One picker, who prefers to work shoeless, knocks
the dirt off her feet and climbs into a minivan where taped salsa music
blares. Other vans and trucks follow, forming a caravan down Baldwin
County 32, heading by lush fields and landscaped verandas, continuing on to rundown trailers and wooden barracks that, until next
month, constitute home.

• • •

"La familia." The family.

The migrant workers who sweep into Baldwin County every year
during May and June, most from south Texas, are not lone, Spanish-
speaking men hunting for pickup work.

They are families who return in vast networks of parents and in-laws and newborns to live in the same houses, year after year, and traipse through the same fields as did the generation before.

Coming in large groups, they tend to keep to themselves, and live out of sight, down red clay roads in camps tucked from the view of sightseers and beach-goers.

Tommy Lee, a black man who drives the two-row potato harvester for Childress Farms, recalls 16 years ago when the Ledesma family started coming to work for the Childresses.

Before then, he says, there were locals from Loxley and Foley who would do the work.

But that local force of agricultural laborers no longer exists, and few young people seem eager to be up with the rooster, toiling hours on end in 90-degree heat. "I remember how, about 10 in the morning, the local folks would be lying out in the fields," Tommy Lee recalls.

Indeed, the economic vitality of one of Alabama's most prosperous terrains rests, in part, in the hands of Martina Ledesma, and in the hands of hundreds of other Mexican-Americans and Mexican nationals. Not only in potato fields and sheds, but in strawberry patches, sod farms and nurseries, these laborers perform a vital task.

"They fill a very needed role in Baldwin County agriculture," says Ed Tunnell, county extension agent. "I don't know how we'd get some of these crops harvested without the migrant workers."

Are these people taking jobs from local folks?

"I don't know of anybody who's been turned down who wants to go out and pick potatoes," Tunnell says.

During summer harvest, the Rio Grande seems to flow right into Mobile Bay. Jerry Contreras, 21, of the enormous Contreras brood that works at another Baldwin County farm, says he knows the contours of Fairhope as well as those of La Villa, Texas. Jerry has been coming to Baldwin County as a migrant since his birth. Now married to Fernando Uresti's daughter, Erika, he lives and works with the Ledesma crew.

The Alabama State Employment Office in Foley even has an officer,

Yvonne Nelson, a Mexican-American from San Diego, whose time is devoted to the migrant workers for four months every year. The only others receiving similar outreach are U.S. veterans.

The granddaughter of an Italian who organized orange pickers in San Bernardino, Calif., Nelson goes out to the fields, making sure workers have sufficient employment. If not, Nelson directs them to a net of social services available, from food stamps, to health care, to educational assistance.

Nelson says that no matter how crude the migrant housing might appear, conditions are vastly improved from her grandfather's era, when migrant barracks had no partitions at all, and everybody slept directly on the floor.

In Floyd Childress' potato shed off U.S. 98, there is a constant din of noise. Phone ringing, men leaning in the office doorway with invoices, women speaking Spanish. Potatoes rumbling down a conveyor belt. Tractor trailers idling engines. Stacked in rows are thousands of sacks of potatoes marked Shrimpboat, the Childress brand, named in honor of the family's tradition of being farmers and shrimpers.

Potato farming in Baldwin County, laments Childress, is a "dying industry." He points to the national glut of potatoes this year, depressing prices.

Extension agent Ed Tunnell says that during the 1960s, Baldwin County had more than 30,000 acres devoted to potato farming, with healthy contracts from Frito-Lay to use Irish white potatoes for making potato chips. The potato chip contracts, he says, are gone.

There are around 1,500 acres in the county now for potato farming. Much of this land is for Irish red potatoes. An average yield, Tunnell says, is 17,500 pounds per acre.

Childress uses 165 acres of his land for potatoes. Of all his crops—corn and soybeans, chief among them—potatoes are the only ones in which he still uses the kind of labor Martina provides.

Some neighboring farms have given up field labor to invest in machinery that picks the potatoes, but the machines, in some ways, are not as effective as human hands, and sometimes scrape the potatoes.

Childress, 58, a laconic man with a dry wit, is no romantic on farming. He says potato work is "dirty work," but that the phone rings constantly with laborers from south Texas or other places asking if he needs help in the fields.

To Childress, providing free housing to workers, and free electricity, sounds like a good deal. One office worker says that, in the past, some migrants have been known to carry the mattresses along when they leave. Childress supplies the mattresses.

Housing workers, Childress says, "is a hassle. A burden."

• • •

Although Martina Ledesma is a native of Matamoros, Mexico, she is a resident alien of the United States. She speaks some English, but will only converse with an outsider in Spanish.

Her five daughters, native Texans, are fluent in Spanish but prefer to speak English. They often converse in a language that one daughter calls "half and half."

At a Sunday picnic, these daughters appeared stylish in gold loop earrings, bright blouses or monogrammed T-shirts, their hair long and curled. They relish Mexican culture, they say, but have no desire to live in Mexico.

Only one of the five daughters is not allowed to work yet in the fields: Vanessa, the youngest. "She is only 13," Martina says in Spanish. "I will not let her work until she is 16."

But other 13-year-old girls say they are already working at farms. Indeed, two raven-haired sixth-graders from migrant families, quite innocently, reveal that they have been making the long trek with their parents to Baldwin County and working in the fields since the age of 9.

"The sun burns your skin," says the first.

"No more fields for me when I grow up," says the second. "It's real boring."

"We work here because my mother and father didn't go to school," adds the first.

"I want to be a teacher," explains the second.

"Me, I want to be a cop."

They explain that, after working in Baldwin County, they will move with their families to Sand Mountain, north of Birmingham, to pick more potatoes.

"I heard about the KKK up there," the first one says.

"They hate us," the second says. "I heard what they said about us on the 'Jerry Springer' show."

"Last year, in Sand Mountain," the first says, "a car stopped in front of where we were picking and there were two men inside who rolled down the window. They yelled, 'Mexicans, go home.' Because my skin is dark they think they're better than me. You know what I will say to them? 'When I die, my bones are white, just like yours.'"

• • •

In her new Ford pickup truck, Martina drives to the workers camp to join the others for lunch. A few years ago, while Martina was here in Alabama, vandals broke into her home in San Benito, "robando los zapatos," she says. Stealing even her shoes.

In south Texas, she says, there are also "gangas." Gangs. One year, they burned up part of her house while the family was away.

With migrants so much on the move, vehicles become homes away from home. She admits she has only begun to make payments on this one.

At the workers camp there is a wooden barracks divided into seven separate dwellings, with portable outdoor toilets at each end. A screen door opens and a woman steps out of the barracks, hurling a tub of water into the dirt. Behind another screen, a haggard man in undershirt looks out.

Across from the barracks are some mobile homes set up on blocks. Tires are piled up. Electrical wires run to each dwelling; televisions drone.

Against one wall are empty beer bottles. Martina says that drinking is a problem among workers. She believes that men drink because their fathers did not give them enough love and attention growing up. She adds that her own husband, Jose, had a bad drinking problem. "Pero mis hijos, no." My sons, no.

La familia.

The Ledesma house, constructed of tin, is larger than all the others, and with indoor plumbing, offers advantages worthy of a crew leader's status. At the door, the youngest, Vanessa, meets Martina.

"Hola, Mama. Estas cansada?" Are you tired?

She shrugs.

Before entering, Martina kicks off her shoes and places them in a chair at the outside. In the chair are the other shoes worn in the potato fields: scrappy lace-ups, muddy boots, Nikes streaked with clay. She goes inside.

In one room is a portrait of Elijio in his graduation cap and gown, his hair long to his shoulders. Elijio's face is angelic; a tortured visage of Christ is painted in faint lines near his.

Martina says that her inspiration to carry on as crew leader comes from her religious faith. "Pido de Dios," she says, I ask prayers of God.

In the hallway leading to the dining room, water stains spread on the ceiling. Tiles are missing.

Martina lives in this worker's house with 15 other family members; she says only kind things about the man who provides this space. A young man who lives in one of the trailers rails bitterly about the shabbiness, about the mosquitoes in the shower stall, about living, with his wife and two children, in cramped quarters with five other family members.

When Martina comes near, though, the young man falls silent. He says he is afraid that if he is heard complaining it will cost him his job.

Martina believes that it is not good to complain; that when children fuss, parents should let them know to behave. It is too late to correct them by the time they are grown.

She says that poor people in America have the fortune to seek aid when needed. "En Mexico, no hay food stamps." In Mexico, there are no food stamps. She says that, as a family, they have what they need. A place to live. Food.

Lunch is "arroz con pollo"—chicken and rice—made in big iron skillets. On the small TV the Ledesmas brought with them, a soap opera flickers. Around the table sit three male members of the family.

There is a news flash about a killer tornado in Texas. Everybody rushes to the TV, but the announcer says the town is north of Austin; a long way from south Texas. They go back to their chores.

Even though the women have worked alongside the men, it is they who prepare the meals. "La mujer trabaja doble," says Martina. Women work twice as hard.

"El hombre trabaja con los manos," says one of the men. A man works with his hands. They laugh.

Outside, one of Martina's 12 grandchildren calls out. With other children, he romps in and out of a small room behind the house. In the room are mattresses with stuffing pulled out, old boards, a torn screen. The children take turns running up a busted mattress propped against the wall, turning flips in the air.

They squeal with delight.

In the kitchen, the arroz con pollo is simmering, and Vanessa comes up behind the woman who is crew boss no longer until after lunch, and siesta, when the potato fields beckon again.

She leans against Martina, wrapping her arms around her "madre" like she'll never let her go.

Helping Hands for Children

She is only 3 years old, and she is waiting for the van.

Even though her mother is barefoot and wears a thin cotton dress frayed at the hem, her own dress, although a hand-me-down, is freshly washed and pressed. There are bows on her shoes and she wears lacy socks. Her hair is in pigtails, with red baubles on the twists.

The sound of a motor rises far off over the fields, and her mother asks, "Estas listo?" Are you ready?

She nods yes, but her tears say no.

A few weeks ago she was in her own house in south Texas, enjoying *fritas papas con tortilla*—fried potatoes with tortilla—in her mother's kitchen, and bouncing on her grandfather's knee.

But now her grandfather, and her father, and her two aunts and an uncle are way out in the fields of this strange place called Baldwin County, and her mother will join them after the van has gone.

"No quiero ir, Mama." I don't want to go.

"Pero tienes." You have to.

"Por que?" Why?

"Necesito trabajar." I need to work. The mother explains that big sister has already left to go to the big school for migrant children at Robertsdale, the one the government pays for, and that is held at St. Patrick's Church.

Hearing the word "Robertsdale" is no comfort, nor the word "Fairhope," where this van for preschoolers will be headed.

She begins to sob as the van turns into the yard and a tall man with long light hair and a ranch hat climbs out.

He walks over, his legs long as stovepipes, and she watches him bend down. His eyes are light-colored; but when he opens his mouth it is not hard American English that comes out—although she understands that, too—but the familiar Spanish of home.

"No llores, chiquita," he says gently. Don't cry, little girl.

His big, pale hands reach down.

She glances up into the van, where there are other little faces. One girl waves.

Now the tall man is lifting her up into the air, high up into a seat of the van where he fastens a seat belt around her.

He cranks the engine, and, before starting a chorus of "The Ants Go Marching In," tells her his name: "Me llamo Ted."

• • •

Ted Henken, a graduate student at Tulane University, is on his way to La Casa de Amigos—House of Friends—a day care center for 75 children from 3 weeks old to 5 years old. Ted's aunt, Sister Sandra Ardoyno, directs La Casa.

Open during May and June, the center sits on Mobile Bay on land owned by the Catholic Church, site of Camp Cullen the rest of the year. It is supported by funds from the federal Migrant Head Start Program and Ecumenical Ministries Inc. of Fairhope, a social-service agency for poor families in Baldwin County.

Sister Sandra has been with La Casa de Amigos since its beginning in 1971. Her mission is deeply personal. "We want these children to know their parents help put our food on the table."

Late each Spring, sometimes before their school year ends, children of the migrant workers are bundled into trucks and station wagons with "la familia" for the trek to south Alabama. Many are too young by law to work in the fields. Taking them under wing is La Casa de Amigos (House of Friends), a day-care program funded by the federal Migrant Head Start Program and Ecumenical Ministries of Fairhope, housed on the shores of Mobile Bay on land owned by the Catholic Church. Under the direction of Sister Sandra Ardoyno, La Casa provides supervision, health care, counseling and fun for hundreds of kids who might otherwise be left to their own devices while their parents are off in the fields. (Kiichiro Sato, Mobile Register)

Next to La Casa de Amigos is Sacred Heart Church, where Spanish Masses are conducted by Father Christopher Viscardi, a priest from Spring Hill College.

On a recent Sunday, Father Viscardi talked with Felipe Martinez, who is a laborer at Woerner Turf, and his fiancée, Celia Zamorano, about their commitment to each other—they will be married in Matamoros, Mexico, get a legal marriage certificate in the United States, and hope to settle in Loxley. At Woerner, and other Baldwin County turf farms, Mexican nationals with green-card status work year-round cutting and rolling endless fields of bright green Bermuda, Zoysia, Centipede and Augustine grass. Some look to make south Alabama their permanent home.

During that same Sunday, several families made plans for their children's First Communion.

Afterward, hundreds of children and their families drifted across the wide lawn to La Casa de Amigos for a picnic, the food provided by area churches.

The Rev. Gerardo Chan, director of Hispanic Ministries for the Presbytery of South Alabama, visited with several men from Cheran, Mexico, talking up a soccer match in Foley. (In Cheran, Baldwin County is known as "Cheran No. 2," and at Mass in a Cheran church the priest asks a blessing for people who have gone to Alabama, to "el Norte.") A counterpart to Rev. Chan is the Rev. Aida Walker, from Oaxaca, Mexico, who directs the area's Hispanic Ministries for the United Methodist Church.

Martina Ledesma took a chair on the porch of La Casa's offices, watching one of her sons play volleyball.

• • •

Ted drives past Baldwin County potato fields and turf farms. Even though the new little girl in his van feels lost, there are a dozen other children who know the ritual. They pull into La Casa and file out.

Pat Preston, a retired nurse from Thomas Hospital in Fairhope, is waiting, along with Fairhope volunteers Drs. William Davis and Paula Drummond. They look into the children's ears, down their throats, listen to their complaints. They give them shots, test for lead poisoning.

Preston says the recurring health concerns of the children are bronchial infection and impetigo from mosquito bites.

At the end of the migrant season Sister Sandra will hand each mother a health-care "continuity record" with a photograph of the child inside. For these families who move from place to place, and have few photos, the records become possessions they are sure not to lose.

Sometimes the children reveal other problems, perhaps turbulence at home. On staff is a social worker, Rosa Cabrales, a native of Colombia who can converse with them in Spanish.

One woman who greets children in the classroom is Rosie Ledesma, a daughter of Martina's. Another is Cristina Vela, whose family are migrants, too. Other classrooms are bright with the faces of college students who take these minimum wage jobs and spend 12 hours a day helping provide the children a home away from home.

Lunch. Snacks. A walk down to the Bay. Sandcastles. Feet in the water.

While their parents are bending and toiling to pick buckets of potatoes far away, here, for now, the children are secure.

• • •

By 5 o'clock, when Ted puts his ranch hat back on and climbs into the driver's seat of his van, the little girl who bawled with fear early in the morning now happily settles in next to him.

He calls out their names, making sure everybody is aboard:

"Francisco?"

"Si."

"Hector?"

"Si."

"Manuel?"

"Si."

Sister Sandra waves good-bye. She touches her fingers to her lips and blows them a kiss.

As Ted finds his way to their trailers and barracks and shanties, he plugs in a cassette tape and a song rings out:

Oh Susanna, no lorres para mi
Vengo de Alabama
Con el banjo
En la rodilla.

After joining Ted in Spanish, they chime in, all-American kids, clapping their hands as they go: "'Cause I come from Alabama with my banjo on my knee!"

On the Asian Coast

❖❖

Khampou's Village

St. Elmo, Summer 1999

Rising at dawn after five hours' sleep, eating a breakfast of sticky rice and water, Khampou Phetsinorath, 55, snugs on his American-flag cap, climbs into his Chevy van, and makes his way toward Grand Bay Seafood to begin his 17-hour workday. Alongside him are his wife, Bounyong, and their eldest daughter, Phousavanh. The night before, Khampou had stepped next door to his daughter's house and watched CNN on her big-screen television, spellbound by pictures of the refugees in Kosovo. He had thought of his homeland, Laos, a rugged landscape of large, close-knit families, where American bombs had rained from the sky. As a prisoner of war he had seen the collapse of his nation. He had witnessed an exodus of his people.

He comes to U.S. 90, where the Laotian Buddhist Temple lies in one direction and the Laotian Baptist Church in another. He crosses the highway, heading down a dirt road to a low building where other Southeast Asians, their hair under caps and nets, plod through a door. Joining them, he enters to face long, metal tables heaped with boiled crabs and ice.

The crabs have been stripped of their outer shells and claws by a night crew; what's left are the underside casements with the hard-to-get-at meat.

The workers roll on their gloves, perch on stools, and begin.

Crack. Cut. Pick. At the start of his 17-hour workday, Khampou Phetsinorath, alongside other Laotians, turns crabs into wages at Grand Bay Seafood. Khampou began his life half a globe away in a nation where, as a soldier with the regular Laotian army fighting against the Communist Laotian army, he was captured and imprisoned for five years. In the mid-1970s, after the fall to Communist forces of three capitals and their nations—Saigon, Vietnam; Phnom Penh, Cambodia; and Vientiane, Laos—Khampou's family became one of hundreds of thousands from southeast Asia that found its way to America, refugees with traumatic stories to tell. Among them were those who made their way to the Gulf Coast, working with seafood. Here in the Deep South the distinctive cultures, Laotian, Vietnamese, and Cambodian, continue to manifest themselves in different ways. (Kate Reali, Mobile Register)

Crack. Cut. Pick. A soft, crushing noise, and Laotian chatter, fill
the air.

Crack. Cut. Pick. With their fingertips they are striving for a stable
life far from the turbulent one they left behind.

• • •

A century ago, the coastal South was refuge for immigrants from
Eastern Europe and the Mediterranean. Merchant blocks in cities like
Mobile, Pensacola and New Orleans were lively with voices speaking
Italian, Yiddish, Greek. Today, in many places along the Gulf Coast,
the voices are Vietnamese, Laotian, Cambodian.

The first wave of Southeast Asian refugees came just after 1975,
when Saigon fell to the North Vietnamese; Phnom Penh to the Cambodian Khmer Rouge; and Vientiane, the capital of Laos, to the
Communist Pathet Lao. More waves came in 1979, after Vietnam
invaded Cambodia on Christmas Day 1978, and there were new
crackdowns in Laos. Who can forget the forlorn faces of the boat
people, adrift on dangerous seas?

Most Southeast Asians settled in California, but several thousand
ventured much farther, to America's coastal South and its familiar
tropical climate, aided by groups like Catholic Charities. Those who
came to Alabama were an especially young population, says Don
Bogie, director of the Center for Demographic and Cultural Research
at Auburn University at Montgomery. They were of childbearing age
in a culture that prizes large families.

In a generation, the families have multiplied. There are new migrants, too, although some of them come from this side of the world.
Laotians tell of relatives in California who have tired of the pressure-
cooker of big-city life and long to relocate to the bayous.

A broad story is sketched by Bureau of the Census estimates for
1997, showing 4,000 Asians and Pacific Islanders in the vicinity of
Mobile, 6,000 near Biloxi, 8,000 in Pensacola and 25,000 in the sur-
rounds of New Orleans.

But the story, in its depth, is revealed in the lives of men like
Khampou Phetsinorath and their families.

• • •

The year was 1974. Home for Khampou (Cam-poo), Bounyong (Boon-yan) and their six children was the city of Savannakhet, Laos, on the Mekong River across from Thailand. Khampou was a master sergeant in the regular Laotian army, long entangled in war against a Communist Laotian army. A cease-fire was declared—a Provisional Government of National Unity sprang up.

Khampou, stationed in the south of Laos, put down his arms. He disappeared.

Bounyong waited months for word of her husband. The months became a year. The cease-fire collapsed. Vietnam fell, Cambodia, Laos—Indochina was in turmoil.

Bounyong held on. Two years passed, three, then five. With war seeming to swirl all around her, she decided that the time to get out had come. She gathered her children together and they stole away from the house, heading to the Mekong River. For any who were caught leaving, imprisonment, or worse, might be the consequence.

They secured passage, and arrived in Thailand. After months in a refugee camp, they were processed for relocation to America, to an unpronounceable place called Montgomery, Alabama.

Bounyong had given up her husband as dead. She filled out her papers for the U.S. Department of State as "widow."

Little did she know that Khampou had been captured by the Communists and thrown into jail; that, subsisting on handfuls of rice (meat twice a year, on Christmas and the Laotian New Year), he had lost more than 70 pounds. Even now he describes, like yesterday, the heavy rains in the Laotian summer that flooded the jail, and the sicknesses that brought low the men; and those who were simply gunned down.

For five years of captivity, Khampou had nursed a scheme. He acted on it one night while cutting bamboo in the Laotian hills, the Communist guards looking on from afar. Deeper he went into the woods, hacking, cutting, until he was alone—and ran.

Through the mountains, south toward the Cambodian border,

west toward Thailand, he made his way. Ten days later, he announced himself to Thai police and was taken to a refugee camp.

At the camp he traced Bounyong to America. To the place named Alabama.

Bounyong received the call from him in Montgomery. "I cry," she recalls, in her simple English, shy about revealing more.

To ready a home for the husband she awaited, she was told through other Laotians of jobs 200 miles to the south, down the oyster-shell roads of Bayou la Batre, Ala. She moved her family there. She worked at night for a furniture manufacturer. In the day, she picked crabs.

• • •

One hour, two hours, three. Crack, cut, pick. One dollar and 60 cents for every pound of choice "jumbo" meat, $1.20 for "lump." It takes 40 crabs, at the least, to give up a pound of meat. Khampou's daughter, Phousavanh, says that when crabs are plentiful, she can work for 12 hours, picking 70 to 80 pounds of meat—more than 3,000 crabs.

Khampou's nephew, John, who picks crabs at the same table, just graduated from Theodore High School and has other ambitions. "I don't want to work seafood my whole life," he says. In the fall, he'll attend the University of Alabama at Huntsville, studying computer information systems.

Up front, in an office hectic with computers and phones, is Dan Viravong, a native of Thailand and owner of Grand Bay Seafood. Dan came to America in the early 1980s to pursue higher education. He graduated from college in Ohio with a degree in aeronautical engineering, and worked for Eastern Airlines. He was living in New York, but sought a bride from his native culture.

Through a network of grandmothers, Dan met Phonekeo "Pon" Sengsiri, whose family had fled Laos and landed in Mobile. In Laos, Pon's family had been wealthy, she says. In Mobile, her mother picked crabs, and her father hauled traps. Pon, who'd been a child when they arrived, learned English, and went on to graduate from Davidson High School.

When Dan and Pon married, they built a house in Grand Bay, and

Dan entered the crab business, taking over a processing plant. Lately, he's been turning to real estate development, planning a new community for Laotians in Irvington. He's making seafood investments, also, but those are in Thailand.

In coastal Alabama, he says, "The children of the crab pickers will grow up and go to college and do other work."

• • •

After working six hours picking crabs, Khampou is ready to start the second part of his workday—11 hours of driving a Grand Bay Seafood truck through south Louisiana where he will load up thousands of pounds of live, crated crabs, then bring them back for the night crew to boil.

The truck is refrigerated in back, but the cab is not. Hot, highway air buffets his face as he shifts gears and rumbles down Interstate 10, making his way to the Mississippi line, an hour later to the Louisiana line, and pulling off at Slidell, La., to gas up.

Along the way he talks about his favorite topic—belief in God. He was raised a Buddhist, and once even shaved his head to become a monk, but he prays to the higher being he found down the back roads of Mobile County, and to whom he and his family lift their voices every Sunday at the First Baptist Church of Irvington.

In Buddhism, he says, with its emphasis on meditation and enlightenment, "God was not clear. God is now clear. Believe in God and you have house, food and money. If you do not believe, you have many bills."

On a recent day, hauling thousands of pounds of crabs, he turned a corner too quickly and flipped the truck. He was not hurt. He says that God was holding him in his hand.

Khampou was converted by the Rev. Noy Paul Phangnivong, a former child monk, who was imprisoned by the Communists in Laos during the war and found Jesus while studying English at a refugee camp church. Noy says that he's brought 30 to 40 Laotian Buddhists to the Baptist way since arriving in Irvington.

The sermon he preached on a recent Sunday was about how the

Laotians, like the ancient Israelites, left their worldly goods behind and set off as refugees. The Israelites, Noy said, knew they were headed to the Promised Land, but the Laotians were not sure of their destination.

Khampou drives on, deeper into Louisiana. Squinting into the harsh, afternoon light that beats on the hood of the truck, he peers out at Lake Pontchartrain far below. He takes a swig of water—only water, no coffee. The doctor told him he has high blood pressure.

After crossing the long bridge over the lake, he pushes on through the industrial stacks, the hurrying traffic, pausing at a dock in Chalmette on the fringe of New Orleans to throw empty crates off the back of his truck to be filled when he doubles back. Again on the highway, he drives farther south, where the industry stops and the little communities begin with their colorful names. Meraux. Violet. Delacroix Island.

He threads down a winding bayou road, past shrimp boats moored against docks, mobile homes up on stilts, the moss on cedar trees moving in the breeze. On the water, like highway markers, are endless floats marking crab traps.

"End of the World," reads a sign at the end of the road on Delacroix Island. Khampou parks. Beyond lie marshlands and the Gulf of Mexico. His is the only Asian face on this slip of land.

Curtis, a lean man who looks like Al Pacino, comes out of a door. He has crates of crabs ready. Curtis says his forebears came from the Canary Islands, off the coast of Spain, and that, for miles around, all of the people have this ancestry. There are no Asians in this part of the bayou, Curtis says. "They stay down in Venice, Louisiana," he says. "We didn't let them settle around here."

Ford, Curtis' brother, handles shrimp at the dock. "Hey, Khampou," he asks, knowing his name from seeing him most every afternoon, "how much it cost to go over to Vietnam?"

"I am not from Vietnam. I am from Laos."

"Oh, you're Vietnamese, you just don't want to admit it."

Khampou begins to make room in the back of the truck for the crabs.

"You went over there, didn't you? How much it cost?"

Khampou says that when he went home to Laos last year to see his aged relatives, it cost him eleven hundred dollars.

"Why don't you stay over there? You don't like it?"

"I like it. America, it is my country."

"You like money is what you like," Ford cracks. "You're greedy for money!"

Khampou smiles politely.

Curtis finishes forklifting crates onto the truck. Khampou makes out a payment—crabs at the dock fetch about 50 to 55 cents a pound—and drives on.

• • •

Money—its value, to the refugees, is counted in several ways. Khampou and other Asian refugees come from countries where wages are far lower than in the United States. Whatever goods they were able to accumulate back home—a house, furniture, clothes, heirlooms— they had to abandon. They gave up possessions, but they saved their necks.

Don Bogie, of Auburn University at Montgomery, says that, in 1990—the last year that the numbers were available—nearly a third of the Laotians, Vietnamese and Cambodians in Alabama had per-capita incomes below the poverty line, but that their family incomes were much higher. Family members, he says, likely have been pooling their resources.

"By working hard and making money," says Khampou's daughter-in-law, Seng, "we make sure the family does not go down."

"I have many children," Khampou says. "I am their bank. Open 24 hours a day. Seven days a week. No interest."

• • •

After 11 hours on the job, when many men would have their feet up at home, Khampou is pressing the accelerator, heading over bayou bridges, watching the Technicolor smog of the New Orleans skyline in the distance. He pulls into the dock in Chalmette where he had left the empty crates.

The dock is owned by Teresa, a petite Vietnamese woman who sports a blue silk shirt, blue slacks, long, red nails and a rice paddy hat. With dramatic flair, she strides the scene, directing the sun-roughened men with a wave of her hand.

When she fled Vietnam in the late 1970s, taking a boat to Thailand, Thai bandits slit her pants to find the purse tied high on her leg, she says. In the refugee camp, she started a coffee shop. Twenty years ago, living in East New Orleans, she sold fish on the street.

When she decided to buy the Chalmette dock, she had no line of credit at the bank. She says she turned to family and friends. "I have ten thousand dollars, you have five, he has five, we put it together," she says.

As crabbers lug their catch from their flatboats onto the dock, Teresa oversees the operation. The crabs are weighed. Teresa scribbles and calculates. Then she climbs on the forklift and commandeers a few thousand pounds of crabs onto the back of Khampou's truck.

While he makes out the payment for the crabs, she is already over hot plates, cooking fish and chicken and rice for her eight children.

"Only working," she says of her life in America. "No lazy."

• • •

Khampou's headlights are turned on now, and an hour later he's riding through streets near downtown New Orleans, kids hanging out on porches in the sultry dusk. He stops at a red light while people cross. "All black people," he observes. "Black people in downtown, white people out of the town." He wonders aloud why this division takes place. "A man of God can be black or white."

He pulls into a motel's parking lot. On the wall is a sign that says, "No firearms." At the back of the lot is a statue of St. Francis and a scattering of empty crab crates. It is eerily quiet.

Suddenly the motel door opens and a man briskly steps out to announce there are no crabs this evening, that bad weather got in the way. The man, Vietnamese, is named Chi. He runs the motel and handles crabs on the side, sent up to him from the coast. He suggests that the crabbing catch, like the weather, is always unpredictable.

"Seafood is a hard life," Chi says.

Khampou glances at his watch. 8:30 p.m. He climbs back in the truck and chugs toward the interstate.

On the way back to Grand Bay Seafood he does not make small talk. He does not sing. He does not listen to the radio. He just clinches the wheel, bears down the accelerator and drives. The noise of the engine grinds through the open windows.

At 11 p.m., he backs his truck up to the plant building in Grand Bay, climbs down and gets into his van to drive home. Before he is gone, the night crew begins to unload, uncrate and boil the 8,000 pounds of crabs, readying them for Khampou and his family who'll plod in the door at sunrise.

• • •

Because Grand Bay Seafood is closed on Sunday, Khampou does not truck in crabs on Saturday evening. Highly perishable, the crabs are always boiled and picked right away. So Saturday is his one afternoon off.

After picking on a Saturday morning, he meets up, as usual, with his family at daughter Phousavanh's handsome brick house—a dwelling he built with other Laotian men during the winter months when there are no crabs.

In the living room, the big-screen television against the wall sits beneath an art object, a giant hand-fan from Laos painted with a scene of huts along a river. A satellite dish brings in Thai television. When Khampou is not tuned to the travails of Kosovo, he watches Thai kick boxing or Asian soap operas.

Laotians have clustered in several places in south Mobile County. Many are in Murray Heights in Irvington, others on Laos Road in Irvington. Khampou's family and others bought 10 acres along Boe Road in St. Elmo, drew lots and constructed their own houses. On Khampou's two-acre lot are his house and those of several of his children. Call it Khampou's Village.

As he leans back on the couch, the front door opens and another daughter appears. In her arms is a toddler. The door opens again: a daughter-in-law. Two preschoolers race in behind her. From a hallway shuffles Bounyong's elderly mother. The women sit and visit on the floor, four generations surrounding Khampou.

Phoulamphone, the youngest daughter, who graduated from Theodore High School and prefers the name Sonya, says she twice moved to Texas, but always came back. "I was homesick," she explains. By home she does not mean Laos.

The daughters go to the kitchen to fix up sticky rice and chicken and the kids tumble on the floor. Bounyong takes her hair out from under the work net. Khampou sinks deeper into the couch.

The toddler, in her colorful dress, climbs up on Khampou's lap. His eyes are closed now, the weight of a 100-hour work week, 1,000 miles of highway, and years of toil to make south Alabama his own seeming to press him down.

As his granddaughter pats him playfully on the cheek he smiles, his family secure and prospering all around him, and begins to doze.

Buddhist Temple

Irvington

Kan Ly studied math and science at a Cambodian college, trained as a paratrooper in France, mastered four languages and served as an officer in the regular Cambodian army—all of which marked him for death in his homeland.

After the fall of Cambodia to the communist Khmer Rouge in 1975, the dictator Pol Pot set out to cut down anyone educated, to eradicate all traces of anything modern. His men murdered military officers, aristocrats, city dwellers, students, artists, intellectuals. "They killed people who drove cars," Kan Ly says. "They killed people just for wearing eyeglasses."

Compact, silver-haired, well-spoken, Kan Ly, 56, tells his story while walking down Angkor Road, a rural lane in south Mobile County. In Cambodia, Angkor is the ancient home of a majestic Buddhist temple secluded in the jungle. In Irvington, Ala., tucked beyond the railroad tracks and neat, suburban dwellings, Angkor is a dirt road coursing through 86 acres of brick houses, mobile homes, vegetable gardens and a small Buddhist temple under construction.

From the years 1975 to 1979, the Pol Pot regime killed a reported 2 million Cambodians—men, women, children, infants. "I have seen one movie in my life, 'The Killing Fields,'" Kan Ly says, referring to the 1984 film about the slaughter of his people. "In reality, what happened was worse."

The loss for Kan Ly and his wife was especially profound. One spring day in 1975, he was in his office in Phnom Penh, a lieutenant colonel in the army, when the communists seized control. On the radio he heard the Khmer Rouge announcement. "They were taking over," he says, "by gun." Military officers were under arrest.

Kan Ly ditched his uniform, slipped on shorts and T-shirt and went outside. The walkways were jammed. To reach home, he had to cross the street, but it was blocked. "Someone tried to cross against orders," he recalls. "They got shot."

Kan Ly claimed to be a poor peasant, a drafted soldier of no importance. He was pushed into a crowd with other townspeople and detained. He says that children were grabbed. Those below sixth grade were taken in one direction, those above in another. His three children were above sixth grade.

"The communists would go into somebody's home and ask, 'Do you want to stay or go?' If a person said, 'I want to stay,' the soldiers put a gun into the person's ear and pulled the trigger. Just like that."

Kan Ly and others were "herded like cows" into the countryside. They walked and walked. If someone tired and fell, he was shot, Kan Ly says. If someone betrayed any sign of being upper class, Kan Ly says—wished aloud, for example, for a drink of coffee—he was shot. It was impossible for Kan Ly to slip away, to hunt for his wife, Ros, or their three children.

He was taken to a prison camp. There, "the soldiers did not even waste their bullets," he says bitterly. "They'd take the men out in groups, strip them, tie them together and crack them on the backs of the heads with a big stick, pushing them into a big grave."

He told the Khmer Rouge guards that he'd worked for the Chinese in Cambodia helping repair buses. "But after eight months, one day I was standing against a tree, like this"—he places his hand on his hip—"and they grabbed me and took me to jail. I'd been standing, they told me, like somebody who watched other people work."

It was nearly his death sentence.

He was asked to write a statement about his background. Shrewdly, he employed a style of language that he'd learned as a boy from a Buddhist monk in the countryside—Old Cambodian. It was a way of putting words down on the page, he says, done only by rural dwellers. He believes it saved his life.

When the Vietnamese invaded Cambodia in 1979—continuing an ages-old animosity between the two nations—there was chaos again. With the Khmer Rouge guards in disarray, Kan Ly escaped from prison with hundreds of others, making a 26-day trek to Thailand. He says he ate lizards, grasshoppers and mice. Miraculously, he heard someone he knew say they had seen his wife—near a train station in a small town.

They found each other. But not their children. "Some teen-agers told us that they were killed, but still we are looking. We have sent money to Cambodia even now, to make a statement on the radio, to hunt for them."

He looks out at the lush, Gulf Coast vegetation, at the oak trees and moss and ferns and kudzu, as though the children might come running from the tangle of green.

Kids do appear, racing down the road on bicycles.

"I know," he says, resolved to heartbreak, "that they are gone."

• • •

Unspeakable losses. Often, they are tucked away behind the serene gazes of Southeast Asians who made their way to America in the aftermath of wars in Vietnam, Laos and Cambodia.

Like others, the refugees who headed south to the Gulf Coast carried these losses deep in their memories.

As the first generation made new lives supported by shrimping, seafood processing, construction and furniture-making, and as the second generation graduated from high school and began going to college, the old losses moved further back on the time-line. If they are not always spoken of, though, they can hardly be forgotten.

"If we go to see this past life," Kan Ly says, "we cannot sleep."

On Angkor Road, a Cambodian lane on the Gulf Coast, victims of one of the most brutal dictatorships of the century now drawing to a close have sought nothing more than a peaceful home.

• • •

In the refugee camp in Thailand, Kan Ly received word that he was being sponsored for relocation by the U.S. Catholic Conference's Migration and Refugee Services. There are numerous refugee-help groups in the United States, among them the Episcopal Migration Ministries and the Hebrew Immigrant Aid Society, but Catholic Refugee Services is the only group operating in Alabama, according to Sandy Etiemble of the Mobile office. It does not restrict itself to helping Catholics. Kan Ly is a Buddhist.

"I asked them, please send me to a place with hot weather."

He received word of his destination. "I got the piece of paper and looked at where I was going. It said, 'Mob.' I asked, Mob, where is that? I looked on the map."

But he did not travel alone. With him was Ros, who'd become pregnant with their fourth child and given birth to the son in the refugee camp. They named him Idona, after the name of the camp. (Their second son, Rosly, would be born in Mobile.) And they brought

other Cambodians with them who could not fend for themselves—
two orphaned girls. They raised the daughters as their own. "We
named them Savory and Sayoeun—the names of two of the children
we had lost."

In "Mob," Kan Ly worked in the shipyards, learned to weld, and
for extra money picked crabmeat, just as his wife still does at Interlan
Seafood, a Cambodian-owned shop on Angkor Road. Now, he's
a caseworker with Catholic Services, helping other refugees—the
newest being Bosnians, Cubans, Sudanese, and still some incoming
Vietnamese—make their way through a bewildering world.

Sometimes this help, on the part of agencies, entails linking
up families with medical care, or helping them find jobs. On the
signboard at Catholic Services are postings for seafood processing,
furniture-making and domestic help.

"We have no welfare people in the Cambodian village," Kan Ly
says. "If we cannot pick crabs, we will do construction. If there is
no construction, we work in welding."

In 1986, Kan Ly banded together with other Cambodians and
purchased the 86 acres in Irvington. Families parceled out lots. The
terms: $500 down, $167 a month for 10 years.

A teen-ager in orange hair now whips by on a bicycle—the son of
Cambodian parents who moved from out west, hoping to create a
more sheltered life for their children. "They were in a bad way in
California," Kan Ly explains.

Another young man drives up in a black 1997 Dodge Avenger and
greets Kan Ly. His name is Vic Dira, the son of a soldier who served
with Kan Ly, and now lives here, too. Vic is home for a few days on
leave—he's a U.S. Marine at Camp Lejeune in North Carolina. He
has a friend with him, another Marine, whose family is from Peru.
Vic is showing his friend around his Alabama home.

"It looks 80 percent like Cambodia," Kan Ly says, gesturing to
the vegetable gardens where Cambodian squash and beans spill in
profusion over wire fences and arbors. Down a row of Cambodian
pumpkins a gardener moves, stick in hand, straw hat turned against
the sun.

But Cambodia itself—now called Kampuchea—is a home to which Kan Ly says he will never return, not even if given the chance to visit.

"Cambodians killed Cambodians," he says sorrowfully, echoing the sentiments of other Southeast Asians who look back on civil wars—Laotian vs. Laotian, Vietnamese vs. Vietnamese—fueled by outside alliances.

"I hate what my country did," he says, while doing all he can to recapture a sense of it here, in the woods of the Deep South.

• • •

Leaving his shoes at the threshold, Kan Ly steps into the house of Huon Serey, the Buddhist monk who lives behind the Buddhist temple on Angkor Road. The house and temple are part of the Khmer Cultural Center, a meeting place, Kan Ly says, for Cambodians from New Orleans to Pensacola.

On the living room walls are photographs of Angkor Wat, the magnificent Buddhist temple in the jungles of Cambodia, originally built as a Hindu Temple; landscape pictures of Angkor; and pictures of statues of the Buddha.

A bedroom door opens and the monk walks out. He is bald; he is barefoot. He wears orange robes wrapped around one shoulder, across his chest. A Westerner steps forward to introduce himself and shake hands, but Kan Ly puts his own hands together and touches them to his forehead and makes a bowing salutation. Silent, smiling, touching no one, the monk continues across the living room.

There's another Westerner, though, in the monk's house who is schooled in Cambodian ways. Indeed, she tutored the monk in English and told him of local customs. Denise Lewis, who did her undergraduate degree at University of South Alabama, is now in a doctoral program at the University of Kentucky in Lexington. She has been living on Angkor Road all summer working on a dissertation. Her field of study is medical anthropology. Barks, roots, teas—Denise describes some of the home remedies popular among the Cambodians. Honeysuckle buds. Banana peels. She names others. She tells of parents who put suction cups on their children's skin to draw out sicknesses, and of a practice called "coining," where, for example, a parent first rubs his child's arm with baby oil, then uses a coin and rubs it briskly over that portion of skin. The idea, she explains, is to draw the blood to the surface, to make it run faster, to speed the healing.

There have been cases, Denise says, where schoolteachers, after witnessing these marks on a student's arm, have thought them to be physical abuse, hitting or whipping. One man has spoken of a situation—involving a Vietnamese family in Biloxi—where a teacher contacted child welfare agencies.

Several Cambodian and Vietnamese adults admit to the practice of coining on their own arms, believing it will restore vitality.

Denise, who grew up in small-town Mississippi, says that there's a quality of life in the Cambodian village reminiscent of her childhood. "There's a strong sense of family here, like we had. We knew who belonged to which family. There's a sense of sharing, too. You have extra beans, you give some to your neighbors."

• • •

On a Sunday morning, the noise of hammering rattles in the pines along Angkor Road. On a foundation built up high above the ground is the Buddhist temple under construction. It rises in an open field near a smaller temple. Kan Ly walks up a board laid from the ground to the new temple's floor.

Cambodians from Florida, Alabama and Louisiana are volunteering their time to build the temple, pitching in a few hours every Sunday morning. Leading the construction is Prek Preay, who escaped from Cambodia in 1978 and lives in Pensacola. He learned to build houses, he says, while working with Mitchell Homes in Mobile.

The structure is 30 feet wide and 60 feet long. The altar, with its Buddhist figures and incense and ancestral banners and prayer mats, must face the east.

Prek Preay says the structure has cost $20,000 in materials so far, a cost they share. "We buy them," he says, "from Home Depot."

On the porch of the Buddhist Temple in Irvington, monk Huon Serey, in saffron robes, turns to the south Alabama sunlight, while 6-year-old Jann Rith, visiting with his family from Boston, lingers at the door. The temple—soon to be replaced by a new one being constructed on an adjacent field—is at the heart of an 86-acre plot of land in south Mobile County, its main street named Angkor Road in honor of the ancient holy site in Cambodia. Dwelling along Angkor Road, in homes deep in tropical vegetation not unlike that of southeast Asia, are dozens of families still traumatized by the brutal Pol Pot regime, a merciless dictatorship that slaughtered more than two million Cambodians. The organizer of this community, Kan Ly, now a caseworker for Catholic Refugee Services of Mobile, escaped after being taken hostage by the Khmer Rouge and was reunited with his wife before coming to America—but his three children, hauled off elsewhere by the Khmer Rouge, were never seen again. (Kate Reali, Mobile Register)

Standing near the entrance to the temple is Hann Hok, visiting from Boston where he lives with his wife, Ra Nung, and their sons, Johnny, 10, and Jann Rith, 6. Ra's parents live on Angkor Road.

Shortly before noon, the door of the monk's house opens and Huon Serey walks out into the full sunlight. He gazes up at the new temple, then drifts toward the old one. It is his time for lunch.

The men climb down the gangplank to the ground and trail behind the monk. The monk, explains Kan Ly, eats twice a day—once upon waking, and once at midday, but not past noon.

On her way to the temple with her sons, Ra Nung, in a beautiful sarong, begins to worry aloud that life in Boston may be too overwhelming for her family. She fears that her two boys might be swept up in a life that is fast-paced, sometimes dangerous. She mentions her concern about gangs: "They dress up sloppy. Their hair's different colors. They hang out on the street."

Yes, she says, there are thousands of Cambodians in Boston, but that may not be the Cambodia she wants. "There's too much civilization," she says, looking around wistfully.

Last year, after the death of her husband's grandfather, they sent his ashes back to Cambodia.

Ra Nung says she and her husband are thinking about moving south, to Angkor Road.

The porch of the temple is beginning to look like a used shoe store—boots and sandals and lace-ups all kicked off out of respect. Kan Ly has already entered. Ra Nung is there.

Inside, the monk takes up a lotus position on an elevated stage to one side, and people are setting dishes down before him. On the floor of the temple, Ra Nung leans down, hands together; next to her is Jann Rith, her younger son.

There is a murmuring of prayerful voices—a call to the spirits of ancestors to join them at the banquet. The boy glances around, looking fidgety.

The monk opens the first dish and spoons up rice. He continues with other dishes. When the monk finishes, the plates are set out for the others and they gather in a circle on the floor, spooning up squid and bean pods and chicken and rice and a dessert of coconut and jelly. Soon they are done, too.

As the group heads back out into the yard, taking up hammers and saws, Kan Ly leads the way to the construction zone. This time, it is the monk who follows, negotiating the gangplank.

The workers have readied insulation wrap, and as they unroll it on the ground outside and try to secure it around the temple, the monk leans out of a window to catch hold. A welcome breeze catches the wrap and billows it like gift wrap, and ruffles the monk's robes so that it looks as if he might suddenly take wing.

He looks down at the road and the gardens and the houses spread out before him, surveying a realm all its own.

PART VII

INTRIGUING PORTRAITS

Anyone's life is interesting if you linger long enough, listen up closely, pay attention to the person's way of talking, thinking, gesturing. Everyone's life touches someone else's—a parent, a child, a friend. Some people, though, by chance or destiny, character or circumstance, impact people in the larger community. Sometimes their actions roll down through time like waves reaching the shore.

These portraits are not meant to be a comprehensive gallery of all the intriguing folks who've ever passed through town. In fact, many faces have already appeared in this collection who could serve as profiles by themselves. In a way, this gallery suggests how many others might have life lessons of interest to others.

Three of the grandest figures I've encountered anywhere deserve their own stories, and these I call our "sage voices." Joseph Langan, a longtime Mobile mayor, who helped this city stay together during the civil rights movement, is now in his 80s. I spent a week visiting with Mayor Langan, and gathering a sense of both his life and that of the city he loves dearly as it found its way through a turbulent era. Albert Murray, also in his 80s, has a tireless intellect, writes buoyant prose, and is a spirited conversationalist, able to converse wittily and incisively on an endless number of topics. Alma Fisher, a petite, delicate woman in her 90s, told a story to me—and thus, to the whole town—that she'd never told before, of surviving the Holocaust, and making a new life for herself in Mobile. The reaction of readers was overwhelming.

"Past Triumphs" looks at a few lives that stay with us today. There's James Franklin, a doctor who was one of Mobile's few black physicians early in the 20th century; Ben May, a very private man who affected public life by his philanthropy; Will Armbrecht, a U.S. Attorney who stepped in to apply Federal laws to a lynching in an episode of Mobile history explored by historian David Alsobrook.

But lives link into a town in other ways, as in the section "Close Ties Far Away"—as far as Morocco, in the story of Joe McPhillips, head of the American School of Tangier; and Tina Allen, a sculptress who "married into" this town, and carries its stories with her everywhere.

Sage Voices

Joe Langan's City Limits

The Mayor and the Peanut Man

Tall, silver-haired, courtly, Joe Langan, 85, once the most powerful figure in Mobile politics, navigates his cart down the grocery aisles. Grits, white bread, bacon—he piles up the items requested. This excursion, one he makes for friends who are housebound or infirm, is on behalf of Lamar Wilson, 79, the Peanut Man.

"It's rough to be old, and alone," Langan says of Wilson, a man who trudges about town on foot, selling bags of peanuts. Wilson's late mother made Langan the trustee of her estate. "Families used to take care of each other, do this kind of thing."

Odd as it appears for a retired brigadier general and former mayor to grocery shop for a street vendor, it typifies Langan's style.

From 1939 as state representative, to 1947 as state senator, to 1953 when first elected city commissioner, until 1969 when a racially polarized electorate finally sent him packing, Joe Langan served as Mobile's most visible, often controversial, and arguably farsighted public official. During an often gloomy era for local politics—Charles Trimmier was killed in a one-car accident, Lambert Mims and Gary Greenough went to jail—Joe Langan has not only survived, he has endured.

Like a candidate making a stump speech, he lists his accomplish-

For thirty years, beginning in 1939, Joseph N. Langan held a succession of state and local political offices, principal among them Place 1, Mobile City Commission, 1953–69, serving his rotations as mayor. He had a vision for Mobile that he tried to realize in pragmatic ways, from expanding the city limits (successful), to merging city and county government (unsuccessful). It was the civil rights movement that called on his greatest talents. Langan was instrumental in bringing together civic leaders, white and black, for meetings on how to push the city forward—emphasizing job opportunities for blacks in formerly all-white institutions—at a time when other Southern cities were set to explode. Vilified as a Communist by old-line whites and a racist by extremist blacks, Langan was finally voted out, returning to his law practice. Here, after a career of public service, and as a retired Brigadier General of the National Guard, Langan gives a patriotic talk at a recent Flag Day celebration in Mobile. (Kate Reali, Mobile Register)

ments: expanding the city limits, revitalizing the economy after the doldrums of the 1930s and '40s, creating a capital budget, paving roads, setting down drainage, building fire stations and a hospital, helping start the University of South Alabama, creating Municipal Park (renamed Langan Park) and the Mobile Museum of Art. He's proud of his work replacing the spoils system—which had enabled politicians to parcel out jobs to supporters—with a merit system.

While Birmingham and Selma were being torn apart by racial conflicts, Langan helped Mobile stay whole. He brought together leaders for sensible dialogue rather than give way to the clamor of the street.

"Langan was key to bringing about nonviolent resolution to the problems," says Robert Gilliard, a retired dentist who was president of Mobile's National Association for the Advancement of Colored People during the civil rights years.

Gilliard adds: "He was a sensitive man, not a total politician."

Although in his mid-80s, Langan sounds like a maverick on issues close to his heart. Blue eyes peering over the rims of his glasses, he harangues you on the need to consolidate city and county government, or how to finance education through an earnings tax. He barely pauses to catch a breath.

He is a study in contradictions. A longtime Democrat who stood down Dixiecrats in order to support Truman, he is now a Republican. He is a practicing attorney who buys mortgages, does estate planning and is a majority stockholder in an insurance company; yet he goes through his office building flicking off lights when he steps out to lunch in order to save precious pennies.

After shopping, now he loads the Peanut Man's groceries into his battered, 1986 Ford LTD. "I don't need a car for a showpiece, a status symbol," he huffs. "This gets me where I want to go." He makes his delivery.

At the door of his enclosed porch, the Peanut Man peeps out, wary at first. In the past, his house was burglarized. Traipsing to church, he was mugged. He is a petite man, bald, with tufts of whiskers down the sides of his face. He speaks rapidly. "My mama died nine years ago. Her name was Addie. My daddy's name was Memphis, he died, too."

It is hot, airless. The Peanut Man's shirt is buttoned at the collar. He wears suspenders. "Mr. Joe," he asks, "your mama and daddy, they still living?"

Setting down the groceries at his feet, Langan shakes his head.

"When, when did they die?"

"My father died 65 years ago. My mother, 20."

"Oh, I'm sorry. I'm sorry to hear that."

"Thank you."

"My mama, she died nine years ago. Her name was Addie." He grabs up the grocery bags. "Well, unless something comes up, I guess I'll be seeing you!"

As the Peanut Man backs into the darkness, Joe Langan wishes him good day and heads back to his law office.

Sons of Ireland

During Ireland's Great Potato Famine of the 1850s, two brothers named Langan decided, like thousands, to set sail for America. "'Langan' means long, tall man," explains Joe, himself 6 foot 2.

One brother came to port in Keene, N.H. The other, Thomas Langan, came to Mobile, settling in the vicinity where grandson Joe, as mayor, would one day help build the Mobile Civic Center.

Joe Langan's mother, Teresa, was part of another Irish brood, the McAleers, whose father was a shoemaker. They took in boarders in their large house downtown, among them Rabbi Alfred Moses. Joe's grandmother often heard the rabbi practicing his sermons in the next room.

Langan says that the powerful Irish contribution to America with its business people, financiers, chemists and intellectuals is similar to that of the Jews.

He speaks proudly of the Irish priests and sisters "who enlightened Europe after the Middle Ages."

"Joe Langan could have been a priest," says John Tyson Sr., an Alabama state senator during Langan's early years in office.

Poor Irish immigrants, Langan explains, had little say in determining their fate; politics became a way to gain power. "Unless you had a voice in the community, you didn't have anything. A lot of the Irish began to organize, to become voters and participate."

Langan, growing up with few material goods, was sometimes dressed in old sugar sacks stitched into clothing, and had to start working in a grocery in fourth grade. From then on, he went to school as he could, graduating from Murphy High in 1931, and Spring Hill College in 1951, after he was already a state senator. He later taught at Spring Hill.

He was of the last generation to qualify for the bar exam without going to law school; in fact, he passed the Alabama Bar in 1936, 15 years before completing his bachelor's degree. He had learned the profession from the ground up, working in the law office of his uncle, Vincent B. McAleer, becoming a specialist in bankruptcy proceedings. His uncle, Joe McAleer, was a bankruptcy judge. His father, David, was a city tax collector.

Politics was Joe's true love. "I always considered law something to do when you got beat."

In 1943, he married Maude Adele Holcombe, a woman from a politically connected family for whom Holcombe Avenue is named. Maude's father, Bob, would be elected sheriff in one term, then Bill, her uncle, would be elected the next. By all accounts, Maude was a great dancer and, together, the Langans went to balls, rode horses.

Mrs. Langan has remained a mystery figure in her husband's career, though. Visible for years on Mobile streets, walking her dogs several miles a day until one pulled her down, she now makes her way on canes. She has chosen to remain deeply private.

They have no children. Langan prizes snapshots of himself surrounded by beaming great-nieces and nephews.

"She doesn't like being in politics," he says, "and she's not part of the activities. It's hard for a person who doesn't want to be part of it.

"She didn't like her daddy being in it, either—the criticism, the campaign rhetoric."

He thinks the public has gone too far in what it expects leaders to reveal.

"Because young people emulate political leaders, we need to

protect their faults and failings to a certain extent. The issue is principles—life, liberty, voting, fairness in employment. These are more important than a person's failings."

Beyond the Limits

When Langan took office as city commissioner, Place 1, in 1953 and served his rotation as mayor, the city of Mobile, he says, covered only 10 square miles. The city limits were at Sage Avenue.

Toulminville, Spring Hill, Cottage Hill—these communities lay outside the city.

In 1955, Joe Langan undertook the expansion that, he contends, was vital to the city's economic future. In one fell swoop, he pushed through annexation of areas that would one day be the locations for Bel Air Mall, Springdale Mall, the University of South Alabama and the subdivisions of west Mobile.

By the time Langan was voted out in 1969, the boundaries of Mobile stretched over 70 square miles.

"If I hadn't done that," Langan says, "Mobile would have gone down the drain."

Leaning over a map of Mobile today, Langan draws red marker over the city boundaries of yesteryear, and those of today. The wider the circle, he says, the larger the tax base and the more chances people have to enjoy a civic effort, for example, like Hank Aaron Stadium.

Cities that expand their limits, Langan says, prevent the "ghettoization" of downtown. He points to the vitality of Charlotte, N.C., Jacksonville, Fla., and Nashville, Tenn.

Mary Zoghby, who served in the Alabama Legislature from 1978 to 1994, points out that Mobile contrasts with Birmingham, "landlocked by 22 municipalities. You start seeing white flight. The affluent move outside." The inner city is left behind.

Langan's massive 1955 annexation of Mobile occurred, however, without a vote of the people. With equal confidence he pushed through the city's first sales tax—1 cent for the general fund—and soon an additional cent to establish a capital budget in a city where there had been none.

"People will never vote a tax on themselves," he says. "You need leadership to show the way."

Not everyone cottoned to Langan's notion of leadership, though, in either taxes or annexation.

Langan's philosophy that the "county should be the city" riled some. As he recalls, laughing with bitterness, he was accused of promoting "one-world government." Although he had climbed the ranks of the National Guard to become a brigadier general, and served in World War II and Korea, he was even accused of being a communist.

His opponents got hold of a photograph of Langan wearing a turtleneck sweater and gold medallion on a chain—a symbol of office given him by a British mayor. Intending to make Langan look like a suave hipster, they reprinted this photo next to one of black community leader John LeFlore on a poster denouncing both as the "Metro Team."

In 1961, during an effort he launched to bring Prichard into the Mobile fold, he received this crudely written telegram:

"Dear Sir: We the people of Prichard and Chickasaw are in great sympathy with you we know that you would like to have these two fine cities but we hope you will never succeed in having any dictorial power of them. . . . All dictators Mr. Langan sooner later die maybe it won't be long with you."

Burning Crosses

Spend a week visiting and talking with Joe Langan, and you will find one subject brings angry tears.

Leaning back in his office chair, hands behind his head, his eyes get wet as he recounts the way black and white soldiers served alongside each other in World War II, but had to go in separate directions back home.

He tells the story of a fellow soldier who had been a buddy of his in the trenches but could not walk into the same restaurant with him back in America.

"It was an illumination for me," he says.

This "illumination" fueled his belief, as a Catholic, in the brotherhood of man; it deepened his appreciation, as an American, of the Declaration of Independence.

When Langan saw a Mobile bus pick up white passengers on one corner of Bienville Square, but bypass black passengers waiting at another, he was astonished. "That night I got on my typewriter and wrote a blistering letter to the head of the Mobile transit system telling them I thought I'd gotten on the wrong boat coming home from overseas and had ended up in Germany rather than the United States."

"After World War II," he says, concerning race, "we all had to take sides."

If George Wallace was on one side, Joe Langan was on the other. In a Look magazine article of April 30, 1968, Alabama author William Bradford Huie highlighted Langan as a vocal opponent of Wallace. The Langan-haters waved the Look article to show why Langan should be voted out.

In the great debate about Wallace—whether he was a diehard bigot, or just a politician riding the tide—Langan ascribes to the latter view. He sees Wallace as part of the downward slide of politics into "doing what the pollsters tell you, instead of having convictions and standing by them."

Not that Langan himself, in his early years, went through the streets of Mobile preaching an abrupt end to segregation. Reports of one political rally in the 1950s show Langan reassuring white voters that desegregation of schools was not the principal issue.

Could Langan have been elected commissioner if he'd demanded the immediate end of segregation? "No," he concedes.

What Langan did, though, according to former NAACP president Gilliard, was to put together a plan emphasizing equality of opportunity. "He took Mobile from the era of rigid segregation to"—Gilliard hesitates—"non-rigid segregation." The emphasis, a pragmatic one, was in jobs and pay—hiring the first black policemen, the first black firemen, encouraging banks to hire black tellers.

Gilliard explains that Langan stuck his neck out plenty in this effort. "My telescope doesn't pick up anybody like Joe Langan on the horizon today," he says.

Langan assembled a monthly gathering of leaders from the black community, among them Gilliard and AME Zion Bishop William Smith, and leaders from the white community, among them Paul Keefe, personnel director of the Alabama Dry Docks, and George Denniston, president of the American National Bank.

Denniston, now 80, and long retired from the bank (now merged with AmSouth) remembers those meetings. He supplied a conference room at the bank, and brought in dinner for everyone. Denniston says Commissioner George McNally, who served with Langan and Trimmier, also played a role.

The gas company, the fast-food restaurants, the clothing stores, the banks—one by one the city businesses were gradually opened to black employees. Considering the buying power of the black community, the move to bring in black employees was practical, too.

"A lot of people in Mobile wanted this to happen," says John Tyson Sr. "But they wanted somebody else to do it." Joe Langan, he says, was that somebody else.

Langan's path became a dangerous one. The Ku Klux Klan burned a cross in front of his home. A member of the White Citizens Council dogged him; an undercover agent found guns under the man's bed.

There were strong counter-forces, too.

Throughout the country, nonviolent leaders like the Rev. Martin Luther King Jr. were being challenged by militant figures like Stokely Carmichael. After the assassination of King, an activist group in Mobile, Neighborhood Organized Workers, dug in its heels.

N.O.W. published a "News Bulletin" in 1969 that contained an article titled "The Racist Three." The article read in part: "The infamous political leadership in the persons of Langan, Outlaw, and Mims are also the moral yardstick (by) which local so-called Christian and Jewish institutions respond to overtures by the white racist community. As political leaders this existing commission, or should we say this perpetuating commission of illegal representation, used the political power and authority to keep black people in the community in a state of total subjection. . . . Whites no matter how liberal they may seem, have a Master mentality."

While being pilloried by whites who thought he'd gone too far on race, Langan was now being reviled by blacks who thought he hadn't gone far enough.

"I was squashed in the middle," he says.

Many black voters stayed home on election day 1969.

Langan believes N.O.W. leaders physically "intimidated" black voters from casting ballots. He suspects that his political opponents spread money around to fuel this intimidation.

The day after Hurricane Camille slammed into the Gulf Coast, affecting the general voter turnout, Langan was defeated by Joe Bailey.

Langan would run again in 1972, unsuccessfully, for Mobile County commissioner.

When the city changed its commission form of government to a mayor-council form, Langan threw his hat into the ring one more time. It was 1985 and he was 73. In the newly formed District 2— with an 80 percent black electorate—he was defeated by the Rev. Charles Tunstall, a black pastor whom he had appointed to his biracial advisory council years earlier.

Straw Hat Day

On the walls of Joe Langan's office, near the manual typewriter and file folders stacked on chairs, are pictures of politicians from the past. Langan can regale you with tales of these colorful characters: of Gov. James "Big Jim" Folsom and his gorgeous, petite wife, Jamelle; of Congressman Frank Boykin, who'd invite Washington VIPs down to his hunting camp, then secretly tie a turkey to a post, letting it loose just before he took his guests out to hunt.

In one photograph are men at the Alabama State Docks, and they are wearing straw hats. April 1, Langan recalls, was "Straw Hat Day" in Mobile.

He keeps his own straw hat and madras jacket on a coatrack in the corner. He puts them on with his white-collared shirt and fish-print tie, blue seersucker pants and white shoes when he steps out to lunch at the Exchange Club.

If a movie were made of Joe Langan's life, he welcomes the suggestion that Jimmy Stewart would have been ideal to play him. "'Mr. Smith Goes to Washington' was one of my favorites," he admits, recalling the movie about the small-town politician who stood up for ideals despite all.

But Jimmy Stewart is now gone.

Only a few Mr. Smiths dwell among us still.

Albert Murray's House of Blues

You can take the "A" train uptown from Forty-second Street in midtown Manhattan and be there in less than ten minutes. There is a stop at Fifty-ninth Street . . . But after that as often as not there are only six more express minutes to go. Then you are pulling into the IND station at 125th Street and St. Nicholas Avenue, and you are that many more miles north from Mobile, Alabama, but you are also, for better or worse, back among homefolks. . . .

Albert Murray, "South to a Very Old Place," 1971

New York

Natty in velour hat, tailored sports jacket and knit tie, Albert Murray, son of Mobile, resident of Harlem, prepares for an outing in Manhattan. Although 80 now, the novelist and blues historian is, as always, on the go. His calendar is packed with readings at Yale, Vassar, and the Library of Congress. For his books ranging from the ana-

Born at Magazine Point near downtown Mobile in 1917, Albert Murray studied at Tuskegee University and later New York University, rose to the rank of general in the U.S. Air Force, and traveled the world—all before publishing his first book, the widely-acclaimed "Omni-Americans," at age 54. Over the next three decades he would go on to establish himself as one of the nation's most intellectually provocative authors, penning memoir, essays, novels. (His newest book turns on an exchange of letters with his friend from Tuskegee days, Ralph Ellison.) The influence of blues and jazz courses through Murray's work; in turn, he has made a deep impact on how the Americans view these art forms. With his book, "Stompin' the Blues," and his passion for the music, he helped launch "Jazz at Lincoln Center" in New York. In this 1950 photograph he relaxes on the streets of Paris. His life there studying literature was interrupted when he was called back to active duty during the Korean War. (Courtesy of Albert Murray)

lytical "The Omni-Americans" in 1970 to the fictional "The Seven League Boots" in 1995, the National Book Critics Circle celebrated him as a "national living treasure." In May 1997, he is being inducted, along with Studs Terkel and select others, into the prestigious American Academy of Arts and Letters.

An American writer—"I am not African-American," he says testily, "I am one hundred percent American"—he shows a visitor the view from his eighth-floor apartment window: the edges of Central Park several blocks south, the spires of midtown Manhattan farther away.

To what Murray wearily calls the "conventional" mind, it may seem like a far piece from little Magazine Point, just outside downtown Mobile, to vast Harlem. But to Murray, a self-described "cosmopolitan," literal time and place offer few restrictions.

As he slides out two small, dim snapshots of his home on the Mobile River and the foster parents who reared him in the 1920s—the father, he points out, "looks like William Faulkner"—it's as though he is a boy again. He remembers the boats in the Port of Mobile, the hubbub on lower Government Street, the activity at Bienville Square, the streetcar that ran to Magazine Point.

Although most people, he admits, look at the literary section of a paper "like they're looking at the obituary page," and "pass a bookstore like they're walking by an undertaker's shop," he relished the literary page, and bookstores.

He also loved sports, recalling one World Series: "It was October 1927 and I was 10 years old and I realized I could read the Mobile Register by myself and could figure out the box scores, the baseball lineups.

"I was in touch with a pretty cosmopolitan atmosphere," he says. "When I got to the third grade and had a geography book, I could see it. It wasn't like I was outside of the world. I was a part of the world."

Part of that world were the honky-tonks along the Mobile River. The music Murray heard there took hold in his imagination. His trilogy of novels set in Gasoline Point—a fictional Magazine Point—and his several non-fiction works, most notably "South to a Very Old Place," are charged with musical rhythms.

"My prose tries to be the literary equivalent of jazz. You do that by reading the greatest books where the language is being used. You can't do that unless you read Pound, unless you read Eliot, unless you read Mann, Hemingway, and Faulkner. That's what a musician would do."

Little wonder that Murray writes his works longhand, then dictates them to a computer operator, carefully tuning the sounds of his prose as he goes. In the apartment filled with books by world authors, photographs of two of Murray's heroes, Duke Ellington and Louis Armstrong, look sweetly on.

"Albert Murray is the greatest living Alabama writer," contends Pulitzer Prize–winning journalist Howell Raines, a fellow Alabamian who puts Murray's accomplishments ahead of even Harper Lee's. From his office as editor of the New York Times editorial page, Raines speaks with delight of Murray's "South to a Very Old Place," recalling "its jazz inflections, the riffs on language, the invocation of the smell of fish frying in his boyhood home near Mobile. It's like you could play it on a trumpet.

"It's interesting, but not surprising," Raines adds, "that he writes about Gasoline Point, Alabama, from Harlem because a lot of Southerners, particularly a lot of Alabamians, find they're closest to home, in a literary sense, when they're away."

• • •

The official name of that place (which is perhaps even more of a location in time than an intersection on a map) was Gasoline Point, Alabama, because that was what our post office address was, and it was also the name on the L & N timetable and the road map. But once upon a time it was also the briarpatch, which is why my nickname was then Scooter, and is also why the chinaberry tree (that was ever as tall as any fairy tale beanstalk) was, among other things, my spyglass tree.

Albert Murray, "Train Whistle Guitar," 1974

On Albert Murray's writing desk are his "reference" books: mythology by Joseph Campbell; novels by Ernest Hemingway, William

Faulkner and Thomas Mann; world histories. Among the "references" are Mother Goose, "Uncle Remus," and a collection of fairy tales. Odd choices for sacred texts?

"If you can't write a fairy tale," he says with mild annoyance—a recurrent mood—"you can't write a novel. If it's got five hundred pages you're trying to make it something as meaningful to a sophisticated reader as a fairy tale. A fairy tale you never outgrow. Journalists' minds are so screwed up with sociology and economics that they don't see you're talking about fairy tales. They spread confusion."

Murray intends to make his literature accessible, and clear. In doing so he returns, time and again, to the geography of his youth, and to heroic characters like Dr. Benjamin Baker, his beloved teacher and principal at Mobile County Training School.

The neighborly street corners of his youth have long been bulldozed over to make way for paper mills. The Magazine Point he knew endures in his imagination. The voice of Scooter, the fictional narrator of his novels, keeps the place alive for others.

"When you deal with your consciousness it's got to have a real base, a point of departure. The meanings begin there. This is where literature turns into romance. The facts are nothing unless they become legend."

Does Murray feel any connection to another black Southern writer of his generation, Richard Wright, author of "Black Boy" and "Native Son"?

"I don't think a novelist should be telling the reader how to vote," he complains. "It feels better to me to be going somewhere with Hemingway than going somewhere with any number of other writers. Certainly going somewhere with Richard Wright, who's depressing to me. With Hemingway I would see the landscape; I would see the streams; I would see the sun; I would see the people; I would hear the language. That's what being alive means to me. That's the earth. You've got to go through race if the guy's talking about a bottle of wine?"

In fact, Murray bridles at being called "black," preferring the term "colored." In America, he argues, black and white are no longer accurate, nor are they valid as distinctions.

He explored the nuances of race and identity in his first book, "The Omni-Americans."

"We don't know who's Negro and who's white," he says. "You don't know who's passing, and nobody cares. People no longer care if a guy's a black second baseman. They care if he's a good second baseman."

Twenty-five years after publication of "The Omni-Americans," Newsweek is on the newsstands with an article titled "In Living Colors," proclaiming that "for this multiracial generation, hip isn't just black and white."

Murray just smiles and laughs wisely when being told he is ahead of his time.

"People are born out of date," he explains. "A kid who was born yesterday, does he know as much as you? A kid who's 15, does he know as much as you? Twenty? Thirty? He's still trying to catch up to all kinds of fundamentals. I don't see why people can't get that straight. I've been there for almost 81 years. I haven't been anywhere else. All this stuff that was happening"—he chuckles—"I was here when it was happening!

"Take a guy who's never even heard of a 78 rpm record. To me, he's ignorant. He doesn't know that the CD came after the LP. See what I mean?"

• • •

The blues as such are synonymous with low spirits. Blues music is not . . . Not only is its express purpose to make people feel good, which is to say in high spirits, but in the process of doing so it is actually expected to generate a disposition that is both elegantly playful and heroic in its nonchalance.

Albert Murray, "Stomping the Blues," 1976

Albert Murray's wife of 56 years, Mozelle, kisses him on the cheek good-bye as time comes to tour the city with his visitor. Mozelle and Albert met as students at Tuskegee Institute. While at Tuskegee, Albert befriended an upperclassman from Oklahoma who also had a passion for books: Ralph Ellison, who would go on to author the great novel "Invisible Man."

Long before he became a famous writer, though, Ellison was a camera buff. Photos taken by Ellison of an intense, young Albert, and a fetching, youthful Mozelle, fill one of the Murrays' many picture albums. In the albums are also affectionate photos of their daughter, Michele, who went on to become an Alvin Ailey dancer.

The names Mozelle and Michele appear in all of Murray's books on the dedication page.

In their early family life together, Albert, Mozelle, and Michele lived in Tuskegee, California, Paris and Morocco. The reason is simple: Before becoming an author, Murray spent a career in the Air Force, retiring as a major in 1962, then moving his family to New York.

At 54, an age when many men and women are biding their time until retirement, Murray started phase two of his life: He wrote "The Omni-Americans" and launched his literary career. His literary sensibility "had been operating" all along. He had taught literature at Tuskegee and had completed a master's at New York University between periods of active military service.

"The Omni-Americans" was reviewed prominently not only in publications like Time and Saturday Review, but also in Air Force magazine. Willie Morris, then editor of Harper's, soon sent him on the journey back to Mobile that resulted in "South to a Very Old Place."

Murray the exuberant New Yorker is now hurtling downtown in a taxi. Before back operations made it difficult to walk, he zipped around town from high culture to low, Lincoln Center to honky-tonks, a familiar presence in cafes and night clubs.

He still takes on New York with zest, directing the driver to the Gotham Bar and Grill in Greenwich Village. He is right at home dining with his visitor where publishers and financiers, all around, deal-make and gossip.

Over lunch he explains how blues and jazz are an "American art form." He tells how his book "Stomping the Blues," and his passion for the music, helped launch "Jazz at Lincoln Center," one of Lincoln

Center's constituent arts organizations. Trumpet genius Wynton Marsalis, its artistic director and a family friend of Murray's, has helped jazz take its place in a world of classical music, opera and ballet.

He discusses a recent "Essentially Ellington" contest. High school jazz bands competed in renditions of Ellington. Finalists had the joy to play music with Wynton Marsalis himself.

With Murray at the event were Michele, and Michael James, Ellington's nephew. Michele reminisced about the time she was 9 years old and was awakened in the middle of the night to meet a friend of her daddy's, Duke Ellington.

Ellington once wrote: "Albert Murray is a man whose learning did not interfere with understanding." He called him "the authority on soul from the days of old."

After lunch, Murray and his visitor head to Strand Book Store. He sidles up to the employees' side door, knocks, and is welcomed like a long-lost celebrity. "Hey, Albert, where you been!"

Around him are "eight miles of books," as the store claims—towering stacks, crowded tables. Bibliophiles roam down endless aisles of used books, remaindered books, hard-to-find books.

One of the clerks hands him sparkling water and a bar of chocolate. "If they see me," Murray teases, "they say, 'We got to keep the old guy from drying up.'" He takes a bite of the chocolate. "Keeps me kissable," he says, grinning.

Murray the philosopher and heady, contentious author is now Murray the bon vivant, the back-porch neighbor.

People come over to him, shake his hand, ask for him to sign a book. "He's like my Dad," one woman says.

He swivels in a chair. "This might as well be Mobile."

"Albert's been coming here for ages," says Fred Bass, owner of this literary cornucopia. "The thing I like about Albert, he's interested in so many things. And he's got an up attitude."

A book clerk carts over a stack of tomes held aside for Murray: Montaigne, Pascal, Emerson, Hemingway. "These are like a reprimand," Murray says, shaking his head at so many books, so little time. "Like you should read Bury's 'History of Greece.'"

It is as though he is a boy again, thrilling to discover a book under the organ lid at home in Magazine Point, or walking into Mobile County Training School, wide-eyed at the intellectual exuberance of Benjamin Baker.

But he is in New York City, the crossroads of international letters, and another clerk brings him a copy of "South to a Very Old Place" to show him, a first edition priced at $90.

Murray turns his head in wonderment: two million books. Even Shakespeare would feel small in this ocean of words.

"I can't figure out," Murray says, meditating on the endless worlds waiting to be explored, "why anybody would want to remain stupid with this stuff around."

• • •

In general, black Mobilians are considerably less polemical than New York-ers on the subject of black heritage. But after all, black teachers in Mobile, like perhaps most others throughout most of the South, have been observing Negro History Week (the week in February that includes Lincoln's and Frederick Douglass's birthday) for decades.
Albert Murray, "Black Pride in Mobile, Alabama,"
from "The Omni-Americans," 1970

Among Albert Murray's many enduring friendships—with artist Romare Bearden, novelist Robert Penn "Red" Warren, composer Duke Ellington—was a lifelong connection to Ralph Ellison.

New York Times editorial writer Brent Staples, author of a memoir, "Parallel Time: Growing Up in Black and White," wrote of Ellison: "With his friend and rival, the critic and novelist Albert Murray, he fought a lifelong battle against black separatism, arguing that blacks were not just deeply American but the most American people of all."

Back in his apartment, Murray lets a visitor catch a glimpse of a stack of typewritten letters to him from Ellison. He is working with the Ellison estate concerning publication of this correspondence.

He does offer a postcard from Ellison typed to Murray. Dated May

14, 1951, it begins: "Dear Albert, You are herewith warned that I have dropped the shuck."

When his visitor asks what that means, Murray shakes his head. "Don't you know anything?" He smiles, translating: Ellison had finished the manuscript of "Invisible Man."

After Ellison's monumental success with "Invisible Man," though, he labored on another. Murray recounts the sad story of how that second novel-in-progress, an original, handwritten draft with no copy, burned up in a house fire. One of the few people who'd heard portions of it read aloud was Murray. Ellison turned to Murray to help him remember those sections.

Ellison died in 1994, having never published the manuscript.

Murray takes out a treasure: a first edition of "Invisible Man" inscribed by the author. He says a collector recently offered him $30,000 for the book.

Murray declined. He says there is nothing he wants now that money could buy—except, maybe, a swimming pool.

In Ralph Ellison's green pen, the inscription reads: "For Albert Murray, My friend who was schooled in the same briarpatch to confound the squares, bears and fools thereabouts. Passion is his, and with its consciousness, but best of all self-acceptance and self-respect. In his my voice becomes richer for his love and knowledge of the experience we both share. Sincerely, Ralph Ellison. Tuskegee, 1954."

Alma Fisher: Out of Auschwitz

In a west Mobile apartment filled with a gleaming grand piano, white birthday roses, and pictures of musicians, there is a woman named Alma Fisher—petite, gracious, 91 years of age—who survived hell. Keen of mind, soft of voice, only her eyesight dimmed, she looks back, with clarity, on terrors of the past.

Adolf Hitler tried to kill Alma—his Nazis and their accom-

A petite lady at a grand piano with an enormity of history on her shoulders, Alma Fisher, at 91, reflects on the barbaric past. Growing up Alma Weiss in Munich, she anticipated her life, as a Jew, unfolding as sweetly as that of any other German citizen from a middle-class family. Among the Weiss's neighbors were a family not Jewish but whose world appeared similar to their own; they even had a daughter about Alma's age, Eva Braun. By 1942, Alma was a prisoner in a concentration camp whose name would become synonymous with death—Auschwitz—and Eva Braun was Adolf Hitler's mistress. That Alma survived four years in "the largest graveyard in human history" and eventually found her way to a new life in Mobile, Ala., is an epic tale, agonizing but at turns heroic—and until now, one she has chosen to keep tucked away deep inside in her heart. (G. M. Andrews, Mobile Register)

plices shot, gassed, tortured and starved to death 6 million Jews, among them Alma's mother and grandmother, and her late husband's mother, sister, brother and two sisters-in-law.

The place that Alma endured from 1942 to 1945—Auschwitz—conjures images of barbed wire, attack dogs, gas chambers, hollow-eyed men and women. "Auschwitz," says the "Encyclopedia of the Holocaust," was "the largest graveyard in human history."

On Alma's forearm there is a scar where the tattoo of her concentration camp serial number used to be. She had it removed, she says, at Mt. Sinai Hospital in New York after coming to America. "Everybody around me stood there crying. They had never seen anything like it."

Alma's story of surviving Auschwitz—and of knowing Hitler's bride, Eva Braun—is one she'd decided never to tell.

After all, the life she made in America was a good one: marriage to a wonderful man, Tony Fisher, whom she'd met in New York; their happy years in Mobile, where they'd moved for his career in lumber export; her successes as a performer with the Mobile Symphony Orchestra and as a piano teacher at Murphy High, Spring Hill College and the University of South Alabama.

"It was easy to get the home feeling here," she says. "We want to live, and we want to forget."

Why has she decided, now, to remember? Perhaps, she says, it was a television documentary she saw on Auschwitz that stirred her. Or maybe it's the anger she feels that some fringe provocateurs claim the Holocaust never happened at all.

Peter Black, a senior historian of the U.S. Holocaust Memorial Museum in Washington, says that the number of Nazi death-camp victims staggers comprehension: half of Europe's 12 millions Jews, half a million Gypsies, 100,000 mentally and physically disabled people, 2.5 million non-Jewish Poles, 3 million Soviet prisoners of war. Tens upon tens of thousands more.

A lone, human voice like Alma Fisher's, Black says, shocks us into recognition when the numbers make us numb.

Alma's voice, gentle yet urgent, is as sweet as any grandmother's, yet unbreakable as steel. Like the tattoo long gone—but forever marking her—her experiences left an indelible scar.

• • •

At the outset of the First World War in 1914, Alma—born Alma Weiss—was in first grade in Munich, Germany. Her father, Moritz, was a businessman; her mother, Vilma, a homemaker. The Weisses were cultured, comfortably off, patriotically German. Moritz served the Kaiser in Vienna during the war.

"We had a king we loved," Alma says. "A princess who walked among us on the streets."

Germany's 500,000 Jews, before the rise of Hitler and the Nazis, generally flourished in the mainstream. In cosmopolitan Munich, the Weisses mingled with Germans of all walks.

"Eva Braun's father was my first-grade teacher," she says. "The Brauns lived around the corner from us, and Eva's mother always said, 'If you need anything, come.'

"Eva's father was a nice man, her mother was nice, too. Before she fell in bad hands, Eva was"—Alma shrugs—"just a girl. They lost their daughter, too, the Brauns. I don't know how proud they were of her."

Alma learned English, French and Italian, and played piano, loving Chopin, Mozart and Liszt.

She wished to attend Munich's Academy of Music, but first secured a business degree at the insistence of her pragmatic father. Going on to the academy, she excelled and was invited to teach. She aspired to be a concert artist.

Like others in her circle of friends, she had not lost sight of Eva Braun.

While working in a Munich photo shop in 1929 at age 17, plump, blonde Eva had been introduced, as she'd later recount, to "a man with a funny mustache," who'd offered her "a lift in his Mercedes." The suitor was the 40-year-old leader of Germany's National Socialist Party, and she soon was meeting him in his Munich apartment. Eva Braun had become the mistress of Adolf Hitler.

"Everybody knew about her," Alma says. "Where Hitler was, Eva was."

Hitler had been a fringe politician in the mid-1920s, when he first lunged for power, landed in prison and began to dictate "Mein Kampf." His book, like his speeches, made Jews the scapegoats for Germany's World War I defeat and its subsequent ills.

As Germany's hard times deepened with the world's depression, Hitler, free by now, had the easy explanations: Why, it was Jewish wealth, Jewish danger, a Jewish conspiracy.

By 1933, Hitler was no longer fringe—he became Germany's chancellor. "His unbearable hatred" of the Jews, as Alma describes it, and his obsession with "Aryan" blood unleashed the nation's basest, and cruelest, instincts.

Books by Jewish writers were burned, cemeteries desecrated, shop windows smashed. Jewish civil servants were fired and Jewish doctors, professors, and lawyers stripped of their credentials. Scientists and physicists who were Jewish—Albert Einstein, among them—were drummed into exile. The Munich synagogue was torched. Nazi strikes against Jews, under Hitler's martial law, resulted in arrests, beatings and murders.

Alma Fisher glimpsed Hitler just once, in the early '30s. A doctor friend visiting Munich invited her to a tea house, the Carlton.

"I didn't know it at the time," she said, "but it was the place where Hitler was seen. He had his own private room there. Suddenly, there was this big excitement and Hitler went through. That doctor wanted to see Hitler, and that's why he took me there."

At the Academy of Music, Alma wished only to teach piano, and study in a master class for honors graduates. The 1930s wore on.

"Then, one day, my teacher came and said I had to write a letter—which was very strange from a teacher, but his character just wasn't big enough for the times—a letter to ask for my resignation on account of health problems. I would not have done it if my teacher, who I adored, and admired, would not have told me."

She adds dryly: "He turned out to be a pretty good Nazi."

Alma's world rapidly changed. Thousands of German Jews managed to emigrate, but a great many more did not. Alma put money down to secure her own passage, but the world's doors were open only to so many. Her sister had married an Italian in 1932 and moved to Italy. Her father had passed away in 1936. Her mother went to live in Yugoslavia with Alma's great-uncle and grandmother, planning to join Alma in America or France if Alma could reach there.

Alma was in Munich on Sept. 1, 1939, when Hitler's army invaded Poland. That same night, the mother and brother of a man she was seeing romantically—he was not Jewish; indeed, he was in the German air force—came to take her to their rural estate.

She stayed with them for several months—the family was soon harboring other Jews—until she sensed problems. "Somehow the people around must have found out they were hiding people," she says.

She remembers, for example, that her hosts, whose livelihood was bound up in farm animals, suddenly had their feed supplies cut off by local authorities. She worried what pressures might come next.

"I knew I wasn't going to stay there and cause trouble."

She moved back to a Munich boarding house.

Alma and the young airman had become engaged, but Hitler's 1935 Nuremberg Laws on German citizenship deemed it unlawful for Jews and non-Jews to wed. So they rendezvoused in secret, depending on friends to provide cover for them.

But the war was pulling them apart.

All around Alma, Jews were being taken from their homes and dragged away. Knowing her turn was coming, she still had one hope—the promise made to her as a child by the mother of Eva Braun.

"When it looked dangerous, that we would all be shipped from Munich, I went to her and asked her if there was anything she could do for me.

"She said, 'I'm going to talk to Eva.'"

The answer from Eva's mother came back soon enough: "Unfortunately, there's absolutely nothing she can do for anybody Jewish."

• • •

As Alma Fisher tells her story she pauses to make iced tea for
her guest and to offer cookies on decorative china. A Liszt sonata
performed by her friend John Browning plays in the background.
Though she has no children, she is anyone's ideal grandmother—
delicate, silver-haired, attentive. Wise.

She takes out a photo album and shows a beloved dog she recently
lost: Tippy, a bright-eyed Westie terrier. On her 90th birthday last
year, friends gave her 90 white roses. The friends showered her with
roses again on her recent 91st.

Macular degeneration makes it difficult for Alma to see, but she
knows her apartment, and memorabilia, by heart. She pulls out a postcard from decades ago and touches the script, returning to the past.

"I had a card from my mother who was about to be shipped out
of that city in Yugoslavia. 'And what will I do?' she writes. 'I won't
even have money for stamps to write to you.'"

She hesitates. "Terrible. The Germans had occupied Yugoslavia in
the meantime. Much later I heard that she was shipped away, together
with my old grandmother."

She whispers their fate: "Gassed."

She puts the postcard away, silent.

• • •

The Nazis seized Alma and shipped her to a compound that had been
a cloister. She became "forced labor," directed by SS guards to toil
in a telephone factory.

She kept her head down and did what she was told.

"I worked well," she said. "I showed them I could do it."

One day a "transport"—a train that loaded up people like cattle—
was readied to carry Jews to Eastern Europe, territory that had fallen
under Hitler's domination. The first transport, Alma recalls, was to
Riga, a town in Latvia where Jews had been shoved into a ghetto of
tens of thousands, marched into the forest and slaughtered.

"One nice day I missed the first transport. To Riga," she says grimly. "Nobody returned from there. Then there came another transport—I had not even heard the word—to Auschwitz."

It was in 1942 when that second transport, Alma aboard, began to make its way to the east, deep into Poland. Crammed into a boxcar, Alma, like the others, was at the mercy of the captors. "They had the guns. We hated the Nazis, but we couldn't do anything. They had the power."

Arriving at the camp, they were ordered out of the train for "the selection"—a delicate word for the cruel, cold decisions made by Nazi SS guards.

"To the left. To the right. To the left. To the right." Alma's voice faintly trembles as she repeats the commands.

Families were split apart, able-bodied workers put into one row, old people and children in another: "We had a whole group of children in our transport. They were all killed. Every child."

Alma was directed "to the left," through the iron gates.

She remembers there were 300 others in her transport—only 50 of them, she was aware of, entered with her. A while later, still innocent of the magnitude of horrors, she asked where the others had gone.

Someone pointed to the chimneys.

Of the 300 in her transport, Alma was one of only three who would survive.

"When we arrived in Auschwitz, they took everything away, clothes, shoes. We were naked. They shave your hair, put a tattoo on your arm. You don't feel anything because you're so numb. Completely paralyzed. You don't realize it can be true."

They were given castoff pants, shirts and dresses: "Clothes that didn't fit and shoes that ruined your feet—that had belonged to the dead."

For months, "sleeping on wooden planks, in stalls," she'd rise, often in bitter cold, and tramp out past a German oom-pah band playing patriotic songs of Hitler's Third Reich. Her labor was mindless— "cutting grass, working in fields. I don't remember what I was thinking.

"The food? Horrible! Potato peel boiled in water."

All the while, she says, "We saw the chimneys with smoke coming out, the people who were gassed and then burned."

Around the camp was electrified wire. "Many people went to the wire to kill themselves—if you put your hands on the wire you were electrocuted. They just couldn't take it."

• • •

Not knowing the fate of her mother, or her fiancé, Alma nursed the hope she would be reunited with both if she could only endure. Little did she know that, even after months of hard labor, the war had three years to go.

At Auschwitz, according to the "Encyclopedia of the Holocaust," a million and a half Jews—men, women, and children—would be put to death. Odds were remote that anyone would survive for very long at the camp.

By freakish luck, Alma was placed in a camp job that could save her. Her lifeline was the business degree from Munich, the one her father had insisted upon.

An SS guard, she believes, had seen her paperwork and knew that she could work with records and files. She lived like the other prisoners, only she reported every day to the Auschwitz office.

She joined a staff of other women prisoners whose job it was to chronicle the gruesome facts of the Auschwitz killing machine.

Under penalty of death, Alma was not allowed to divulge anything of what she saw.

When Alma realized that SS guards, in the office, did not long endure the presence of foul-smelling prisoners—"they were afraid they'd catch a sickness"—she contrived a way to wash up, regularly slipping into a shower-closet near her quarters. It became part of her strategy of survival.

The depth of misery in the camp was so great that the tiniest gesture of kindness was seen, by Alma, as "a miracle"—a German soldier, who'd been transferred to the Auschwitz office after suffering a war wound, handed Alma a gift from his wife one day. "It was," she remembers as though speaking of a treasure, "a piece of apple."

Some days later, she took a risk. She asked the soldier to send a message to the family of her fiancé, telling of her whereabouts. Remarkably, he did, bringing word back of their acknowledgment.

By January 1945, Russia was pushing deeper into Poland, beating back Hitler's forces. As the Red Army neared Auschwitz, the Nazis began to abandon the camp, taking with them the 58,000 victims who were still alive.

Alma Fisher was suddenly outside, on the open roads of Poland. The SS guards were directing her and the others—frail, hungry, exhausted, and beaten-down—to walk, without stopping, hundreds of miles back to Germany.

"They put us," she says, "on the death march."

• • •

"For seven days and seven nights we were running from the Russians. Anyone who could not walk anymore, or was sitting down, was shot."

She tells of the death march in a blur. From other camps across the crumbling German empire, Jewish survivors were being herded west. Thousands, who lagged, were killed and left in roadside ditches.

Alma thought she was going to become one of the fallen.

"I was close," she says, "to giving up." Then another prisoner, a stranger beside her—"Somebody I never knew before, and never saw afterward"—picked her up and carried her.

Those who survived the march arrived at another camp, this one deep inside Germany, just north of Berlin—Ravensbrueck. That camp had held women, and served as a training ground for women in Hitler's SS guard.

At Ravensbrueck, in April, Alma heard that the American president, Franklin Roosevelt, had died.

"We thought that was the end of the world," she says. "All we had hoped for was that Roosevelt would save us, then he was dead."

Within days, Alma was set on a death march again; Ravensbrueck was being evacuated. On this march, chaos ensued. The SS guards, fearing their own capture now, abandoned the prisoners, threw away their uniforms and fled.

Alma and the others began to wander on their own.

"We went into houses that were left alone, opened the doors, went in, slept, and tried to feed ourselves. We dug potatoes out of the earth and ate those raw. The Russians came and left, fortunately, after awhile.

"Then the Americans came."

With the Allied forces victorious, Alma made her way back to Munich. But there was nobody for her there anymore. She soon learned the fate of her mother.

She went to see her fiance's family in the countryside. Toward the end of the war, they said, he'd been killed in action.

● ● ●

The story of her life that Alma Fisher recounts is a tragic one up until 1945. She was, by then, only 38 years old.

Looking back, she grieves for the loss of loved ones, and for the nameless millions, too. She puzzles, like anyone else, about what drove, in the deepest sense, the madman.

"There was this tremendous hate, this envy, that's what must have happened to Hitler. This unbearable hate. How anybody could choose a place and kill 6 million people. Not anybody in his right sense! And so many thousands of thousands followed him."

She has been back to visit friends in Munich, "but not to live there, never. If that's possible in a country as beautiful as Munich was, and Germany was, no, I would not go back."

But she remembers those who showed kindness: the youthful fiancé who risked himself to see her, the man in the death camp who handed her a piece of apple, the stranger, on the death march, who lifted her onto his back.

Alma was given a government job in Munich right after the war. Soon, as a "Displaced Person" under the Truman Act—which brought

Holocaust survivors to America—she boarded a ship and crossed the Atlantic.

In New York, she was invited for coffee by friends from Munich on the same evening as a Yugoslavian named Tony Fisher, also scarred by the Holocaust. He was working in the lumber business in North Carolina.

Tony kept calling on her, and soon asked her to marry him. They moved south, to Mobile, where he had connections. One day, when she was practicing piano in her new home, a stranger passed by, heard her and told educators at Barton Academy about her.

On May 1, 1951, in a ceremony conducted by Federal Judge Dan H. Thomas, Alma took the oath of U.S. citizenship along with 40 others in Mobile. Thomas talked to them about American ideals, according to an account in the Mobile newspaper: "The heart and soul of those ideals is the profound conviction that the right of the individual to life, liberty and the pursuit of happiness rises above the arbitrary demands of the state."

The judge's words proclaimed the exact opposite of the demands of Nazi Germany.

"We were happy," Alma says of her life with Tony, who passed away in 1991, at age 90. In Mobile, they were active in social and civic affairs. Tony was president of the local theater company, the Joe Jefferson Players; Alma was Mrs. Frank in the play "The Diary of Anne Frank."

"Life made it up to me," she whispers, exhausted from her tale, yet unburdened of it now. "God made it up to me."

The girl who lived around the corner from Alma in childhood—and once coldly denied her help—of course found a husband, too. On April 29, 1945, in a wedding ceremony in the fuehrer's bunker beneath Berlin, Eva Braun finally became Eva Hitler.

One day later, as the world would cheer, the bride put poison into her mouth, and the groom a bullet into his head.

Past Triumphs

Dr. James Franklin: Healing Us Still

As Thelma Shamburger remembers it, the man came to town after being chased out of Evergreen, Ala., for doctoring a white woman.

In her yellow house in the Plateau community in North Mobile, sitting next to a basket filled with home remedies, Mrs. Shamburger, 85, recalls the long-ago afternoon.

She was 8 years old that day the train ground to a halt at the Plateau station and a nicely dressed stranger got off and started walking toward her home. "He was coming down the street and had a brown satchel in his hand."

The stranger asked Thelma's daddy if he had a room where he could put up for the night. "My daddy asked him what that bag was in his hand. 'It's a doctor's bag,' he told him. My daddy said, 'We need a doctor in Plateau.'"

The stranger's name was James A. Franklin and the family invited him to stay that night, and heard his story.

He'd grown up in Tennessee, went to medical school at the University of Michigan, and had served in the Armed Forces during the Great War. He'd just come from practicing medicine in Evergreen, where a flu epidemic had taken its toll on the town. Dr. Franklin, 33 at the time, had tended more than black patients.

"A gang was mad at him 'cause he doctored a white lady," recalls Mrs. Shamburger; little matter that the white woman, in fact, "was cured." The woman's husband came to Dr. Franklin's rescue, bundling him off on a train. Plateau is where he landed.

After spending that night with Thelma's family, Dr. Franklin set up his office on the corner. "He stayed for two or three years," she says, taking nominal fees or food for his services.

Even when he moved his office over to Davis Avenue—now Dr. Martin Luther King Jr. Boulevard—he'd return to Plateau to tend folks in the community.

As Mrs. Shamburger stands from her chair and slowly walks out to Front Street, she points to the now-vacant lot where Dr. Franklin had patients "lined up out the door."

Like others Dr. Franklin got to know after he stepped off that southbound train, Mrs. Shamburger speaks of him not only as a doctor, but also as mentor and friend.

Mrs. Shamburger herself went on to be a midwife, delivering more than 3,000 babies of all backgrounds and hues. "Dr. Franklin," says Mrs. Shamburger, missing him still, "was closer to me than a dime is to you."

• • •

The story of James A. Franklin (1886–1972) is one of a soft-spoken but tough physician caring for Mobile's black community, and inspiring others.

From Dr. Judkin Robinson, who made house calls as a student of Dr. Franklin, to Sister Marilyn Aiello, M.D., who founded a clinic in impoverished Marks, Miss., Dr. Franklin's legacy has taken hold.

Dr. Franklin practiced medicine for decades in a city where black patients, through the 1950s, were admitted in the back door of area hospitals—if admitted at all—and were confined to segregated wards. Even Mobile General, formerly a tuberculosis hospital, had separate areas for blacks.

The Catholic Church opened Martin de Porres Hospital to accommodate the black community.

"Martin de Porres was very small," says Dr. Robinson. "Before

Doctor bag in hand, James Franklin makes his way down a dirt road in the Plateau community of Mobile. The early photograph of Franklin (1886–1972) offers a glimpse into what the daily rounds might have entailed for one of Mobile's few black physicians, as he traipsed to house calls. As Thelma Shamburger, a midwife in her eighties (now deceased) recalled of Franklin's first appearance in town, "My daddy said, 'We need a doctor in Plateau.'" While tending to the needs of Plateau, the Michigan Medical School graduate also set up an office in downtown Mobile, seeing as many as a hundred patients a day, doctoring as he might at a time when hospital access was often limited for blacks. Throughout Mobile today, a series of Franklin clinics, named in his honor, receive patients with no insurance or on Medicaid, part of Franklin Memorial Primary Health Center Inc. (Photographer unknown)

Martin de Porres, Negroes were often not admitted to hospitals at all—many were turned down in the emergency room. They would be tended at home, and many died."

In our age when economic means, not race, determines where patients seek medical care, Dr. Franklin would surely be proud to have his name on a series of clinics that turn no one away at the door.

Sixty percent of the more than 25,000 patients who walk through the doors of Franklin Memorial Primary Health Center Inc. today have no insurance at all, says current director Charles White. Thirty-five percent are on Medicaid.

Dr. Franklin made no Nobel Prize–winning discoveries, healed no president. His good works were the sum of thousands of patients who came to see him looking for care. And, as with many doctors, he achieved a comfortable style of living, eventually buying a seven-bedroom house a couple of blocks from his Davis Avenue office. His second wife, Marguerite, lives there still.

But as a physician, along with others like Dr. E. B. Goode and Dr. Robinson, he carried more than a brown satchel in his hand; even though he practiced in the middle of a city, like a rural doctor he tended an entire community, sometimes seeing as many as 100 patients a day.

Mary Walker was one of Dr. Franklin's patients.

"There was nowhere I could have gone to get the kind of care Dr. Franklin gave me," she says, remembering his office when she was a young woman with a passel of babies and money was scarce.

"You'd try to do everything you could with home remedy—remembering what your mother did, and others told you—but that wasn't always good."

Her visits to Dr. Franklin were to a man who gave her advice not only about getting well, but staying well, too. She tells of the signs in his office exhorting patients to eat right and exercise, and of the comfort she felt just talking with him.

"Dr. Franklin was caring about people. He took time with his patients. He would do whatever he could to help you."

When her youngest child was only 2, she found herself alone. "My husband died, and I had all nine of them on my shoulders," she explains.

Although her husband had gotten insurance on his job, Mrs. Walker retained none. "I worked as a cook and a maid. Anything that would earn me an honest dollar."

With Dr. Franklin no longer living, Mrs. Walker began to take her children to the Franklin Clinic, the first one established at the site of the doctor's original office. "For people like myself, with a lot of children and a small income, it was a godsend. I couldn't afford going to a regular physician. There wasn't no 30, 40, 50 dollars a visit, so I could afford going there.

"My grandson had a big sore and he said he couldn't go to the doctor. I told him, 'You go there and they'll help you. Tell them you don't have a job.' When he went to the clinic they sent him to the hospital and he had a blood clot in his leg. And they saved his life."

• • •

In 1928, at age 13, Judkin Robinson went swimming in the Mobile River. He caught a splinter in his foot and pried it out. Two days later his neck got stiff and his head began to pound.

He went to Dr. Franklin, who diagnosed lockjaw. He remembers how Dr. Franklin came to his parents' home, morning and night, to check on him when he was ill from that infection, and how when he started having spasms he was there to doctor him as needed.

Eventually young Judkin went to Meharry University in Nashville, one of the nation's prominent black medical schools of the day. When he returned, he made rounds with Dr. Franklin in his horse and buggy.

"Dr. Franklin's bedside manner was very calm. He had a strong mind; you couldn't distract him."

Dr. Robinson planned to practice with Dr. Franklin, but decided to go into pediatrics. To this day, thinking back to the day he went swimming in the Mobile River, he credits Dr. Franklin with having shown him direction.

"He treated me for tetanus and I survived," says Dr. Robinson, who still practices at 81, serving the same neighborhood as Dr. Franklin. "He was my inspiration."

• • •

Dr. Franklin and his first wife, Dora, who died in 1950, had 10 children. Among them were two daughters, Evelyn and Joycelyn, who married two brothers, John and James Finley.

The Finley brothers wanted to become pharmacists. When no college in Alabama would admit blacks for this study, John went to Xavier University in New Orleans.

In his home today, John Finley keeps a portrait of the Xavier class of 1950, the year he graduated. Mr. Finley, although retired, still volunteers his services to the Franklin Clinic Pharmacy in Prichard on afternoons.

During his long career on Davis Avenue, the Finley Pharmacy, next to the Booker T. movie theater, was the meeting place of Central High students. From the pharmacy in the back, John and James Finley made up prescriptions, many for their father-in-law's patients.

Although Finley Pharmacy was not the first on the Avenue, it was the first one that was owned by residents of the community. The others were owned by whites.

Even as the small pharmacies in town began to fold, unable to match the competition provided by the big chain drugstores, Finley Pharmacy persisted. Only recently did Mr. Finley close it.

His brother was deceased, and his son, John Finley III, also a pharmacist, decided to head out to work for one of the chains. In his comfortable suburban home, John Finley explains that his life as a pharmacist has been good, and that Dr. Franklin gave him advice he never forgot.

"He'd say, 'Don't worry about anything, because what's for you is what you'll get.'"

• • •

The Franklin family, as generations unfolded, would produce numerous descendants in the health-care field, among them Coleridge Taylor Franklin Jr., a doctor in Louisiana. And friends of the family were inspired too.

Sister Marilyn Aiello grew up in an Italian family in Chicago and came to Mobile to teach at Most Pure Heart of Mary School on Davis Avenue, an all-black parochial school, in 1962. While teaching on the Avenue, she came to know the Franklin family.

Alarmed by the lack of sufficient health care in that neighborhood, Sister Marilyn made a brave decision at the age of 38. She enrolled at the newly opened medical school at University of South Alabama.

While still a student, she enlisted the help of other students, and some professors, to begin the Franklin Clinic. Dr. Franklin had died and the Franklin family agreed to lease the doctor's office as a clinic for $1 a year.

A Dominican nun, Sister Marilyn—now known to her patients as "Dr. Sister"—left Mobile to do her residency in Chicago, but did not return here. Instead, motivated by the work of Dr. Franklin, she traveled to the Delta town of Marks, Miss.

In her clinic there, she and one other "Dr. Sister" serve a county of 10,000 residents—the only health care available.

As she and her colleague and staff see up to 60 patients a day, she marvels at the commitment, and energy, of Dr. Franklin. "I don't think I would have ever gotten off the ground if it weren't for Dr. Franklin and his family. You never know when you're planting a seed. His life goes on."

• • •

Marguerite Franklin, chatty and elegant at 91, sits in her spacious home two blocks from the office where her husband walked to work every day except Thursday.

Turning through a photo album, she remembers how he'd breakfast at 8, tend to his patients, come home at 3 for lunch, then go back again until well into the evening. On his day off, though, he'd often "slip back" to the office.

As a prominent physician, Dr. Franklin often made his home the place for others to meet—some of them national celebrities who were black and unable to find lodging in Mobile's restricted hotels.

Mrs. Franklin talks spiritedly of the sometimes romantic world she and her husband moved in, of their lively bridge parties, of friends in the Utopia Social Club, of how Marian Anderson, the great opera singer, was in town to sing at Big Zion AME Church and sought lodging with them.

She laughs as she recalls the day they received a call from Jackie Robinson, who was playing with the Dodgers in a touring game in Mississippi, and how Robinson, Roy Campanella and others came to spend the night.

She walks through the rooms of the house, remembering where they stayed, and how the next morning she fixed them a ballplayer's breakfast.

"I never cooked so much bacon and eggs in my life."

And when the civil rights movement began and she joined leaders like John LeFlore to protest racial injustices, she recalls how her husband was quietly supportive, but anxious for her safety. When she protested an all-white lunch counter in town and a white man, afterward, kept bumping his car into hers on her way home, Dr. Franklin became frightened.

"'You'll get hurt,' he told me. 'Someone has to do it,' I told him."

Turning the pages of the photo album, she remembers her husband's intensity—how, "when he was angry, he wouldn't say anything but you'd know it, and how he sometimes spent evenings at home with his head in a book."

But mostly she remembers the quiet, steady sensitivity of her husband to his patients.

Even in his later years, he'd go visit the elderly ones at home. Mrs. Franklin would drive him to see them—in Mobile, Prichard and on the blocks surrounding Thelma Shamburger, the streets of Plateau.

"He was just as humble," says Marguerite Franklin, closing her photograph album, "as he could be."

Ben May: The Quiet Philanthropist

On November 24, 1972, Nobel laureate Charles B. Huggins, of Chicago's Ben May Institute for Cancer Research, delivered a funeral oration in Mobile for his friend, Ben May. At the Springhill Avenue Temple, Huggins stepped to the pulpit and began, "We assemble to say farewell to the earthly habit of our friend. . . . Fortunate beyond words are we to have been transmuted by contact with Ben May."

Huggins told how Ben May, owner of Gulf Lumber Co., had first written him in 1944 offering support for his research on prostate cancer. In 1947, Huggins came south to visit May, and the two men met in true Mobile fashion—during a hurricane. In 1951, May's funds established the Ben May Institute at the University of Chicago, Huggins among its faculty.

Huggins recounted how May had aided others: from the United Jewish Appeal, to the Boy Scouts, to "the penniless widow of a Protestant clergyman with four small children."

Among the mourners that day were some who had known May through his early involvement with the shipping industry; or had tromped through piney woods with him in his work with timber. Others knew him from the magnificent hunting preserves he owned.

A few remembered him from his festive bachelor years in Paris—his only dalliance, it seems, with extravagant living.

Others knew him as the quiet man in hat, glasses, vest and tie, slipping into a modest office at the First National Bank building.

How many, though, really knew him at all? He was generous with his money, but cautious in his interactions; a passionate reader of journals who never wished to see his name in print; a copious letter-writer who, in person, often had little to say.

"We are vain enough to think," Huggins said in his eulogy, surely bringing smiles, "that Ben May liked us—at least he tolerated us.

"We come together with a common bond. We loved Ben May."

In his heady youth as he roamed the world, Ben May, in hat, tours Istanbul, Turkey, with his traveling companion to right, Victor Pintel, and Victor's mother. The man at far right is unidentified. May (1889–1972) betrayed little sense of romance once he established himself as a somewhat eccentric, behind-the-scenes businessman and philanthropist in Mobile, having made a fortune during WWI in an unusual business venture involving the shipping of timber to Europe. As owner of Gulf Lumber in Mobile, May was in possession of land chock full of wildlife—sites now of the private hunting camps Choctaw Bluff and Bull Pen—but he had no interest in the sport. His obsession was medical research, and he aided it as best he could through financial contributions. Well north of Mobile, at the University of Chicago today, thrives the Ben May Institute for Cancer Research. (Courtesy of Irene Pintel)

• • •

"Dear Alexander Fleming: I have not found any way of taking my money with me, nor do I feel at all certain that I shall be able to use it on the other side of the Styx. I shall get more fun out of it if I can employ it in the service of things that are worthwhile."

Ben May, 1947

Ben May was born in 1889 in Atlanta, the son of Pauline and Meyer May, Jewish immigrants from Alsace-Lorraine, France. His was a modest home, hardly the kind that would inspire him to believe that one day he'd write the likes of Alexander Fleming, discoverer of penicillin, offering financial support. (Fleming would accept.)

But in the art of business, Ben May was creative, and he was inspired.

At 15 his father sent him to a summer job in Alabama, working with timber on the plantation of a former Yankee navy captain named Stimpson. On the same job in Marengo County was young Fred Stimpson, the same age as Ben.

The teen-age friendship between Ben and Fred would one day blossom into a vibrant business partnership: Ben the owner of Gulf Lumber, Fred and his sons responsible for running the business and, on Ben's death, exercising the option to buy the company as stated in May's will.

But that was yet to come.

In the meantime, there was the First World War—and Ben May's inspired idea.

During the war years, Europe had a high tariff on lumber being shipped from America to its shores. At the same time, ships needed lumber to line their containers to keep dampness from rotting cargo; and for packing and crating.

Ben May said he'd offer lumber, for free, to the ships. When it arrived in European ports, agents contracted by May would unload the lumber and sell it, tariff-free, as second-hand timber.

By the war's end, May had made $7 million.

• • •

"Henry Ford had enough money to employ 10,000 or 20,000 doctors, but his son died of cancer because there was nothing in the reservoir of knowledge which told how to really cure him."

Ben May, 1952

In the 1920s, the poor boy from Atlanta, now a wealthy bachelor in Mobile, decided to see the world.

Through a concert pianist he knew in New York, Ben May hired the musician's son, a bon vivant, Victor Pintel, to show him Europe. That's the way Irene Pintel recounts it. Eighty-nine now, still lovely and dignified, she sits by the window in her Spring Hill home, remembering when she first met the men.

Turning the pages of an album filled with snapshots from Europe, some taken by Ben May, she tells how she was born in Russia, and came of age during the Revolution. Her family, White Russians in opposition to the Communists, became scattered and she was soon a schoolgirl, alone, in Czechoslovakia.

When she went to Paris to visit her sister, she was invited to a party at Ben May's. In the elegant smoking room of his flat on Rue de la Faisandre, she came to know Europeans who'd gather there, among them expatriate Russians. One of the group, Victor, had a Turkish mother; he spoke Russian to woo her.

Irene would bide time in Paris while Victor and Ben made trips to Mobile; she'd take English lessons paid for by Ben May. Once, Victor sent her lilies of the valley in advance of their return. She still keeps a vase of the flowers on a mantel.

Not yet 20 years old while in Paris, Irene was too young to marry without parental consent. Victor took her to England, where she was turned away, accused of being a Communist. Through the Irish Ambassador to France, Ben May orchestrated their journey to Ireland, and a church wedding there. Then he brought them to Mobile.

Years later, when Hitler marched through Europe, May would bring other families from Europe to Mobile, Jews fleeing Nazi death camps. Among them were the Tensers, Czechoslovakians he'd met through the lumber business. When they got off the train in Mobile, refugees with one battered suitcase, he took them to Metzger's store, where they were elegantly outfitted. Madame Rose Palmai-Tenser, a singer, became a legend in Mobile opera, founding the Mobile Opera Guild in 1946.

Ben May would always love opera.

Irene tells a melancholy story of Ben May's romantic life. She recalls how, when single, he'd loved a legal secretary in Mobile. His family disapproved. They arranged a meeting with a young, small-town girl still living in France—a second cousin, Yvonne.

Ben and Yvonne married in 1928 and started their life together in Mobile.

They were divorced in the last year before Ben May died.

• • •

"Perhaps more people would take interest in medical research if only they understood the practicing physician's relationship to research, and every person's own likely dependence on medical research for health and even for life itself."

Ben May, 1952

Billy Stimpson, who took over ownership of Gulf Lumber with his brothers, and has now passed it on to the next generation of Stimpsons, remembers Ben May well.

Billy is sitting in the office he still maintains at Gulf Lumber, photographs of African safaris on the wall, the giant sawmill in the next lot buzz-sawing timber.

It was in 1925 that Billy's father, Fred, approached Ben May and asked him if he wished to go in on shares of a vast hunting preserve upriver. When Ben understood the land, filled with hardwood timber, would prove a good investment, he offered to purchase the thousands of acres on his own. He gave Fred and others lifelong hunting rights, and an eventual piece of ownership if they'd manage the land.

The hunting camps, Choctaw Bluff and Bull Pen, are said to be a hunter's dream, filled with wildlife and offering comfortable housing. Part of the land is today owned by the Stimpsons; part is in the Ben May trust.

In 1940, as World War II began changing the face of the globe, Ben May established Gulf Lumber, hiring different managers, among them his wife's brother, Andre Picard, to manage the business. In 1952, according to Billy Stimpson, the Stimpsons came aboard to run the company for May.

"Ben May didn't like to be out front," Billy explains, saying how May, providing money and vision, allowed the Stimpsons to manage the operation. Ben would come in on weekends, though, to walk through the sawmill, checking over details.

Did Ben May like to hunt? "Not at all," says Billy.

What Ben May liked to do was read—journals on timber, journals on tax law, journals on medicine—and speculate on ways to invest and help the world.

Sister-in-law Muriel Picard remembers lively conversations at the weekly dinners she and her late husband Andre shared with Ben and Yvonne.

"He could talk about Schopenhauer, or he could talk about baseball." She says he was preoccupied with physical fitness, only acquiring houses that had steps he could use for exercise, or plots of land big enough to accommodate his vigorous walks. He was obsessive in taking a nip of whiskey "for medicinal purposes" before eating, and taking vitamins B12 and C.

He was a man who, according to Billy Stimpson, "was honorable enough to do business with a handshake." Ironically, May was known by some to shy away from shaking hands for fear of catching influenza.

Muriel tells of the lifelong care Ben provided for his only child, a son who struggled with mental illness from a young age.

In a 1946 address to the Rotary Club at the Battle House, May called for greater care, on a national basis, for patients suffering mental disease. In 1959, May was named a trustee of a voluntary health agency, RISE Inc., Research in Schizophrenia Endowment.

• • •

"The three million dollars we spent on cancer research last year was not enough. I was shocked to learn that we spend five million dollars a year on goldfish and some 50 millions a year on electric toy trains—all this despite the fact we have a stake in cancer."

Ben May, 1949

In Dr. Martin Perlman's office at Mobile Infirmary, there is a 1975 photograph of himself standing before a picture of Ben May. The occasion was the induction of May, posthumously, into the Alabama Business Hall of Fame.

Perlman accepted on his behalf. Ronald Reagan, then governor of California, gave the keynote address.

Perlman, an internist and oncologist, speaks with deep affection for his friend, old enough to have been his grandfather; but whom he came to know treating him as an internist.

Perlman says that great medical researchers like Charles Huggins, and Elwood Jensen (who focused his research on breast cancer), owe thanks to May for support. He opens a biography of Alexander Fleming, and points out several letters exchanged between the great scientist and May. The book is inscribed from Amalia Fleming, Alexander's wife: "To our dear friend Ben May with my gratitude for so many things."

Perlman explains that it was May's funds to the Southern Research Institute that caused it to add medical research to its industrial mission.

The Ben May Institute for Cancer Research, started in 1951, has become one of the premier cancer research institutes in the United States. The Ben May Charitable Trust continues as its principal donor.

As Dr. Howard Skipper, cancer researcher at the Southern Institute, wrote of Ben May in 1955: "Ben May's heart is about the size of a washtub. . . . His desire to help his fellow man appears to be boundless."

· · ·

"Real property, and particularly cut over lands on which timber is growing, go through long periods of depressed valuations when little but distress property is being sold, and that at very low prices, but at long intervals there develops strong demand . . . and then sales may be made at excellent prices. I wish to impress upon my Executors and upon any Trustee not . . . to sell it when values are depressed, the demand small and prices low."

Ben May, Last Will and Testament

A business genius to the very end, Ben May left instructions for making sure the realm he acquired during his life was not frittered away afterward.

While it is true he had become wealthy, he maintained the sensibility of one who recalls what it means to be poor. His secretary, Joyce Tanner, says he would send worn shirts off to have the collars reversed, then wear them as new.

He left a large portion of his properties in the Ben May Charitable Trust, its assets managed by AmSouth Bank, its distribution committee made up of Mr. Vivian Johnston, Dr. Martin Perlman, and Judge Brevard Hand. While setting up broad mandates that the trust "aid hospitals, schools . . . and research institutions," and "the advancement of human knowledge and the alleviation of human suffering," it made specific recommendations for such institutions as University of Chicago's Ben May Institute and the American Friends of the Hebrew University.

Vivian Johnston remembers that Thanksgiving, 1972, when he heard the sad news. He'd been hunting with his sons at Choctaw Bluff camp, and was suddenly in the midst of young turkeys. His son was about to take aim when a truck came roaring down the road, honking, scattering the turkeys.

It was a camp worker, shouting that Ben May, at age 83, had suffered a fatal heart attack.

Charles Huggins was soon on his way from Chicago to eulogize his old friend.

To Ralph Chandler, Publisher, Mobile Press Register, June 7, 1951, "Dear Ralph: When the time comes, you might fix an obit which just says, We hope this party finds the peace that he has sought for so many years."

Ben May

U.S. Attorney Armbrecht: A Matter of Will

April 1998

The Library

From David Alsobrook's office at the George Bush Presidential Library in College Station, Texas, it is a far piece to Mobile, Ala. As director of a library-museum with 38 million pages of documents, Alsobrook, who grew up in Mobile, supervises a staff of 31 and does research at the behest of President Bush. When the workday is over, however, Alsobrook turns to finishing a research paper of his own— about a black man, Richard Robertson, who was lynched in Mobile in 1909, and how Mobile's U.S. attorney, Will Armbrecht, in maneuvers rare at the time, tried to employ federal laws to bring justice to bear.

Alsobrook, 51, who came to the Bush Library after being at the Jimmy Carter Library in Atlanta—"I'm not political, I'm a civil servant," he explains—has a native son's fascination with Mobile. Graduating from Davidson High in its last all-white class, Alsobrook watched desegregation break over the horizon. For his doctorate in history at Auburn University, he wrote about Mobile's progressive era, 1896 to 1917, a period, he says, that witnessed racial violence, including the lynching of two black men in Mobile's Plateau community in 1906, and another in 1907.

When Alsobrook returns to Mobile shortly to address the Alabama Historical Association on Will Armbrecht and the 1909 lynching, he will be standing, he notes, only two blocks from where the oak tree loomed that served as the gallows.

The Lynching

Turn to Mobile Register accounts and imagine that night.

It is 1 a.m. on Saturday, Jan. 23, 1909. Richard Robertson, accused of killing Deputy Sheriff Philip Fatch two days before in a shoot-out in downtown Mobile, crouches in his jail cell. He hears rising voices, and a crowd of footsteps. The front doors of the jail have been left open—the voices, and the footsteps, get closer.

He is already in pain, having been shot in the right arm and side in the fray; but he says nothing. The men coming into the jail compound are wearing masks. They have taken keys from two guards who seem to be sleeping; and have threatened two other guards with pistols.

The padlock is opened and Robertson is led out. He makes no noise. The men, 20 strong now, gag him, lift him, carting him down the street. They are only a block from the police station on St. Emanuel Street, heading toward Church Street, but no officers appear.

The men set Robertson down on the ground and the gag loosens; he begins to cry out.

"Shoot him!" someone says. A gun explodes three times and he lurches from being hit.

There are hands grasping him again; a rope is hurled upward to loop over the fork of an oak tree. A noose is pulled tight on his neck.

An hour or more later, two policemen, arriving on the scene, take his body down.

The coroner, H. P. Hirshfield, in consultation with a coroner's jury, determines, "We, the jury, find the deceased came to his death by being hanged by parties unknown to this jury." The newspaper initially misspells Robertson's name, leaving off the "t."

As that weekend unfolds, there is curiosity-seeking by some— people come to the tree and chip pieces of the bark, taking them home as souvenirs.

There is outrage by others—Harry Pillans, a prominent lawyer, writes in a letter to the Mobile Register, "The dreadful assassination of a prisoner by a group of self-constituted executioners last night calls for prompt and stern punishment, and I hope that the grand jury to assemble next month will be at pains to discover the identity of the criminals and bring them to justice."

On Sunday, Jan. 24, there is preaching—the Rev. H. H. McNeill, pastor of the St. Francis Street Methodist Church, proclaims, "The horrible crime of Friday night is not a sporadic case. It was not born of itself; it is only the logical outcome of the spirit of this age."

And there are retaliations, like a hand-scrawled letter mailed to the Mobile Daily Item: "Dear Sirs, We are sending you this letter hoping you will publish it in your paper so the public can read it. We the lynchers of Richard Robertson want to warn the good citizens of Mobile not to have anything to do with the lynching of this blood thirsty brute. We think that we did the right thing by doing this. We are going to protect our town against such crimes, hoping that our bros. citizens will let it drop where it is because we do not want to have to do anymore of this work in the city of Mobile. Now we hope every one will heed to this good warning. We are yours very truly, Lynchers."

Will Armbrecht

Were it not for David Alsobrook, we might never know Will Armbrecht's role in the events of 1909. Even though some of the lynchers were thought to be well-heeled—they drove away in cars—no members of the mob were publicly identified. A citizens committee, led by former Mobile Mayor Joseph Rich, a friend of Armbrecht's, called for Gov. B. B. Comer to bring pressure to bear on law enforcement leaders. The Register of that year is filled with these stories.

Will Armbrecht's name does not appear in these articles.

Armbrecht was born in Port Chester, N.Y., in 1874, the son of Caesar and Anna Kraft Armbrecht, German immigrants. Caesar Armbrecht had enlisted in the Union Army after arriving in America and was wounded at Antietam. The Armbrechts moved to the South when Will was young and he went to school in Tennessee. They eventually settled in Mobile, Alsobrook suspects, because a German community flourished in the city.

Will studied law through apprenticeship to the general counsel of the Mobile & Ohio railroad; he was U.S. attorney, appointed by President Theodore Roosevelt, from 1904 to 1911. Later, in private practice, he was president of Mobile's Chamber of Commerce. There is a 1913 photograph, taken in the Battle House Hotel, of President Woodrow Wilson at a breakfast, seated next to Will Armbrecht. Judging by another picture of Will—a portrait in the home of his grandson, William Armbrecht III, a retired lawyer in Mobile—Will was a lean, handsome man, distinguished in his bearing.

Armbrecht's political leanings were unusual for the Deep South at the time. As a Mobile Register editorial would note in 1941 in mourning his passing: "Mr. Armbrecht was a leader of the Republican Party in Alabama, and although his political faith is not common to this section, his opponents always looked upon him as a fair, but hard-hitting foe."

David Alsobrook was doing research in U.S. attorneys' files when

When a white mob lynched a black man in downtown Mobile in 1909, U.S. Attorney Will Armbrecht (1874–1941) struggled behind the scenes to intervene with the weight of federal law. In the view of historian David Alsobrook—a Mobile native formerly in charge of the George Bush Presidential Library in College Station, Texas, and now director of the Clinton Presidential Papers in Little Rock, Arkansas, as of October 2000—Armbrecht's little-known work in that lynching case may have anticipated the civil rights movement of the future. As a young attorney here in high collar and spectacles, Armbrecht was a founder of one of Mobile's distinguished law firms. That firm, in celebration of its centennial, chose a week coinciding with historian Alsobrook's presentation of his research on Armbrecht to the Alabama Historical Association. (Erik Overbey Collection, University of South Alabama Archives)

he stumbled across information that Armbrecht was working behind the scenes to wield federal laws to punish the lynchers.

At that time, lynchings were viewed as matters for local law enforcement. "In 1909," Alsobrook explains, "it was unprecedented for the federal government to become deeply involved in any racial matters at the state and local levels."

But Will Armbrecht was clearly outraged.

David Alsobrook found another threatening letter, this one sent to H. H. McNeill, the Methodist minister who had decried the crime from his pulpit. The authors, the "Committee of 100," claimed to be members of the lynch mob. Misspellings and all, it began: "My friend, You are medling in other peoples buisness too mutch and I want to say to you that you and some of your friends are going to get a rope around your necks if you don't keep your mouths shut about that negro lynching."

Armbrecht sent a copy of this letter to the U.S. attorney general, Charles Bonaparte, and wrote a long letter of his own, discovered by Alsobrook in the files. Armbrecht lamented, "No investigation worthy of the name 'investigation' can possibly be hoped for from either the sheriff's office or the city police force."

Indeed, Armbrecht reported to Bonaparte that a woman who'd seen a ruckus outside her house on Church Street the morning of Jan. 23 had telephoned the police only to be informed that a lynching was taking place.

Armbrecht continued: "I understand, of course, that the federal courts have no jurisdiction of matters of lynching, but it occurs to me possibly the mailing of this letter is a violation of the federal laws."

Armbrecht asked Bonaparte to send postal inspectors from other cities to Mobile to see if they could determine who mailed the letter to McNeill and if the contents of the letter incited violence or murder.

Postal inspectors soon arrived. Their investigation, on the surface, appeared to be for naught.

But David Alsobrook believes that, "while Armbrecht was not successful in his quest to prosecute any guilty parties through the postal laws, his concerted efforts contributed to the public furor in Mobile and across the state."

Armbrecht's efforts, Alsobrook concludes, "eventually led Gov. Comer to direct his attorney general, Alex Garber, to initiate impeachment proceedings against Sheriff Frank Cazalas."

The Mobile Register, in a dateline from Montgomery on June 3, 1909, reported: "A majority of the justices of the Supreme Court decided today that Sheriff Cazalas of Mobile County had committed a breach of trust in allowing a mob to lynch the Robertson negro, and made an order removing the sheriff from office."

Hanging Tree

At the corner of St. Emanuel and Church streets, across from the massive beauty of Christ Episcopal Church, there are no oaks and no houses as there were in 1909. There is a parking lot; beyond it is the entrance ramp to Interstate 10, and the approach to the Wallace twin tunnels.

The legacy of Will Armbrecht takes a great many forms beyond his actions in the Robertson case. Armbrecht's efforts to apply federal laws to local crimes presaged the civil rights movement of the 1960s, Alsobrook believes.

What occurred was not about politics. "His actions," Alsobrook says, "were simply those of a man of great honor and integrity."

The day before Alsobrook presents his paper to the Alabama Historical Association there will be a centennial luncheon of the firm that grew from Will Armbrecht's legal practice, now Armbrecht, Jackson, DeMouy, Crowe, Holmes & Reeves.

Law firms, says David Bagwell, a member of the firm, are not unlike family trees branching off to create new families. A time-line constructed by Bagwell shows, for example, that in 1906 the firm was Inge & Armbrecht, in 1926 Armbrecht & Hand, and in 1930 Armbrecht, Hand & Twitty—all prominent names in Mobile's legal profession, some spinning out firms of their own.

Bagwell, who had done extensive reading into Mobile history, did not know about Will Armbrecht's role in the Robertson lynching.

It took David Alsobrook to conjure up that fateful oak near Christ Church; the man who hung beneath it; and the demand for justice that emerged from its shadows.

Close Ties Far Away

❖

Morocco to Mobile: Paul Bowles' Secret Journey

Fall 1996

From the time of his first visit to Tangier, Morocco, in the 1930s, American Paul Bowles—who moved to Tangier for good in the 1940s—has returned to the United States only rarely. At Lincoln Center in 1996, where the author and composer was honored for his music, he told friends he was never coming back again.

But late that same year, then 86-year-old Bowles flew from Tangier to Amsterdam to Atlanta, and on to his destination, Mobile.

That Bowles was in Mobile was an international secret.

Although he is not as widely known as others in his circle—among them, over the years, Tennessee Williams, Truman Capote, William Burroughs and Allen Ginsberg—to legions of serious readers, and music-lovers, he has cult-like fame. Since his 1949 novel, "Sheltering Sky," was made into a 1990 movie starring Debra Winger, his public recognition has also been on the rise.

Sixty years ago it was Gertrude Stein, in Paris, who suggested to Bowles that he travel to Tangier. Now it was a Point Clear, Ala., native, Joseph McPhillips III, headmaster of the American School of Tangier, who suggested Bowles fly to Mobile for vascular surgery by Dr. Frank McPhillips, Joe's brother. The hope was the operation would ease the excruciating pain in Bowles' right leg.

When Bowles was in Atlanta the previous year for another medical procedure, followers besieged him from around the nation. Those who sheltered Bowles during his Mobile visit, and tended him through recuperation, gave the author an assumed name, screened calls, and made sure fans did not come, from all over the nation, pounding on his door.

Dapper in sports jacket and tie, author Paul Bowles—internationally famous resident of Tangier, Morocco—relaxes at the Point Clear, Ala., home of Lynn Meador with Lynn's brother, Dr. Frank McPhillips, a vascular surgeon, sitting at his feet. Bowles inscribed a copy of this photograph, "For Frank with gratitude, Paul," referring to surgery the doctor performed to clear up an excruciating pain in Bowles's right leg. Bowles's sojourn in Mobile was unknown to his devotees, many of whom seek him out on his rare visits to the U.S.; he would later record his impressions of the trip and fax them to Mobile, as printed here. The secret journey was orchestrated by Lynn and Frank's brother, Joe McPhillips, headmaster of the American School of Tangier, and a close friend of Bowles, Yves St. Laurent, and other renowned artists. By phone from Tangier Joe McPhillips explains, "I live in a beautiful home with furniture from Alabama." (Courtesy of Stella McPhillips)

"He was under wraps," explains Andreas Brown, an archivist in charge of the literary papers of Bowles and his late wife, author Jane Bowles. The papers are housed at the University of Texas.

"He wanted it quiet, and private. They protected him." Brown, also owner of the famed Gotham Book Mart in New York, says even he was unaware of Bowles' visit.

But literary critic Regina Weinreich, also in New York, had heard that the author might be traveling to Alabama for medical attention.

"There's a Paul Bowles rumor mill," says Weinreich, co-producer of the film "Paul Bowles: The Complete Outsider." "He's part of the biggest picture, not only in American literature, but world literature. His writing is really beautiful, with a sinister edge to it. It's in the tradition of Poe and Joseph Conrad."

• • •

Paul Bowles has no phone. As legend has it, he tired of being bothered by people calling and ripped it from the wall.

Those who seek him out from around the world must climb the steps to his small apartment in Tangier and rap on the door, or they must send him a fax.

One evening he receives a fax from Mobile asking about the visit he made in November. Even though many of his stories explore characters in extreme psychological states, Bowles, in person, is known for his courtliness and charm.

He faxes back:

> *Dear Mr. Hoffman,*
> *I apologize for sending what will prove to be a chaotic message. I'm writing in bed, and with insufficient light.*
> *It is difficult for me to give you my reactions to being in Mobile. I had two days of sight-seeing before hospitalization. One day included a visit to Dauphin Island, and the other a visit to Point Clear, where I was served a magnificent gumbo. The hospital was distinguished for its food. I've been in many hospitals in many countries, and the meals everywhere are famous for being unappetizing.*

*The Providence Hospital clearly cared about its patients' palates.
After leaving the hospital I was invited to begin my recuperation
at the home of my surgeon, Dr. Frank McPhillips. The house is ex-
quisitely decorated, and my hostess, Stella McPhillips, could not have
been kinder and more charming.*

*To give you my impression of Mobile is a different task. I got the
impressions that it is a very pleasant place to live in. I doubt that
I ever saw the city itself. I was most impressed by the miles of heavy
traffic. There seem to be more cars than people in the vicinity. The
lasting image is that of an endless suburb that stretches in many
directions. One doesn't know whether the center of the city is ahead
of one or behind one. All this is said objectively, and certainly not
disparagingly, for I like the place. I even saw a little Spanish moss
at one point!*

My best,
Paul Bowles

• • •

At 3 o'clock in the afternoon in Mobile, it is 9 at night in Tangier,
Morocco, and all that connects the cities, at this moment, is a tele-
phone call. On the Tangier end is Joe McPhillips, in his house by the
Straits of Gibraltar.

"I live in a beautiful home with furniture from Alabama," he says.
"I'm sitting on a bed my great-grandfather owned and I'm looking
out on Spain."

Joe's forebears came from Ireland to Mobile before the Civil War.
In the late 1800s, on the McPhillips side, they flourished in the grocery and liquor business. They even had a street named for them,
McPhillips Avenue, near Ann Street. On the Heustis side of the family,
there was a famous Mobile doctor, James Heustis (1829–1891), for
whom the Eichold-Heustis Medical Museum is named in part.

As Joe talks on the phone tonight, sitting on his bed from Mobile,
across the room is a rocking chair also from the old family home.
The house, as he describes it, seems an exotic blend of North Africa
and south Alabama.

After going to University Military School as a boy, Joe went to

Andover Academy in Massachusetts, then Princeton. He traveled to Tangier after college, met Paul Bowles and other "Tangerines" in the international arts community his first night there, and fell in love with the country. A photograph shot by Life magazine in 1967 shows Joe McPhillips hosting a party for the Bowleses. The guests clap hands while turbaned Moroccans play flute and drums.

As headmaster of the American School of Tangier—a position formerly held by Omar Pound, son of poet Ezra Pound—Joe is in charge of an institution that, while not an American Embassy school, does receive some funds from the Department of State. Most of its 340 students, grades kindergarten to 12, are Moroccan. The school's emphasis, he explains, is on classical education.

"There's no gum chewing here, no 'Hey man,'" he says. "Students stand up when a teacher walks in. There's a tremendous reverence here for intellectual work. These students haven't grown up on television."

Of America's enthusiasm for computers in schools, he adds: "It's very sad to want to put a computer with every child. What they need is a book of Shakespeare in one hand and a Bible in the next."

Joe's first love is theater, and, in addition to his work as headmaster, he directs plays for the school. Remarkably, he has engaged Paul Bowles to compose music for several of the works. He argues that "Bowles is the best theater musician of this century," and admits, "my position at the school is enhanced by Paul Bowles."

As if it were not impressive enough to enlist Bowles for a recent production of Oscar Wilde's "Salome," Joe attracted an internationally famous designer to make the costumes—Yves St. Laurent.

Joe loves Bowles' writing, too, describing his friend's fiction as "precise, keen, lean. It's like watching a greyhound race in Pensacola. But I don't share Bowles' deep, dry, negative view of humanity. I'm a fairly drenched-in-the-blood Southern optimist."

Having lived in Tangier for 34 of his 60 years, and heading up a school that can summon the support of artists like Paul Bowles and Yves St. Laurent, Joe McPhillips is part of a Moroccan world. "Yet," he admits, "I'm devoted to Mobile."

"It's quite weird because I love it now more than ever in my life. To walk from the Grand Hotel to my parents' house—it touches me more now than ever before. It's the biggest emotional resource I have."

• • •

According to Dr. Frank McPhillips, the vascular bypass operation to remedy the bad circulation in Paul Bowles' leg—acute ischemia—was a success.

McPhillips had traveled to New York to first examine Bowles' leg when the writer was there for the Lincoln Center tribute. He says that Bowles, although "an icon" to his followers, was like any other patient, except that no other patient had ever told him stories about Gertrude Stein's dog.

What Bowles did not mention in his fax is that in the home of Frank and Stella McPhillips there is a strong flavor of Morocco in the furnishings and art.

"While we were shipping furniture from Mobile to Joe in Tangier," Stella says, "a shipment of Moroccan furniture was coming to us here."

Stanley Ellis, the interior designer who worked with Stella on her home, went to Morocco as part of the Mobile connection.

In fact, Joe McPhillips keeps a small but steady flow of Mobilians traveling to Tangier. His sister, Lynn Meador, who fixed the Point Clear gumbo Bowles hailed, has a photograph of herself in Tangier. She is standing next to Paul Bowles with several of her Mobile cousins —Lucy Lyons, Ellen Thomasson and Genie Inge.

Who knows if the Thanksgiving dinner Paul Bowles ate at Mobile Country Club with Frank and Stella McPhillips, or the first visit in his life to a McDonald's with Stella, will one day be revealed, in some bizarrely transmuted way, in the fiction of this master?

What we do know is that the Paul Bowles rumor mill, from Manhattan to Marrakesh, will hum with the news that he traveled to the realm of Point Clear gumbo, Spanish moss, and the "endless suburb that stretches in many directions."

We also know that Bowles, according to Stella McPhillips, took something from Mobile back with him. Not pecans, or pralines, or fruitcake, but something unobtainable even in the exotic bazaars of Morocco—a suitcase of Grape-Nuts cereal.

• • •

Fall 1999

Joe McPhillips was on his way from Tangier to Mobile for Thanksgiving when he got word, while stopping over in New York, that Paul Bowles, on Nov. 18, 1999, had passed away.

Joe headed right back to Morocco to bid farewell to his old friend.

Monumental Talent: Tina Allen's Heroic Sculptures

New York

Like Jack climbing the beanstalk, Tina Allen makes her way up a folding ladder and comes face to face with a 2-ton woman who is 12 feet tall.

Tina, mid-40s, has a tangle of long, dark hair, an effusive smile, and, at work today, wears sneakers, sweatpants, and a University of South Alabama sweatshirt. The giantess she scales has a noble visage, wears a shawl, has short, crinkly hair under a bonnet and enormous spectacles perched on her nose.

Tina's statue-in-progress is Sojourner Truth, ex-slave, abolitionist, campaigner for women's rights, orator, guest of President Abraham Lincoln for a meeting in the White House. Working on principal commission from the Kellogg Foundation, Tina brings Sojourner to life at Sculpture House Casting, one of several studios around the country where she transforms her maquettes—small, precise figures made at her home studio in California—into enormous clay replicas.

A visual artist from the time she was a child growing up in New York, Tina Allen's esthetic vision became focused—portraying the human figure with monumental sculpture—after she married a man from Mobile and began to study art at the University of South Alabama. The city girl was astounded by the intricate knowledge folks in the "small town" had of one another, likening it to "an African village, where people keep copious notes on families." Here she touches up a hand of one of her creations in progress, Sojourner Truth, a former slave who became a spokeswoman for abolition. The monument would soon be unveiled in Battle Creek, Mich., joining her list of sculptures, such as "Roots" author Alex Haley in Knoxville, that dominate outdoor plazas. "There are enormous souls," she explains, "encased in bodies we never expected." (Allen Studios)

After Tina sees the huge, clay woman through the involved process of being transformed to bronze, Sojourner will be transported for unveiling in Battle Creek, Mich.

Guided by photographs of Sojourner from the 1860s, Tina is rendering her subject at age 70, but there are no wrinkles on the face. "African-American women don't really get wrinkles," Tina explains. But the passage of time, and the weight of many years, suggest themselves in other ways.

Tina reaches out and touches the damp clay of Sojourner's eyes—a wide, solid gaze. She has been bringing this statue to life, on and off, for a year, and has mastered the sensibility of real, human eyes, eyes that have seen a turbulent world, known pain, gazed out in hope.

"I demand good-looking eyes," Tina says, brushing her finger over the clay. "Eyes that have intelligence behind them."

Tina Allen is a sculptor working in the great American tradition of monumental-size figures. A native of New York City who married into a prominent Mobile family, studied fine arts at USA, and in many ways, she admits, "grew up" in Mobile, Tina largely draws on African-American culture and history for her subjects.

In the spring of 1998, Tina's 13-foot statue of "Roots" author Alex Haley, seated and holding an open book, was unveiled in Knoxville, Tenn. The "CBS Sunday Morning" show featured the event and also showed a bust she made of diplomat Ralph Bunche on display at the United Nations in Geneva, Switzerland.

Tina has begun planning a magisterial statue of Martin Luther King Jr., for a park in north Las Vegas, and on the drawing board are plans for a statue in bronze of Sammy Davis Jr.—a 25-foot-tall "action pose" of the Rat Pack entertainer, which will dance forever in front of a Las Vegas hotel.

In all her works, Tina says, she is after a lifelike quality, and beauty—of the soul. "There are enormous souls encased in bodies we never expected," she says as she leans from her ladder, holding a hand tool called a "loop," to shave away a sliver of clay from Sojourner's shoulder.

"Spirits hang out in different bodies. Some come crippled, some in unpopular shades, some fat. Real beauty is an inner thing."

She picks up a mallet, its end covered with chicken wire, and begins to pound the statue's dress. The clay keeps the impression of the chicken wire—cross-hatching that renders the appearance of coarse fabric. She climbs down from the ladder and gazes up at the heroine towering overhead. Sojourner's right hand is poised just above a Bible on a lectern; her left hand reaches out, imploring an audience to heed her words.

"It's about achievement," Tina says, "about a well-lived life."

• • •

Born in New York City and raised first in Queens, N.Y., later on the Caribbean island of Grenada, Tina Powell had an unusual early childhood. "I grew up in the Ed Sullivan Theater."

Her parents divorced when she was a child, and the weekends she spent with her father, Gordon "Specs" Powell, were at his place of work. Specs Powell was a musician. Saturday night meant dress rehearsals for a television show where he played in the orchestra, which on Sunday evenings played during a live broadcast. It was the "Ed Sullivan Show."

Tina became aware not only of her father's vibrant talent as a musician, but also of how, in the midst of the Ray Bloch Orchestra on the show, he was distinctive in another way. "He was one of the first blacks to cross the color line in TV and radio."

Tina's own art seemed to spring full-blown from her head. While most sculptors, she says, first draw, then make objects, she started working in three dimensions from the start. "Sculpture is my first language."

As a teen-ager, when a teacher assigned the class to model ashtrays from clay, Tina went home and returned with a bust of a philosopher she'd been reading—Aristotle. "'Where'd you get that!' the teacher asked me." Tina laughs.

"I like the physical labor of sculpting. I'm not an illusionist. I make objects that are physical, concrete. It's the same feeling of being in a kitchen and cooking. It just feels natural."

She enrolled in New York's School of Visual Arts, but her instructors encouraged abstract work. She wanted to do figures—realistic, old-fashioned.

Soon she would find herself in a more supportive environment— far south at the University of South Alabama. At USA, she studied with James Kennedy, an art professor who affirmed "the validity" of her ambitions. "Kennedy developed me," she says. Her journey to Mobile, though, was set in motion by matters of the heart.

• • •

In the early 1970s Roger Allen had just finished his MBA at the University of Chicago and was on a visit to New York. In a recording studio in Greenwich Village he saw a beautiful young woman singing back-up in a band. She was a fledgling visual artist who enjoyed music, too. He took her picture. Her name was Tina. They started dating.

Roger had not grown up in Mobile, but his family roots ran deep in the Port City. Roger's father, Clarence Allen III, had been one of the U.S. Army Air Corps' "Tuskegee Airmen," an all-black combat unit in World War II, and had taken a leadership position in the family business in Mobile. He beckoned Roger to move south to join him.

That business was a venerable institution established by Roger's great-grandfather, Clarence Allen Sr.—Johnson-Allen Mortuary and its subsidiary, Unity Burial and Life Insurance, which became Unity Life. At a time when white-owned insurance companies did not offer coverage to blacks, Roger explains, the presence of his great-grandfather's insurance company was vital to the black community.

Clarence Sr. and his wife, Josephine, were important figures in Mobile circles. When Booker T. Washington visited Mobile he made a sports outing with Clarence. In a well-known photograph from Mobile's history, the two men are shown at the resort of Coden, formally dressed, showing off a string of fish they have caught.

Josephine B. Allen founded the Allen Institute, an early, independent school in Mobile for black students. Roger remembers his great-grandmother as a loving but demanding, and very stern, educator.

Other visible names would become associated with Unity Life. One of the early officers was Alex Herman, whose daughter, Alexis, would become U.S. Secretary of Labor in May 1997.

Roger and Tina soon married and moved to Mobile. They named one of their three children Josephine Allen, in honor of the great-grandmother whose name still graces a housing development in the Plateau community.

Coming south surprised Tina in many ways. "I never got to know people so well in my life as when I came to Mobile," she says. She describes the city in terms of "an African village, where people keep copious notes on families. I got to know two hundred years of family histories. I knew everything about people when they walked up, practically their DNA."

She marvels at the beauty of Mobile—and reminisces about its lovely, old houses, particularly the Creole cottage on Stanton Road where she lived.

Mobile provided high drama, too, colorful escapades that Tina heard about through the intricate web of families—people falling in love, out of love, committing crimes, running away, making their fortunes, losing their fortunes. "I couldn't believe so much was happening in such a peaceful town!"

The couple live in California now.

• • •

When Tina had first headed to Alabama, she had entered not so much a strange land as a familiar, and inspiring, one. "The giants were right there. Martin Luther King Jr., Rosa Parks, Vivian Malone." She adds the names of other civil-rights figures, and cities:

"Birmingham. Selma."

In talking about the civil rights movement, Tina includes George Wallace—a man whose about-face on issues of desegregation she accepts as genuine. "Being wrong is part of being human," she says.

"The South has a way of dealing with humanity like nowhere else."

Affected deeply as a teen-ager by the assassinations of both Robert

Kennedy and Martin Luther King Jr., Tina early on had realized the importance of aspiring to the heroic qualities of great men and women. There are heroes in our midst, she firmly believes. "We just don't always see them."

Her desire to uplift a new generation with stories of these heroes in part drives her enormous energy as a sculptor. By making monumental pieces, she believes she is able to "energize the new generation" who gaze up at the works. She likens her sculpture to the booming voices of opera enchanting listeners with vast reach. Indeed, she often plays a tape of Luciano Pavarotti as she works.

Because of the expense of making these pieces—she estimates the Sojourner Truth statue will cost in the vicinity of $350,000—she works only on sculptures that are commissioned, or on works for which she competes, creating maquettes as an example of what the big statue will be.

She is not interested in doing vanity sculptures of celebrities or the wealthy. By contrast, she is exuberant, and a little nervous, she admits, about the possibility of launching into the biggest sculpture of her career—a 10-story statue of Nelson Mandela. If all the pieces come together in this vast undertaking, the independently commissioned statue will rise on Robben Island in South Africa, where Mandela was jailed.

Tina can sculpt heroes who are white as well as those who are black, but she believes she has a mission, as an American artist, to "sing the song of my people. By showing the beauty and potential of African-Americans you help two groups at the same time. You reduce the feeling of invisibility, the feeling that because of this or that physiology you can't succeed." In doing so, she explains, Americans of all backgrounds are able to move along in "the healing process of a long-torn-apart nation."

As Tina takes a dry paintbrush and adds a few lines to Sojourner's fingers, she explains: "I want people to look at this woman who had 10 children and came through that particularly unfortunate period of our history and managed to stay with her head together without

Prozac, without benefit of psychotherapy, without anyone throwing a warm blanket over her shoulder.

"She never bit the apple. She never descended into hate."

• • •

At the end of her work day, Tina steps back to regard her creation. Tomorrow, she must fix the folds of the cloak. The shoes need another crease or two. When she finishes this stage, the clay figure will be cut into pieces along designated lines, and the artisans of the Sculpture Studio will begin a process of casting molds from the clay, first in rubber, then in wax. The molds will be shipped to an industrial site where bronze, 2010 degrees Fahrenheit, will be poured into the cavities.

When the pieces are reassembled, she explains, the figure will be loaded onto a truck for transport. "It looks like a scene in 'Gulliver's Travels.'"

Tina remarks that she once heard historian Kenneth Clark say that great cultures can be measured by how they build objects to last. There are bronze statues made by the Greeks that endure magnificently to this day.

Tina is a firm believer that there is an element in her art that comes from elsewhere. Speaking in a way that is not so much mystical as matter-of-fact, she says, "I'm a conduit for the spirit."

She turns off one of the lights of the studio and takes a step back, still looking up at the statue. "I feel like her spirit is longing to be released. To come back."

Tina turns off another light, leaving a single bulb overhead. The enormous, durable, wise face of the giantess is steady.

Tina does not move. She keeps her gaze focused on Sojourner's. She turns off the last light now.

Through the pale darkness the spirit inside the clay gazes back.

PART VIII

THE SEASONAL ROUND

❖

A rainstorm, a bike ride, a trip to the post office—the simple activities of daily life, the seasonal round, help provide the texture of a place, the experiences we all share but too often take for granted. For several years I have felt compelled to write short, personal essays inspired by nothing more than an event of the hour, of the holiday or season. Some came about through the joy of watching my daughter—5 years old as this collection begins, a pre-teen by its close—grow and flourish. Without her in our lives, I might never have had occasion to set foot backstage at Danny and Pam Molise's Playhouse-in-the-Park, or in the rehearsal studios of Winthrop Corey's Mobile Ballet, or to listen to top-40 rock on WABB on the way to school at 7 A.M.

A selection of personal essays—a few dates circled on a calendar—are included here. Going ballroom dancing with my parents, the heat of summer, the first music of fall with school bands blasting their sounds, the gathering of families at Thanksgiving, the magic of a rare, Deep South snow—these make up both ordinary comings-and-goings, and life's deep mysteries. Before long the city and countryside are shimmering with holiday lights, and we count the minutes down until the new year—all the way to the millennium and now beyond—until we start out, blessedly, all over again.

As the Calendar Turns

❖

Rain Town, U.S.A.

Once upon a time, in a town called Mobile that was built on the water, with a road called Water, downtown streets were paved with wooden blocks. Coated in creosote, the blocks were hammered down tightly, creating a waffled surface where horse hooves clopped and carriage wheels rattled. The creosote enabled the blocks, ideally, to withstand the rains.

But Mobile rain is unceasing, insistent; it finds a way to seep into shoes, socks, books, and hair-dos. It takes the life out of crunchy cereal and makes mold go crazy on the underside of armchairs kept in storage bins. It turns lawns into rice paddies, and brings out otherwise elegant neighbors, barefoot, to fetch the morning paper.

The Mobile rain, my father remembers, found its way, too, into cracks between the street's wooden blocks. Along Dauphin, after a deluge, the blocks swelled, popped up and were scattered on the street. When a horseless carriage came bumping along, a tire edge would catch the edge of displaced blocks and flip them into the air.

"They'd fly like tiddlywinks at the windows of the Dauphin Street stores," he recalls. "People on the sidewalk had to be nimble to duck the flying blocks. Store windows would get broken, but the city of Mobile would not pay for the damage, calling it 'an act of God.'" After endless storms one summer, containers floated down the street —the packing crates of storefront merchants who sold their wares on Royal.

While the farmers would stand forlornly during downpours, next season's cotton already rotting in its bolls, business would be good for somebody, though. Playing in the rain as a boy, my father watched grown-ups scurry to the store of Henry Baumer at Government and Royal. Baumer Umbrella Shop made and repaired umbrellas—large-arced, heavy-ribbed.

Since the time, eons ago, leviathans rolled through the seas above the land that would one day rise to provide a foundation for our drive-up banks and drive-thru cleaners and drive-by restaurants, Mobile has been a town of water. If the "Guinness Book of World Records" were to establish a category "Windshield Wiper Activity," Mobile would be a contender. Even though countless short stories have been written about a South where broiling sun beats down on dusty fields, they were most likely penned by authors, if anywhere near here, who tracked mud over the rug.

That life-giving rain can turn deadly we know all too well. That substance which nurtures crops also creates breeding grounds for infectious mosquitoes; that which cleanses our bodies can also, if not purified, carry amoebas that wreak havoc in our stomachs. That which rushes gloriously by in streams can turn drainage ditches into watery graves. For some, today's rain marks an endless sorrow.

But most of us trust, knowing life in this tropical place, that today's rain will blend into yesterday's; that, before long, our shoes will dry, our hair will settle, our lawns will reappear, and Noah's dove—our gull—will laugh and swoop as the sun breaks through.

Azaleas at 8 mph

In Mobile's sweet Spring, when roads are finally dry and mosquitoes not yet hatched, I love to climb on my bicycle and take off down the road. Pavement whirring under the tires, wind running over my face, I am again speeding under the big oak trees near Murphy

High School, taking a curb—bounding skyward—expecting to find E.T. peeping from the handlebar basket. Beneath me the city—from Spring Hill to Mobile Bay—is spread out. The azaleas, wildly, are in bloom.

That setting off on a bike is always a journey into childhood comes as a mixed blessing. In kindergarten I broke my collar bone when another boy and I ran headlong into each other on bikes; I remember the swerve, the crash. But cycling meant freedom, too. Long before I could see over the steering wheel of a car, I was allowed to navigate my bike, alone, to Mr. Snow's Barber Shop at the Loop. I can still see the tall, silver-haired man in white apron stepping out the door to survey my wheels. "Mighty fine horse you got there," he said, reaching out and patting the crossbar.

I came to associate bikes, too, with luck. In a Little League raffle, I won my only contest prize to date—a hardy, bright-blue Schwinn. Early one Saturday morning I lined up at the store on Dauphin Street with a few other Little Leaguers waiting for the spoils. Sometimes when I ride downtown streets now on a weekend afternoon, whooshing by empty windows where cars also used to be sold, I see the boys leaving the store again thirty-five years ago on their prizes, heading pell-mell for the playgrounds.

I now have more gears than I know what to do with—twenty-one, in all—mountain trail tires and an aluminum frame. Rather than sit up I lean over, and the seat is as hard as a ledge. I wear a helmet, carry a titanium lock, and brake by squeezing my fingers rather than slamming back with my foot. I'm burning calories and working my heart—concepts that never entered my mind when cycling to Mr. Snow's at the Loop.

As a cyclist I'm distrusted by some pedestrians, like a woman I know who was race-walking on a rural highway when a bicycle zipping by sent her crashing to the ground. Some folks in automobiles don't seem to care for us much either—you can hear the ones bearing down who refuse to slow or give up one iota of road.

Despite highway contentiousness—and the fact there are not enough bike paths in our area—Mobile, in its floral ease, endures, come Spring, as a place to be cycled. Taking an evening stroll is a Southern art—but new neighborhoods often have no sidewalks. Jogging is America's fitness pastime; but it's hard to appreciate historic homes—Creole cottages, Queen Anne houses—when you're sweating and pounding the pavement.

Behind the wheels of their automobiles, drivers brush their hair, talk on their phones, argue aloud with Rush and Dr. Lara haranguing on the radio.

Traveling by bicycle, however, seems just right.

Azaleas gliding by at 8 mph offer joy, and solace. And when you shift into high gear and pump hard down a winding, country highway, you earn the sensation of pure, heart-pumping freedom.

Point Clear P.O.

Of the 28,189 post offices in America, 545 are in Alabama, and one of them is up the road from me—Point Clear, 36564. There may be 1,749,970 home deliveries of mail to Alabamians, but not to us. Like residents of Montrose and Stapleton in Baldwin County, Bucks and St. Elmo in Mobile County, and 19 other south Alabama towns, we fetch mail for ourselves. Daily, after checking my "e-mail" at home, I head out to the small brick building with the large American flag for my "snail mail." Cubbyholes there are stuffed with postcards, power bills, store ads, newspapers, magazines, and an old-fashioned letter or two.

"There's never nothing," says Helen McCants, who lives in a trailer on a side road in the district, and says that peeking into her post office box provides a "highlight" of her day. "People tell me, 'Oh, you live in Point Clear with the money!' But there's a back side to Point Clear, too. We all come together at the post office."

"It's like the old country store," says Marc Miller, a retired businessman who chats with friends near the newspaper rack.

Jack Edwards, who served as U.S. Congressman for twenty years, has used this post office for the last fourteen. "If I ever run again, I'll just come here and get a chair."

Kaye Campbell was postmistress of the Point Clear station, but just transferred to Magnolia Springs. She tried to say good-bye to everyone, but that was impossible.

"She's gone?" asks Alice Calloway, sounding a little saddened. "I used to always stick my head in and wave." Calloway grew up going to school in Point Clear, when it had a school, and remembers when the original post office, in the Broadbeck-Zundel store, distributed mail that came by ferry to Zundel's Wharf.

"It's better for Angie 'cause they live near Magnolia Springs," explains a man, looking up from his post office box.

They're talking about Angie, Kaye's grown daughter with Down syndrome. Everybody came to know her, the Crimson Tide's greatest sports fan, sitting in the post office's bay window waiting for her school bus. Jack Edwards says Angie often asked him to relay messages to former 'Bama Coach Gene Stallings.

Angie liked men's whiskers. Once, as I was getting my mail, she appeared from behind the counter and reached up, running her finger over my moustache. She tucked back to where Kaye, while affixing "Priority Mail" stickers to an envelope, was quietly nodding as a woman sadly told about a loved-one in the hospital.

Kaye held people's stories in confidence, but she passed along important news. When Keldrick Wasp, a Fairhope High School student, was killed in a car accident, she grieved for the family. Wasp Lane, a rural road named for the family, sits inside the postal area.

Kaye told me where a makeshift shrine had been built to the student-athlete. I drove down the highway, finding his photograph pinned to a pole, flowers and messages beneath it.

• • •

John Metzger, 80, used to be postmaster. Snappy in corduroy jacket and hat, he arrives this morning to get his mail pedaling a bicycle. "It's got one speed, flat-out." During his years on the job, from 1956 to 1983, the post office was located alongside a general store on the Marlow Highway, now a dirt lane close by. A bus to Mobile—also a ghost of the past—stopped there.

There are 819 rented boxes at the Point Clear post office today, but far fewer were needed then. Metzger once received a letter addressed, "Zelda, Point Clear." He knew where to put it.

He also recalls when stamps were 3 cents and "Air Mail" hurried a letter to its destination. For local mail, a letter from Point Clear to Daphne, ten miles away, was dropped off en route; now it's first sent to a processing plant in Tillman's Corner before being routed back across the bay—a considerable voyage.

Dorothy Pacey, 78, appears for her mail. She says that her mother, Bessie Broadbeck, was postmistress prior to Metzger. "People called her 'Aunt Sam.' They couldn't very well call her 'Uncle Sam!'"

Pacey, who delivered "Special Delivery" for her mother in 1935— she got 10 cents for every run—says letters are prized possessions. She describes the joy, during long-ago courtship, to find letters in her box from the man she would marry.

Pen-and-ink still carries emotional weight. "I'm just learning to use the telephone when someone dies," she says.

• • •

There is a petition circulating among some residents requesting home delivery of mail. If Jack Edwards is correct, home delivery might spell the eventual doom of our little crossroads. Even though Edwards likes the fact that the U.S. postal service is "no longer political"—it became a quasi-governmental, self-supporting business in 1982— that change means elected officials can no longer fend for their post offices.

"Someday it will go and be part of the Fairhope route," he believes. "If there's no post office, there's no Point Clear."

Jerry Pond, 61, remembers when there was a Battles Wharf post office. There is little recognition, anymore, of a distinct community by that name.

Pond bridles at the thought this same fate could befall tiny Point

Clear. "Too many things are getting swallowed up by larger municipalities!"

If that day ever comes for the Point Clear post office, few will celebrate. "It's part of our history," reflects Bill Allen, 74, who taught law in the business school at Auburn University before retiring here. Ironically, Allen and his wife live within the jurisdiction of Fairhope delivery, but prefer to spend $12 a year for a Point Clear box.

Years ago, Allen explains, they lived in Newbern, Ala., in Hale County, and picked up their mail at the Newbern post office. When the Newbern postmaster heard they were moving south he recommended Kaye Campbell and a box at Point Clear.

Leaning on his cane, the sunlight bright on his green madras jacket, Professor Allen clutches his mail on a bright April morning and chats with others.

He looks right at home.

In My Parents' Dancesteps

It may be sunny outside, but in a Gulf Coast dance hall the ball reflector throws out its own sparkle of light. The combo is playing "Fly Me to the Moon," and I am dancing with a woman thirty years my senior, trying to make small talk while sparing her feet. Across the floor I see my mother dancing lightly with a gray-haired gentleman, while my father nearby turns his own partner then gives a little shake. The whistle blows; couples fall apart, find new partners. As the band strikes up "Misty," a retired nurse from Biloxi takes my hand. I explain I am visiting this tea dance with my parents; that, beyond a basic box-step, I am not good for much at all. She nods politely, awaits my lead. In a mild sweat I watch my father for inspiration: he is smoothly fox-trotting his new partner across the hall.

On the dance floor my father is a better man than I. When the sax starts in to yesteryear's melody, he is out there, having a ball on the polished floors. Whereas I may balk at the meringue or, faced with the prospect of a new partner, feel cloddish and shy, my dad can blithely fake a Latin move or, given a whistle dance—"OK, everybody, change partners!"—do a friendly cha-cha with a woman he hardly knows.

Mostly, of course, he is dancing with my mother. From the time he first cut in on her sixty years ago—marrying her not long after—they have gone cheek-to-cheek, from dude ranches to fancy cruises, from Mardi Gras balls in Mobile to a "Gone With the Wind" party in Atlanta. They are not choosy about where they cut the rug. Not long ago, in the basement of a friend of theirs I watched them swaying to taped John Denver. They could not have looked happier in the Rainbow Room.

Not that my mom's grace on the dance floor isn't also to be admired. She deserves as much praise as Ginger Rogers, of whom it was said: "She did everything Fred Astaire did but backwards and in heels." But my mother's finesse on the floor is not surprising. Having danced with her a thousand times myself I know for a fact: she is light as a feather, gracious and winning. If you met her you would guess as much.

When you meet my father, though, you don't necessarily think *dancer*. He is a bald-headed, elder attorney who keeps his silver sideburns closely trimmed and could stand to shed a few pounds. After six decades of practicing law, he still enjoys scrambling in court. He is good-natured and talkative, and relishes a corny joke, but cross him and he'll bridle, insult him and he may well have you by the collar. Ambling down Mobile streets, he will most likely be eating peanuts and pausing to chat with friends. He can certainly *hurry*, but it's not his preferred style. For a show with an 8 o'clock curtain, he will just make it in time for the overture.

Strike up a dance band, though, and he's the first one on the floor, starting in to a brisk two-step with my mother to get the party rolling. If I am watching from the sidelines he will shoot me a bemused look as if to say, "Why don't you and your wife get out here, too." While I am fortifying myself with a drink he may show me up by asking my wife to dance. As he twirls her to some old show tune, the look on her face is unmistakable: she is having good plain fun.

My Uncle Louie seemed much the same. I remember two versions of him: the easygoing, slow-talking furniture store owner who loved his rocking chair; and the white-shoed, tangoing fool said to have "a heart like a hotel." Their father, my grandfather Morris, never danced much except at Jewish weddings, but then did so with abandon. My father and uncle grew up in the day of the big band when dancing brought out the style in men's hearts. What did my hay years, the 1960s and '70s, do for dancing save make it a loose-limbed prelude to sex?

Perhaps it's just that a slow-quick-quick step still seems daunting. Eighth-grade cotillion remains all too near: the boys and girls walking up the middle of the gym in a grand march, turning to each other ("Boys, keep your right hand placed firmly on the girl's lower back, left hand up to meet hers!"), and beginning to lurch about. And more than one childhood afternoon I spent compliantly jitterbugging with my big sisters, Fats Domino crying off a 45 rpm. It is ironic that the dance floor is the last place in America where a woman will ritually concede to a man, "Where you lead me I will follow."

Whatever rhythm the drummer is laying down, the dance floor becomes a refuge for the part of us that too often gets hidden away. The banker who finally loosens his tie when the horns are blaring in, the English teacher who lets go to the drummer's riff—they are revealing more of their true souls than in a dozen male-bonding trips to the woods. In a Louisiana dance hall I once watched an otherwise solemn friend do exuberant Cajun swing with any girl willing. At an outdoor band shell at Jones Beach in New York I have marveled at portly, loud-shirted men changed to lumbering Gene Kelleys on a summer's eve.

I have learned much from my father: how to try and be a loving husband, an understanding parent, a reliable friend. There are some secrets, still, he has not yet revealed, among them where to find the fountain of youth. He has other things on his mind, after all. There is a new dance band playing down the coast tonight, and he is already there, taking my mother's hand, ushering her out. The rhythm is his favorite, a slow swing, and he holds her close a moment before giving her a twirl.

The End-of-Year Recital

When you see ballet students on stage their movements are airy and elegant. Up close, though, at a ballet school, they bend and stretch, twirl and leap, and leap again—a workout as strenuous as any athlete's. Poised on a stool in the corner is the ballet teacher, herself a graceful dancer, and demanding as any coach.

I catch glimpses of this world of young dancers when I drive my daughter to Mobile Ballet. By age 11, Meredith has already made forays into modern dance, jazz dance, and ballet.

Wherever we have lived, my wife, usually, and I, on occasion, have shepherded her to big, mirrored rooms where music soars. On the way to class she may have been a pop culture–loving, middle-school student, spinning the radio dial to rock, country, and rap, but after arriving she digs into her dance bag, takes out leotards, ballet shoes and scrunchy, and reappears as a young woman about to spin through the room to Tchaikovsky.

On roomy couches at Mobile Ballet we even pause to rest a few minutes, peering through the curved windows at the studios where our children, jumping and twirling, remind us of the years when we, too, could go to school all day, expend physical energy all afternoon, and lug a sack of books home to study half the night.

Some of the older dance students may well go on to pursue careers in dance or the performing arts. Some of the younger ones, though, may find themselves barreling down a soccer field this time next year, or deciding they'd rather take hip-hop, gymnastics, or Tae-Bo.

• • •

The end-of-year recital. It is a ritual of growing up; and of being a parent. Do you have enough film for the camera? Is the video cam charged up? Did you remember to get flowers?

On a Saturday morning before the Sunday evening showcase, there's a run-through, and I cart my daughter. The lobby is crowded with other parents—my favorite spot on the couch is taken—but the studio's picture window offers everyone a view.

In charge is Mobile Ballet's artistic director, Winthrop "Wink" Corey, a tall, poised gentleman who used to be a principal dancer with the Royal Winnipeg Ballet and National Ballet of Canada. Wink runs the 250-student school, teaches high-level classes, choreographs and mounts full-scale ballets. He works with the company's ballet mistress, Ann Duke. Every summer Wink heads to New York to teach at the Joffrey Ballet's school in Greenwich Village.

For this morning's rehearsal the hallways are crowded with dancers —the vast majority, girls—little girls in light pink leotards, middle-school girls in navy blue ones, older dancers in black. The teachers—known as Miss Lori, Miss Zoe, Miss Jenny, and Miss Sydney—ready them.

For the showcase, Wink tells me, dancers with long hair will wear it up with bobby pins. This morning, though, they can keep it out of their faces as they choose—plaits, ponytails, pigtails; rubber bands, purple scrunchies, butterfly barrettes; hairpins, dragonfly clips, bows. If their leotards create uniformity, their hair says, "Hey, I'm me."

The taped, orchestral music begins and the littlest ones prance out. Arm-in-arm they begin galloping, a line of children linked to one another, feet busy to the music. A group of students, slightly older, replaces them, and then another, each group looking more elegant, more balletic—a leap, a pirouette—as they mature.

By the time my daughter's class comes out I realize how beautifully they use their arms and hands, reaching into the air, cool and elongated. As they run and spin I know they're getting winded and sweaty, but through the glass they appear artful, composed.

The next class comes on, bigger students who've reached the level of going "en pointe," up on their toes. I have a sense of their challenge. I once read a magazine article, "Dancer's Feet," about the punishment inflicted on the toes and insteps and heels and ankles of the ballet dancers who give the illusion they are suspended in air. (And you think your feet get tired!)

Dancer after dancer the students are reflected in the mirrors on the studio walls, as though each has an identical twin dancing along. In the reflection we also see ourselves in the lobby, not-quite-in-shape parents, slumped on the couches, milling by the door.

When the rehearsal ends, the vibrant youngsters pour into the lobby and hallway. Meredith, among them, disappears a moment and returns, dance bag over her shoulder, back in street clothes. "Ready," she announces.

In the car she reaches to the radio, and I imagine that classical music will finally accompany us. We have, after all, just spent a morning in the enchanted realm of ballet.

Rock music fills the air.

Summer Heat

In Mobile's sultry summer, beneath a spreading oak, I settle into "American Summer, 1929—Secrets of a Southern Porch," by Eugene Walter, in the New Yorker magazine.

"In my childhood," Walter says, "the porch was a concept as well as a place. In Mobile, Alabama, everybody would always sit on the front porch shelling peas and exchanging the neighborhood gossip."

As Walter continues with memories of "a passing parade of street venders and peddlers of all kinds pushing their wagons and carts down Conti Street," I can hear again the late Mobilian's soft and lilting voice—with good reason. The piece is excerpted from a colorful oral history of Walter conducted by author Katherine Clark.

"Of all the stories about summer collected here," writes Adam Gopnik in an introduction to the New Yorker issue—and others are by Jack Kerouac, Stephen King, and Arthur Miller—"only one gives us, naturally and unironically, an American summer of the kind that we like to think about. Eugene Walter describes a summer of ice men and watermelon and porches."

If Walter were still alive he might say that the fact of growing up in a hot, damp, coastal town like Mobile ensures that summer, always, will be one of "ice men and watermelon and porches."

Outwardly, of course, there have been changes. Our ice men have been replaced by the ice cube makers on the doors of our refrigerators. We pick our watermelons from the bins of stadium-sized grocery stores. After the brutal sun sinks we linger on our porches chatting with friends—sometimes via cordless phone.

We try to cocoon ourselves against the heat. The hum of crickets on the lawn as tropical night falls is matched by the thrum of compressors up and down the block—the noise of bedrooms cooling down, of power bills going up. In the morning we suit ourselves up in our central-air homes only to feel pasty again, cotton shirts clinging to our backs, by the time we get into our cars and blast the a/c to high. My grandfather's store on Dauphin Street had a radio jingle until the 1950s that went, "We have ceiling fans and window fans, one-room fans and three-room fans, any old fan, even a baseball fan." Today, the term "oscillating" sounds not modern, but quaint.

To ward off the late-night Mobile summers, Eugene Walter remembers the joy of drinking Cuba libres, a rum-and-Coke mixture, "a Southern drink for a Southern climate," he says.

Freon is now the single additive we require.

But we can't keep cool 24 hours a day.

When the Mobile BayBears try to sock the rawhide out to BayBear Mountain there will be fans in the stadium who will note that, even though the sun is setting, the temperature continues to feel Costa Rican. There will be wedding parties out-of-doors where brides and grooms feel torrents of love, and trickles of sweat. When Father's Day comes, there will be children at the beach who wonder why daddy's slathering himself in 30-grade sunblock.

And we will feel thankful—for not having forest fires, or a sky choked with haze. For not living in the other hemisphere of the globe where Mardi Gras, in February, would be in the middle of summer. For being able to look out just before dawn at the day star, Venus, and not having to worry about how hot it must be to live there.

Summer fogs our eyeglasses, wilts our shirts, coaxes us to cross the lawn barefoot; it reminds us how pleasant it is to eat cold fruit; how dangerous it can be to labor outdoors at noon; how good it feels to float in salt water. It enlivens the meaning of "wilt," "crumple," "scorch," and "simmer."

Henry James once said that the words "summer afternoon" were the most beautiful in the English language. The two most beautiful words inspired by "summer afternoon," it seems to me, must then be "afternoon nap."

"Old men with sugarcane stalks over their shoulders," Walter says, "children selling cut flowers stolen from that morning's funeral wreaths at Magnolia Cemetery, and the pot mender, with his strange tools and spirit lamp and bits of lead and solder, would pass by. The postman always stopped for a word. Conversations went on, rice was picked over, coffee was ground, beads were re-strung, and paper wicks were folded for next winter's fireplaces. Somehow, a whole world was encompassed, seized, dealt with, and all before noon."

I relish Walter's summer of 1929. I head to my own porch to read it again, making sure the sliding windows are closed tight, and the thermostat turned comfortably low.

The First Music of Fall

On Grand Boulevard in midtown Mobile there is a gray stucco house with wide porch, the ghost of a swing, and vast rooms echoing with the memory of pianos—the house of Thelma Perkins. When I was a boy I learned to play piano at that house.

Once a week, after the bell rang at Augusta Evans—then a neighborhood, primary school—I'd loll across the grassy field behind the classrooms, wend through the elephant ears, and arrive on Grand Boulevard near my destination. When I neared the porch I could hear the tinkle and boom of the pianos.

Dr. Perkins was a thin woman with brown hair and slender features. She was stern, but kind. I remember her standing over me as my 7-year-old fingers crawled up the white keys of the "C" scale, and, before long, began to add black keys too.

I was told to sit up straight; to cup my hands over the keys.

Sometimes I'd turn away from the piano and clap along with her. One-two-three-four—a lesson in keeping time. "Steady," she'd say.

She'd set the metronome going, a needle that wagged back and forth. Clik-clok. It was the sound of a creepy house in a scary movie. Clik-clok. It was hypnotic, too; the rhythm of a nap.

Back at the piano I learned the song of the Volga boatmen. Folk songs. Holiday songs. I progressed to sonatinas. Sometimes Dr. Perkins would sit alongside me and we'd play a duet.

Then, I'd learn of the fate that awaited me in the Spring—the music she wished me to perform in the yearly recital.

To this day when I enter Bernheim Hall in downtown Mobile I feel a slight panic. Will I be able to master the work?

It was a hot night, the hall was still, the girls were in fancy concert dress and the boys in blazers and neckties. Over the door was a sign that said exit, but for those of us whose names were printed on the program—next to the titles of our recital numbers—there was no way out.

When my turn came I walked across the stage in a daze and sat down before the ivories of the gargantuan grand piano and forgot everything I knew.

But my fingers remembered. With amazement I watched them swiftly giving life to "The Flight of the Bumblebee." From the high notes, to the middle, to the bass, I somehow trilled my way downwards to the dramatic flourish. I lay the back of my fingernails on the keys and swept upwards over the notes—a glissando.

Exalted, I bowed. The audience clapped. As I stepped off the stage another student passed me, nervously, on his way to the piano, fearing that he, too, had suddenly forgotten all Dr. Perkins had taught him.

• • •

All over town the first weeks of fall, students take out their clarinets, trombones, snare drums, French horns, tubas, violins, cornets, flutes, bassoons, violas, and electronic keyboards, starting lessons again. A lot of students play in school bands—I piped a clarinet at Sidney Phillips Junior High, ting-tinged a glockenspiel at U.M.S. It's an uplifting experience to be part of a crowd, no matter how screechy, sending John Philip Sousa marches into the south Alabama air.

There are many students, as well, who go to homes for private sessions one-on-one. Bach Inventions are struggled through, Chopin Waltzes are pounded out—and, sometimes, expressive playing, like a wildflower through a sidewalk, breaks through.

In the tradition of Mobile's Thelma Perkins, Dorothy Tonsmeire, and Alma Fisher—accomplished musicians who raised a generation of piano students—today's teachers, patiently, do what they can to inspire.

I suspect their task, like that of most teachers, never gets easier. In a time when so much music is available to hear—from Walkmans, boomboxes, car radios, cable television—the art of music, to some kids, must be like orange juice. "Why," they'll ask, "go to the trouble of making it at home?"

For those who do struggle to learn instruments, the classical repertory faces the competing appeal of pop. You can hear Arthur Rubenstein playing Beethoven's "Moonlight Sonata" on one radio station in Mobile, WHIL. In the course of a weekend, by contrast, Madonna will be all over the dial.

Whatever kind of music they play, though, students who keep at it know the joy of what it means to learn an instrument. It may be a chore, as a youngster, to practice; but for a grown-up there's no livelier therapy than to get lost in music of one's own.

• • •

I myself have a weakness for popular piano—from cocktail music, to blues, to barrelhouse, to the standards that draw folks to the edge of the keyboard, glass in hand, pretending to be Tony Bennett or Liza Minelli.

Not long after my last grammar school performance at Bernheim Hall, I left Thelma Perkins to study with Pat Byrne, an affable man with an eloquent voice who taught out of a house on Old Shell Road. In his studio I learned showy tunes like "The Old Piano Roll Blues" and "Stars Fell on Alabama."

I moved on to a house on Government Street, where Tom Decker taught me how to "fake." By faking, a pianist with only a melody line and a chord progression can improvise a song. Decker, an inventive musician who had a room of electronic gadgetry at the time, was always looking for innovative ways to teach. He still plays piano at clubs in town.

From faking, it was only a short distance to learning to play by ear—hearing a song, then picking out the melody and chords.

I explained to a friend who wanted to hire me to play a birthday party that I was a lousy choice; that I had a limited repertoire. He hired me anyway, explaining the music budget was only twenty dollars. Since I knew how to fake and play by ear, the party-goers got their money's worth, so long as they did not mind singing every song in the key of "C."

Over the years I've gotten my share of barstool applause and drinks on the house—wherever a piano beckons from the corner of a lounge or cafe, unused and unloved. Untuned.

One summer during college, when a buddy, Carl Root, and I ventured from Mobile to Alaska, there was a piano lounge aboard the inland waterway ferry. By the time we got to Ketchikan I got the nerve to sit down and play.

A moment later a rumpled dollar was stuffed into the tip jar.

The guy asked me where I'd learned to play. I began the story back at Dr. Perkins' door.

Already Home for the Holidays

On Interstate 10 over Mobile Bay the travelers zip by me, their license plates showing a Florida orange; a Texas Lone Star; a Georgia peach. The November light sparkles on the hoods of the compacts and coupes and sport utility vehicles. One low-slung, red two-door has a tag that suggests an especially long journey home: "Hawaii: The Aloha State."

Much as the Thanksgiving holidays give rise to the picture of a large family gathered around the table, they conjure another image, too—the suitcase. A celebration that resulted from a trip—the Pilgrims' sojourn to Plymouth Rock—is now one where Alabamians travel to Texas, Texans to New York, New Yorkers to California, and Californians to Alabama. When the weekend winds down, the leftovers are gone, the bargain sales are over, and credit cards are maxed out, everybody packs up and travels back to where they started.

Then they plan to make journeys home all over again.

Having resided far from Mobile for many years I've logged my share of holiday miles. During our years in New York my daughter never went over the river and through the woods to grandmother's house, but she did travel through the Queens Midtown Tunnel to La Guardia Airport—and grandmother's house, from that point on, was only three hours away.

It's been at the Atlanta airport during holidays like this one that I've glimpsed the faces of the New South—intent, youthful, in a hurry. Thousands of folks with plane tickets in one hand and frozen yogurt in the other scan the departure boards. Realizing their connections are two terminals away, they break into a run. I've entered this Atlanta Olympiad myself, dodging rolling suitcases and luggage carts.

But even in that airport I'd feel the Gulf Coast getting close at the connecting gate to Mobile. A friend of my Dad's, or a guy I knew from Little League baseball, or a girl I once took to a high school dance—familiar faces would emerge as we'd trundle down the ramp onto the plane.

The next hour would be spent talking about where we had moved, our work, our mutual acquaintances. Out the airplane window south Alabama would soon revolve into view—the red clay, the pine trees, the bay.

It was the holidays. We were closing in on home.

• • •

Mobile is a town some people define by leaving. Whatever people yearn for—riches or fame, anonymity or glamour—seems to lie beyond the far hill. At holidays there are few families who do not welcome back someone who has left the fold to quest for his or her fortune—or simply to get away from the familiar crowd.

In some cases better opportunities really do exist far away. It's hard to be a ski instructor, a Broadway dancer, a major urban planner, or a Fortune 500 executive and live year-round in Mobile. Philip and Mary Hyman are authoring "L'inventaire Du Patrimoine Culinaire de la France," a 26-volume history of edibles in French markets, from sausage, to snails, to croissants—a project, financed by the French, easier to commandeer from their apartment in Paris' Montmartre district, than from where Philip grew up in Mobile.

Some people leave because they prefer mountains, others because they tire of the heat, others because they fall in love with somebody from Oregon, Oklahoma, or Spain.

In some cases, though, leaving home is really about going far away in order to come back again. On the other side of the mythic hill it may not be much different at all.

Besides, Mobile itself is a destination for young people from other towns—particularly small Southern towns—who want to move somewhere with a university, job possibilities, a ball team, shopping malls, movie cineplexes, and rock music blaring at midnight in downtown clubs.

Right this moment there may be two cars passing each other in opposite directions. One holds a person who must depart this city in order to thrive, the other a person just arriving here to flourish.

• • •

As a result of all this movement, people with south Alabama connections turn up in the unlikeliest places.

One morning when we lived in Brooklyn, N.Y., I was jogging in my neighborhood and passed a pastry shop. I decided to pause and pick up croissants for breakfast. I thought nothing of my T-shirt— "Redneck Riviera, Gulf Shores, Alabama"—until the lady behind the counter said, "Oh, my husband and I have spent time in Gulf Shores!" It turned out she was a native of Montgomery, was married to a Frenchman, and they'd opened "Marquet Patisserie" in Brooklyn as well as in Manhattan's Greenwich Village. I stopped in regularly after that.

One afternoon during Thanksgiving holidays many years ago my wife and I were strolling through downtown New York when a homeless man asked us for a handout. He was clearly down on his luck, but personable. We gave him some change; he inquired where we were from.

"Alabama," we told him.

"Durn," he said wistfully. "Home people!"

"Home people" seem to turn up everywhere. While registering for a card at the Library of Congress in Washington, D.C., I showed my Alabama driver's license. The administrator exclaimed, "I grew up in Fairhope!" We talked about a plot of land she'd inherited near Greeno Road, just big enough to build a house on one day if she decided to move back.

Across the continent last summer I was buying stamps for vacation postcards in San Francisco's Haight-Ashbury district. I chatted with the postal worker about the South. As I was heading out the door a young man came over.

"I overheard you say 'Alabama,'" he said, explaining he'd grown up in Washington County.

He, too, had recently come into a small piece of property; he told me it was at a rural crossroads where there was not much else anymore. "There's a building on the property that used to be an old post office," he said. "I'm thinking about moving home one day and turning it into a cafe."

He wanted to know what I thought of that idea.

A cafe? In a rural Alabama ghost town? "Maybe," I offered.

What I didn't tell him—he was a stranger, after all, except for his upbringing amid the sweet sound of drawls and the crisp smell of pines—was that he had probably lived away too long.

• • •

For my part, when it came time this year to make Thanksgiving pilgrimages from one relative's house to another, I was happy to watch the odometer rack up merely low double-digits.

Not that I mind travel. As even bigger holidays await us in December, chances are we'll even celebrate by doing something we never felt free to do when home always beckoned—take a trip somewhere we've never been.

Snow!

The tea kettle is on, the furnace is roaring, and snow is falling on azaleas outside my window. Throughout the town, schoolchildren romp, poinsettias are in shock, and Santa Claus doesn't look uncomfortable in a long beard.

For twenty years I lived up north, slogging through snows knee-deep in the streets of Brooklyn, or sledding down it on the hills of Vermont—and now I have traveled back south to watch flurries, unbelievably, paint lawns white. The word "Mobile" might conjure thunderclouds and bourbon and funky music and damp air redolent of flowers and cooking—but never snow.

Down it falls, though, flecking moss, outlining fences, turning ordinary streets into calendar lanes. The roads, of course, are a mess—nowhere here are sanitation trucks where brawny men hurl salt onto the concrete, keeping the streets from becoming sheets of ice. Normal drivers become nervous slowpokes on the Bayway; along the Interstate, drivers wipe at their fogging windshields with one hand; up ahead, police car lights whirl.

Here one wants to be just where I am—at home, by the window, the tea kettle beginning to rattle.

There is the phone, of course. Like a man tucked into an Alaskan cabin, I phone my mother who reports, like one tucked away in another cabin, that the snow is falling at Williams Court. "Like pieces of white from Heaven," she says.

On my parents' lawn, I'm told, the neighbors' children are playing; their own parents want lawns where the snow is undisturbed, and daddies are driving home early from work, cameras at the ready, snapping next year's holiday shots. I am reminded of my father's old 8 mm home movies with their footage of that legendary afternoon of my own childhood—the other time it snowed. Tomorrow, throughout the city, the film labs will be humming.

I hang up the phone and, making contact from my snow cabin again, plug in my computer on-line. I tap into the newspaper's bulletin board. With the exuberance of people sighting UFOs, my colleagues are posting reports of snow out-of-town, in town, in Semmes, in Bay Minette. They are like kids on cyberspace's front-lawn, kicking up virtual snow; I expect to be hit by a virtual snowball.

I click off the computer and watch the snow, and listen to its hush. Because it makes no sound in this time when everything does—radios and TVs and video games and automobiles—it is loud in its silence. By tonight it will be noisy again with the sound of wet boots being yanked off and people dragging out electric blankets and kids staying up late because school will start late tomorrow, if at all.

But now, gracing the car hood, tracing the swing, and swirling around the mailman's feet, it is still silent, and pure.

Even the library, usually the quietest place of all, was closed "due to weather" when I went there a while ago. There was a novel, Truman Capote's "Other Voices, Other Rooms," I wanted to browse through again.

But I find it, dog-eared, on my own shelf; perhaps I'd been saving it, for years, waiting for this snow.

I turn to a scene where a young man, Joel, and Zoo, who works for Joel's family, are talking. Zoo has told Joel that she wants to leave Alabama and move to Washington, D.C. When Joel asks her why she doesn't move to New Orleans instead, she answers, "Aw, I ain't studyin' no New Orleans. It ain't only the mens, honey: I wants to be where they got snow, and not all this sunshine."

A moment later, when Zoo asks Joel if he's ever seen snow, he fibs and says he has, but thinks: "It was a pardonable deception, for he had a great yearning to see bona fide snow: next to owning the Koh-i-noor diamond, that was his ultimate secret wish."

Like Joel and Zoo, I suspect that many have nursed a wish to see snow—not on flights to Colorado, or car trips to the Smoky Mountains, but here, where azaleas pop forth ahead of the game. If we saw it all the time, we would go on about our business, thinking nothing of wearing short-shorts one week and wool socks the next.

As it is, though, mid-December, with snow swirling down, becomes extraordinary. Even so, it probably won't be with us tomorrow. As my tea kettle sings (I never even think about tea until it snows), and my daughter comes stamping in the back door, like she's switched places with her best friend, Kai, in Maine, she cries with annoyance, "It's already melting!"

Quick! The camera!

Holiday Lights

Every Christmas for half a century the residents of Siena Vista, a block in midtown Mobile, have decorated their homes with lights—

lights draped off eaves like icicles, lights entwining the grillwork of porches, lights blinking down walkways. When cars lined up to view those decorations during the 1960s, I'd ride along as a youngster, waiting to see the house of my aunt and uncle. Inside their home there was no tree but a Hanukkah menorah, and their own lights blended joyously with those of their neighbors.

Like the Siena Vista of my youth, I see the lights of our city, in this holiday season, shining from different sources.

There are the menorahs that burn brightly in the homes of Jewish families. In an African-American holiday, one drawn from African traditions, there are the candles of Kwanzaa. The first candle is called "Umoja," meaning unity.

And there are, of course, the lights of Christmas.

I have seen those lights in many places beyond Mobile. Some are spectacular, like the gigantic Christmas tree of Rockefeller Center in New York, where ice skaters loop and swirl beneath the glittering magic. Some are expressions of American pop culture, like those at Graceland, Elvis' Memphis home, where an illuminated guitar, piano and harp sit at roadside, part of the decorations that go up the day after Thanksgiving and come down on Jan. 8, Elvis' birthday.

I have never been to Atlanta's light display on the campus of Life Chiropractic, but I'm told that, for those willing to creep along in perpetual Atlanta traffic, there are Santas, Christmas trees, and packages all ablaze in the Georgia woods.

For a tropical Christmas—bay air, poinsettias, and illuminations— we have to go no further than our own Bellingrath Gardens. For Yule lights of a bygone era, Oakleigh. For theatrical Christmas lights down main street, U.S.A., Foley.

But I have an affection for the lights that people display in their homes. Some are elaborate, like those of houses on Government near Broad, where lights wrap columns like candy canes. Others are religious, like the creche before a Dauphin Street home at midtown, where the figures of the nativity stand bathed in light.

Some lights show the way. While driving one night on Highway 98 from Lucedale, Miss., to Mobile, I watched the Christmas lights of rural Alabama brighten the countryside—the outlines of shrubs, porches, garages, mobile homes. I've seen those same lights on Highway 27 in Baldwin County, where, at dusk, farmhouses look like strands of pearls on the horizon.

Firemen, whose workplace is a home away from home, seem to have a special appreciation of lights. From Dauphin Island Parkway, to Lafayette Street, I have seen firehouses where reindeer and Santas and elves blink red and green.

People who live alone, too, like the residents of a retirement home in downtown Mobile, also send out their messages of welcome. In the windows, in bright rows, are lights that signal to the street below that the season of peace and joy has descended, in a hush, on the town.

• • •

Sometimes the simplest lights shine the brightest.

When I became old enough to drive I'd sometimes give a ride to the woman who'd worked for my family since I was born, and who'd helped raise me in the old-fashioned way of the Deep South. Alberta West, a member of El Bethel Primitive Baptist Church, was devout in her faith—one that was far different from mine, but that was as clear as the blue skies when she clutched her Bible and read aloud from its well-thumbed pages.

It was toward Christmas Eve that I parked the car before Alberta's house at the Orange Grove project just north of Beuregard Street and went inside with her to visit. I sat on the sofa next to her and looked at the pictures of her many children and grandchildren in a photo album, and I enjoyed a piece of her pecan pie.

On a table near the window was a small tree with some presents underneath. With some effort she stood—she was tired from a long day of work—and went over to the tree. She reached down and flicked a switch.

As she turned to me her face was caught in a glow, her single strand of lights suddenly radiant as all the stars of heaven.

Marking Time

On New Year's Eve, a day in which we contemplate time, I think of a story my father tells me about a clock that hung outside the old Mobile courthouse on the corner of Royal and Government in the 1930s. Legend has it that the clock was always wrong. One day an inmate at the county jail next door offered to repair the clock—if the county reduced his sentence.

After repairing the public's time, the inmate was allowed to serve less of his own.

To think of an era when we depended so critically on our town clocks is, well, to turn back the clock. There was something haunting yet reassuring, like the sound of waves at the Gulf, in the sweep of clock hands around a vast, numbered dial. Even small clocks were appealing. I always imagined that long-bearded Father Time, traipsing his tired way to midnight, carried a pocket watch in his vest. Even the Grim Reaper, scythe over his back, moved to the hands of a clock—never the luminous dial of a digital watch.

Time never weighed more heavily, though, than one afternoon at the corner of Dauphin and Royal, in the 1950s. A truck, taking a sharp right turn to head to the river, careened into the public clock that stood ten feet tall at the corner. The clock fell onto a woman, injuring her badly.

I have far rosier associations with the four-sided clock that stood across from Bienville Square in front of the First National Bank, long a popular meeting place for associates, and lovers. A young attorney, Charlie Hoffman, and Evelyn Robinton, a bookkeeper, once rendezvoused there and drove to Florida where they were married sixty-one years ago—on New Year's Eve.

That my parents' marriage has outlasted the First National clock is both testimony to the power of love—and to the evanescence of clocks. Yes, time flies, but so do time-keeping mechanisms. My brother-in-law, a medievalist at the University of North Carolina, tells me that the invention of mechanical clocks in the 14th century may have had a more profound impact on society than did the industrial revolution of the 19th century. Where we were once informal in our culture, saying, "I'll do this at sunset," we became exact, saying, "I'll do it at 5:15."

"We started to do things," he explains, "that fit the arbitrariness of time." School by 8, work by 9, appointments at noon—hurry, don't be late!

His son, and my daughter, both born the same day—although several hours apart, they remind me—would have been lousy schoolkids five hundred years ago. Like most of their classmates, they are obsessive time-keepers, sporting digital watches with the hour, minute, second, tenth of a second, in this time zone and twenty others. They are happy in the realm of fast-forward.

And why shouldn't they be? Whereas light years have passed, in their minds, between last New Year's and this one, for me it seems like only last month that my family was dancing foxtrots until the countdown to 1996.

I begin to understand why Oscar Wilde's Dorian Gray wished, whatever the cost, never to grow old.

On New Year's Day, of course, from bowl to bowl, millions will watch teams butt heads on gridirons where clocks, imperiously, count down time. Perhaps my preference of baseball to football comes from its being a game without clocks—those long summer evenings where the contest is not between man and time, but between man, chewing tobacco, and stitched rawhide. In baseball, nothing much stops the clock but a fistfight or thunderstorm; in football, basketball, and boxing, time is a factor.

Around town today we can still see the time—often, in bright electronic lights, exchanging places with the temperature. Phoning in to our voice mail, we can hear it repeated by a friendly if disembodied voice; scrolling through our computer menus, we can see it turning inexorably, second by second, whether our screens are flicked on or not.

Nowhere, of course, will time be as comforting as the tick-tick of my father's pocket watch, the one his own mother gave him when he graduated from Barton Academy. Nor will the flash of digital time on a screen ever compete with the lulling of a grandfather clock like my wife's parents keep in their dining room, the names of their grandchildren and birth dates listed up the side, the gong pealing appealingly on half hours.

On New Year's Eve, I can still see the four-sided clock in front of the First National, the young couple, romantic and headstrong, meeting below, heading off to get married, time bountiful before them, little troubled at the prospect that the clock hands would go round, and round, and round. After all, it was just 1935!

With a copy of H. G. Wells' "Time Machine" on my bookshelf, the Rolling Stones singing "Time on my Mind" on the stereo, an ad for a time-share condo in a stack of mail, and a reminder from my wife that it is time to get ready for the party, I concede that, whether we grieve or celebrate or weep or wear funny hats, tonight, at twelve, those hands will go round again.

PART IX

MARDI GRAS DRUMS

$\diamondsuit$

Of all the festive noises in the world—firecrackers, party horns, whoops and hollers—none matches the spirit of Mardi Gras drums. I'll be an old man combing a ratty beard in the 21st century, but I'll be a kid when I hear those drums.

They grow louder, stealing up the sides of buildings, climbing the balconies like an acrobat. They herald the horses, plumes dancing, the riders flinging doubloons to the crowd.

Leading the riders are the Braswells, known to kids at Braswell Stables as Uncle Bob and Aunt Helen. In his cowboy hat and fancy shirt Uncle Bob looks like a leathery Roy Rogers; Aunt Helen like Dale Evans with a dash of grit. Bob rides Silver Allen; Helen's on Queen.

Next come the majorettes, sleek and high-stepping. Their banners ripple; their batons flash. They are beautiful in their leotards. But aren't they cold?

The drums are buzzing the window panes.

As a college student in New Orleans I relished the French Quarter on Mardi Gras Day. The movie "Easy Rider," with its depiction of shaggy youths roaring into town on motorbikes, turned New Orleans' Mardi Gras into a Woodstock in masquerade.

On the streets of Mamou, La., at another Mardi Gras, a Cajun band, Dewey Balfa and His Musical Brothers, played sad waltzes on a flatbed truck. I delighted in dancing with women of the town—I tried to lead, but had more than one swing me around.

I even celebrated Mardi Gras in New York City, often seeking out a Gulf Coast–style restaurant. I wrote a New York Times essay that

From the early 1700s when French settlers in Mobile marked Boeuf Gras by carrying a boar's head down a lane, to 1830 when the Cowbellion de Rakin' Society marched with rakes and hoes downtown, to 1866 when Joe Cain's Lost Cause Minstrels revived Mardi Gras after the Civil War, to the snare drum rat-tat-tatting of today, Fat Tuesday has been celebrated in Mobile in many colorful ways. Setting the beat here is Jeremiah Mosely, 14, of Vigor High School, as Vigor's marching band advances down Government Street during the Infant Mystics parade. The Infant Mystics, founded in 1868, takes to the streets on Monday nights as the second oldest mystic society. The final parade on Tuesday, Mardi Gras Day, is reserved for the oldest, dating from 1867, the Order of Myths. (Kiichiro Sato, Mobile Register)

ran with a drawing of jester Folly chasing skeleton Death. My by-line: "Roy Hoffman is celebrating Mardi Gras in his apartment." Friends came over to share a 6-pack. What we missed were the drums.

The drummers are up to where we're standing now, and folks around us are finger-snapping and hip-swaying.

This is not the Macy's Thanksgiving Day parade; nor the Rose Bowl parade; nor a Fireman's Fourth of July procession. That drumming is orderly, something John Philip Sousa would be proud to claim.

The beat here is syncopated, and the bass drum shakes your chest. This is a sound that makes your feet itch, your hip-bones move.

There are drums ahead of us and behind us, the streets lit up with snares and tom-toms. Saxophones and clarinets and trombones start up. Trumpets blare in. Cymbals crash. Drums—flashy, rhythmic, heart-thumping—fill the air.

Let the Good Times Roll

❖

There's an old saying in town that you're not really a Mobilian unless you're born under an azalea bush in Bienville Square on Mardi Gras Day. Although my grandparents were Eastern European immigrants to Mobile in 1907, and I was born a couple of miles from Bienville Square in the sultry heat of summer, the sense of Mardi Gras was often hovering in the air.

On Mardi Gras Day my sisters, friends and I would camp out all day long on the balcony of my grandparents' furniture store on Dauphin Street. This was the heart of Mobile's shopping district until the 1960s, when it suffered a precipitous decline, losing out to the cloverleaf highways and shopping malls. Then, on Mardi Gras Day, a balcony of Dauphin Street was the place to be.

As the marching bands thundered and the horses clip-clopped and the floats rolled close, I remember leaning far out, waving my hands, looking down at the men in their 1950s fedoras and the ladies in scarves like bright helmets against the February wind, and the children, all standing on their tiptoes, craning their necks to see. I could glimpse the tops of the floats turning the corner at Broad Street and heading up our way. Alongside the floats young men called "Flambeaus" carried gas-lit torches.

Even as a child I knew that, in Mobile, we enjoyed the best Mardi Gras throws. In New Orleans, I'd heard, only brightly colored beads were hurled from the floats—skimpy fare. Ours was a cornucopia pouring forth from the floats: rubber balls, Cracker Jack, rolls of serpentine, bags of confetti, candy kisses, candy bars, stuffed animals. As the floats got closer—all of a sudden they were a block away, rocking back and forth near the general mercantile stores and shoe repair shops and Army-Navy stores of old Dauphin Street—the sidewalks became a sea of hands reaching up. The music of the bands competed with the din of the shouting crowd: "Hey, hey . . . Over here . . . Throw me something . . . Cracker Jack . . . Throw me a ball!"

Every float had its practical joker, a masked rider who kept a prize throw—a roll of serpentine—attached to a rubber band and hurled it at the grasping hands only to bring it back like a yo-yo. Throw and snatch back. The crowd roared.

From the balcony of my grandfather's store, the parade seemed all for me.

• • •

Mules pulled the floats in the 1950s, now motor vehicles do. Back then Dauphin Street was the main thoroughfare for the parades, now it's considered too narrow, and parts of it are forlorn, many once-vibrant family-owned businesses boarded up. My grandfather's store is still there, run by my cousin, but the balcony, getting rickety, was removed. The parades now pass along Government Street, a much wider venue, where police barricades are easily set up along the sidewalks for crowd control—an unheard-of restriction forty years ago.

But gigantic and colorful floats still rock and saw through the city streets come early February, and the tradition of Mardi Gras endures. I am happy that it does.

There are plenty of sensible reasons why my hometown would be better off without it. Mardi Gras makes a mess of the streets. Mountains of money are expended on candies and trinkets, parties and costumes—an impractical expenditure of hundreds of thousands of dollars. The celebration maintains, indeed codifies, social divisions along lines of money and class. And in our gun-crazy era there can be outbursts of violence on the street, usually between drunken acquaintances, that throw the vast majority of safety-minded, convivial townsfolk into a panic.

Mardi Gras is also decried by some for religious reasons. A few conservative-minded churches tending to Fundamentalism—it is, of course, a Catholic holiday—contend that it is decadent, and billboards annually sprout up far from downtown claiming that the spiritual ruination of our town is at hand.

But Mardi Gras brings people who otherwise are strangers out to mingle amicably on the street. It revitalizes our sidewalks as public spaces where grown-ups can become children again, loosening their neckties and shouting for candy. It gives us a calendar that, outside of New Orleans, is distinctively our own—schools are closed for Mardi Gras, many offices and some banks, too. It's good for our mental health to be relieved now and then of our 9-to-5 jobs.

The celebration, in the deepest sense, helps us retain our sense of place. Much of Mobile has been lost to development, Sunbelt sprawl, and the eagerness to be modern. Mardi Gras, like Mobile Bay, reminds us where we live and helps define who we are.

• • •

On the Sunday before Mardi Gras, at the Church Street Graveyard in downtown Mobile, the widows are weeping. Dressed in black, covered in veils, the women bow down to the resting place marked "Joe Cain." They keen and sway, theatrical with grief.

Among them is a figure in mock Indian headdress, Chief Slacabamarimico, a mythical Chickasaw warrior. Looking on are revelers in clownish hats and painted faces—a crowd waiting for a procession to begin. The voices of the widows rise. Bereaved over the same husband, it's no wonder they begin squabbling. One brandishes a cane; another hurls an invective. An onlooker lifts a beer can and takes a swig.

Joe Cain Day is one of the many oddities of Mobile's carnival. Like New Orleans, Mobile is heir to the French Catholic tradition of the Boeuf Gras—literally "fat beef"—the ancient celebration on the Tuesday before Lent of eating and drinking heartily before six weeks of abstinence. (Mobile and New Orleans share not only a culture, but also a founder, the explorer Jean-Baptiste Le Moyne, Sieur de Bienville, who set foot in the territory of the Mauvila Indians, the city's namesake, in 1702.)

New Orleans may have the most famous Mardi Gras in the country, but Mobile claims the first. The French celebrated Boeuf Gras by carrying a boar's head through their early settlement. Our modern tradition got started on New Year's Eve, 1830, when a youth, Michael Kraft, and friends grabbed up rakes and hoes from a hardware store and marched with spirited racket through Mobile streets. Their procession, known as the Cowbellion de Rakin' Society, became an annual event, and soon took place on the Tuesday before Lent. But Mobile's celebrations were suspended during the Civil War.

Enter Joe Cain, who was born in 1832, the son of Philadelphia shipbuilders who'd arrived in Mobile by covered wagon. In 1866, Cain brazenly defied Yankee occupiers by deciding to revive the processions of Mardi Gras Day. He appeared on the Mobile streets dressed as Chief Slacabamarimico and led a group of ex-Confederates as the Lost Cause Minstrels. It was no coincidence that he pretended to be a Chickasaw, a tribe that had gone undefeated in battle. Slacabamarimico, to Joe Cain, became a symbol of both revelry and defiance—the party must go on.

Mardi Gras took hold again, and mystic societies began to unfold: the Order of Myths in 1867, Infant Mystics, 1868, the Knights of Revelry, 1874. These three groups would dominate carnival until after World War II when there was an efflorescence of new societies and parades.

In the oldest parade, the Order of Myths—which rolls through Mobile to this day—the lead float holds a figure dressed as Folly chasing the persona of Death. Folly holds a string of inflated pig bladders and beats Death around the head and shoulders with them. The symbolism is unmistakable. In this festival with deeply Catholic traditions, the triumph of life over death, joy over suffering, is paramount this day before Lent.

Cain was soon forgotten. It was not until the 1930s that a writer emerged in Mobile, Julian Rayford, who had a romantic notion of the old Mardi Gras. Rayford found romance in much about Mobile, publishing a novel, "Cottonmouth," about the city that was praised by the legendary editor, Max Perkins, and published by Scribner's.

"It was a civic safety valve, people let off steam, during those five days, people relaxed," Rayford wrote in his novel. "And not only the kids put on comic dress, hundreds put on make-believe. Dignified businessmen who were austere all year round in the countinghouses came out in satin and gold and velvet and purple to dance on floats and fling confetti. And people wore breathtaking formal dress, the men in swell evening clothes, the women in expensive gowns. Thousands gathered on the Wharf to see the Queen and her maids. And the maids walked out one by one, and a little ripple of clapping increased to a cyclone of cheering as they kept on coming forward in those astonishingly lovely dresses. And King Felix and his knights, all of them wearing phony costumes of some pseudo-European court."

By the time Rayford published "Cottonmouth," Joe Cain was buried in an unmarked grave in Bayou la Batre, near Mobile's Gulf waters. Rayford, a lover of folktales and tall-tale figures, decided to revive Cain's spirit. He had him disinterred from Bayou la Batre and moved to the historic Church Street Graveyard. The reburial was done in 1966, and gave rise to the first Joe Cain Day. In a procession to the graveyard behind a somber brass band, Rayford played the part of Slacabamarimico. Rayford himself passed away in 1981 and was buried next to Joe Cain.

Rayford loved a party, I'm told, and the tradition of Joe Cain's widows became part of the histrionics at the graveyard. If there were to be a procession, there'd have to be a widow, after all (although Joe Cain's wife was reburied with him). Soon other "widows" joined the quirky day of mourning, their identities kept secret.

Before the "widows" leave today, and begin their march through downtown Mobile streets, they cease their squabbling and remember Joe Cain one last time, draping Mardi Gras beads over his headstone, and across Julian Rayford's, too.

• • •

Mobile's second oldest society, the Infant Mystics, parades on the eve of Mardi Gras Day, the oldest, the Order of Myths, takes to the streets the night of Mardi Gras Day—the last parade of the season.

Historically, membership in these societies and others was meant to be secretive—thus, the masking of the members in the Mardi Gras parades. But those secrets are little kept anymore.

From families who are long part of the ranks of the oldest groups, typically, are drawn the kings and queens who rule over Mobile's Mardi Gras. The best way to become king or queen is to be the child of a king or queen. The annals of Mardi Gras royalty show an interlocking network of names; often, a queen's last name becomes the first name of the next generation's king. You could cross-list those names with the law firms, insurance companies, and business organizations in the city and have a pretty good idea of the power structure of this town. You could then cross-list those with addresses in upscale Mobile neighborhoods, private schools, and summer houses on Mobile Bay—a portrait of Old Mobile.

Each parade—and there are at least two dozen—is sponsored by a mystic society. Some mystic societies are old money, some new money. Some are more socially prestigious than others. Some welcome Jews as members, others welcome them only as friends and guests. There are men's organizations—the older ones—and women's organizations.

The Mardi Gras organizations are racially segregated. However, there's little if any political or social tension in that fact. The parades all draw mixed crowds to the streets for what is a weeklong city-wide party. Mobile's black Mardi Gras organization, parading in the afternoon on Mardi Gras Day, ties into its own power structure in the African-American community. The most famous queen of Mobile's black Mardi Gras was crowned in 1974 as Queen Alexis—Alexis M. Herman, who'd become U.S. Secretary of Labor in the Clinton administration. Alexis' father, Alex, was king of the organization in 1940, the year it began.

As a public celebration, Mardi Gras has had a way of adapting to the times. My father was one of the charter members of the Mystics of Time in 1949, one of the post–World War II societies formed by men prominent in Mobile's civic life—businesspeople and professionals—and who were not, by Mardi Gras' standards, from

Mobile's socially reigning families. Fifty years later, the Mystics of Time parade is on Saturday night, with its signature dragons winding through the streets. There are women's parades with telltale names—the Maids of Mirth (better known as the Moms), the Polka Dots, the Order of LaShe's. One group puts on a gay Mardi Gras ball, the Osiris Ball.

In staging its parade, each society picks a different theme. The floats—craftsmen have already begun building next year's—are like chapters in a story. The 1999 Knights of Revelry parade, for example, had the theme "Mobile Memories—Things Mobile Has Lost in the Last 25 Years." The floats were still-life pageants of yesteryears' icons—a well-known park, a popular drugstore, a beautiful garden, a gargantuan globe in the lobby of a downtown bank.

Mardi Gras continues to evolve. Parading societies have sprung up where recent transplants, even Yankees, have moved to the area. On the salty barrier island of Dauphin Island, for example, close to Mobile's Civil War fortress, Fort Gaines, a Mardi Gras parade takes place three weeks before Fat Tuesday. There are parades in the now-upscale resort town of Fairhope, even a parade at Gulf Shores, part of the coastal strip of "Redneck Riviera."

• • •

Not all the city's mystic societies parade, but most stage balls for members and members' guests at the Municipal Auditorium or Mobile's new Convention Center. White tie and tails for men, long dress for ladies, is *de rigueur*. No matter how much money you have, no matter who's your daddy, you won't get into a ball in anything less than the stipulated dress. It's little wonder that Mobile has one of the largest formal wear markets in the nation. For inaugural events in Washington, D.C., I've heard, planners turn to our city for back-up rentals.

I've also heard it said that Mobile, for the same reason, lags behind other Southern cities in charitable contributions—all those bucks spent on Mardi Gras parties and outfits and throws. Friends of mine confess to spending well into four figures on the holiday. Membership in the societies, the costs of the floats, the expenses of ball tickets for guests, the moonpies and necklaces—it adds up.

When societies do parade, some members—usually the younger ones—don shiny jester-type suits and plastic masks with sinister eye-slits, and ride the floats. After the parades, non-parading members arrive at the balls in formal dress, while parading members stay in costume for the big bashes, which typically offer a rock band in one room, orchestra in another, tables of food, and an endless river of booze.

As a guest of different mystic societies, I've downed my share of bourbon and wandered from room to room, bumping into folks I've known since grade school, who themselves are often deep in the Mardi Gras sacrament of liquor. Some balls begin with a procession akin to high school "call-outs," with officers and members presented on the stage—and some put on "tableaus," short, theatrical presentations, to start the balls.

As the evening wears on, a Mardi Gras ball begins to suggest a senior prom; the party goers are simply older, broader, grayer. Guys are slapping each other on the back, their starched shirts getting rumpled; gals are looking for their dates or their husbands, and stopping to catch up with old friends, forgetting their dates. If the band is close by, everybody has to shout over the music. But then couples reconnect and stumble out onto the steps of the auditorium, drunk and happy with several hours of music and frivolity, falling against each other and wrapping up like teen-agers again. As the Cajun song has it, "Laissez le Bons Temps Roulez," "Let the Good Times Roll." When they fall away from each other, the time has come to debate who's sober enough to navigate the car home.

• • •

As the drums got louder and the cornets rang out and cheers from the street rose higher, the floats arrived beneath us. The balcony of my grandfather's store was now a bright stage for hauling in carnival loot.

The masks of the men on the floats made a single, ghoulish expression, a wax museum of features, as the costumed creatures danced and rocked, often keeping time to the marching bands. Sometimes a hand would rise and a finger would point at me and my name was called. It would be a family friend, or a dad of one of my school buddies, although I could never make out just who it was behind the mask. Throws would be heaped on us from that float.

The parade that comes back to me most vividly, though, is the Mystics of Time, whose three dragons slithered through the streets, breathing fire. To this day the bright flames flickering at their tongues cause kids to squeal and grown-ups to shrink back and laugh. Whenever my father got to ride one of the dragons, we'd come down from the balcony onto the street and wait for him.

I can still see the dragon looming over my head, turning Grendel-like on me, transforming the street into a Beowulfian battle between float and boy. A creature in a phantasmagorical mask rises from the dragon's back and hurls a bag of throws right at me. Other kids grab at the sack of bean bags and rubber balls and taffy twists and necklaces, but I wrest it free. The dragon curves away; the phantasmal creature turns to stare at me one last time, then blows me a kiss.

WELCOME MILLENNIUM

On nice afternoons, in Mobile's winter sun, I walk through downtown streets and try to look into the past. Even though the Crown Theater on Dauphin has been restored as a dance club, the Van Antwerp building at Dauphin and Royal is now home to a restaurant, and the Battle House Hotel on Royal is still boarded up, these locales are picture windows into the ways we once lived. In their doorways lean the shadows of our forebears, the men and women who lost loved ones to yellow fever, welcomed their sons home from the Spanish-American War, nodded appreciatively as electric bulbs, switched on by pull cords, brightened rooms at night.

The first day of the new millennium brings the recognition that, as time unrolls like a vast Turkish carpet, we will soon be someone else's past. Our great-grandchildren, a hundred years from now, will amble by the buildings that provided the stage for our lives, and try to envision who we were. Much as we look at the abandoned GM & O terminal on Water Street and see an era of passenger trains, so our descendants will visit the lobby of the AmSouth building at Bienville Square, and wonder about the world where we made transactions with the 20th-century artifact called cash.

In their photo collections, we will look odd, even comical. Just as we thought of the handlebar mustaches and top hats of our grandfathers as overly formal, they will see us as trying to look forever young. In our slacks, open-collar shirts and athletic shoes, we will be clad in uniforms of the past.

The family heirlooms handed down to us—Civil War swords, and Tiffany lamps, and music boxes—will be relegated to ancient history.

Our vinyl record albums, our fountain pens, our rotary phones—even our CDs, laptops and cell phones—will become the bric-a-brac by which we are known.

A famous Mobilian, baseball great Satchel Paige, once advised, "Don't look back. Something may be gaining on you." One of our New Year's hopes must surely be that, 100 years from now, folks will heed Paige's advice as little as do we, and, glancing back over their shoulders to spy us waving from the past, appreciate what they see.

• • •

They could do well, come to think of it, to recall Satchel Paige, said to be the best baseball pitcher of all time—but who spent the height of his career in the Negro Baseball League, in the era before Jackie Robinson broke the color line. Studying his career alongside that of another Mobile Hall of Famer, Hank Aaron, would provide an epic view of the 20th century.

They could do well to explore the political rise and fall of Joseph Langan, who served as Mobile's mayor from 1953 to 1969, helping the city cross the bridge from a segregated to a desegregated South, and doing so with a minimum of violence. But Langan, in his last election, was turned out by the electorate—caught between extremes on both sides, and often vilified by both.

It would serve them well to study the career of Fred Whiddon, who began as a dreamy boy in the wiregrass country of southeast Alabama, became a philosophy professor, and founded—indeed, built—a breakaway academic institution that became the University of South Alabama. Whiddon's career as one of the longest-serving university presidents in the nation ended in controversy and acrimony.

They would find other stories to write from the lives of the three men who lie alongside each other in Church Street Graveyard—Joe Cain, Julian Rayford, and Eugene Walter. Three men of fanciful notions, colorful and eccentric, their imaginations were oddly and quintessentially Mobile. Not everyone loved them, either.

There are countless others, of course—doctors and lawyers and architects, chefs and teachers and clergymen, engineers and scientists and musicians—whose names will be turned up, whose lives will be examined. People who supported their families by picking crab-meat, or scrubbing floors, or pumping gas may not alter history, but their offspring's offspring will remember them for how they selflessly toiled.

No matter our contributions to the future, what we share today is the calendar, a fact that, as time moves on, will bond us ever closer. "The past is a foreign country. They do things differently there," wrote the English author L. P. Hartley in 1953.

"What country did they come from?" a resident of the future might ask of us.

"They came," the answer will go, "from the 20th century."

• • •

At the outset of the millennium we can plug into the Internet, sur-round ourselves with high-definition television, palm-size computers and digital cameras, and feel like we have arrived, finally, on the brink of tomorrow.

"The past is never dead," William Faulkner said, "it's not even past." Could the same be said of the future? Since we now take for granted that the technology arriving at our doorstep through "e-shopping" will be outmoded as soon as we open its box, has the future, arriving so quickly, finally rammed into the present?

Are we moving forward? Backward? Staying in place?

Did we build our superhighways only that we could sit in traffic jams at the concrete confluence of Bel Air and Springdale malls?

Did we purchase our customized home computers only that we should worry that our children might disappear in them like Alice through the looking glass?

In 1904, the Irish poet W. B. Yeats realized in a poem: "O love is the crooked thing, / There is nobody wise enough / To find out all that is in it, / For he would be thinking of love / Till the stars had run away / And the shadows eaten the moon."

With "microchip" and "cloning" and "genetic engineering" and "cyberspace" now part of our daily vocabulary, have we come any closer to finding out "all that is in it" concerning love?

• • •

Sometimes on my walks through town, I imagine composing a letter to the readers of 100 years from now, or even later. I've even taken notes—pen on paper, an old-fashioned concept even to us, by now—but am short-sighted when it comes to envisioning the future. I suspect that citizens of the future will continue to live amidst sharp contrasts, as do we. Just stroll through the De Tonti Square neighborhood of downtown and see where the historic elegance of the Richards D.A.R. House backs up to the late-afternoon melancholy of the Waterfront Rescue Mission. It's a symbolic picture of the state of the world.

The people of the future will also face the upside, and downside, of progress. Drive to Dauphin Island and see how the gas rigs, just offshore, have changed the look and feel of what was once a wind-swept barrier island, the most beautifully isolated place anywhere around. Good? Bad?

Travel to picturesque Daphne, on the eastern side of Mobile Bay, and look at the construction going on. Good? Bad?

"It was the best of times, it was the worst of times, it was the age of wisdom, it was the age of foolishness," Charles Dickens wrote in "A Tale of Two Cities" in 1859, and the same could be said of today—and a century from now.

"Dear Future Readers," I would say, "A hundred years ago, at the start of 2000, a community of well-intentioned folks wanted to send you their greetings. Few, if any of them, are around today, but their salutations are no less heartfelt. Dependent on computers for the first time in history, they worried their heads off about entering the new millennium—like primitive peoples fearful of an eclipse of the sun—but then relaxed, and being a good-natured people, had a pretty good time.

"Some of them accomplished great feats, others met tragic ends. Most enjoyed what might be considered, in terms of history, 'ordinary' lives, but which felt downright extraordinary to those folks living them.

"All we ask is that you pause to consider our stories; above all, that you not delete us from your bank of memories.

"If, on the transition of your own century to the next, all your fancy, hyper-speed computers should experience glitches and return you to the year 2000, congratulations!

"On behalf of the 21st century, let me be the first to welcome you back to what are surely, by now, the good ol' days."

Acknowledgments

Any book, in part, is a collaborative effort between author and editors. This is especially true of a collection of works like "Back Home."

At the University of Alabama Press, I want to thank Nicole Mitchell, Curtis Clark, and Mindy Wilson for helping take this book, with persistence and patience, from concept to reality. Jennifer Horne, Suzette Griffith, Kathy Cummings, Michelle Sellers, Elizabeth Motherwell and Priscilla McWilliams have also been key to this process.

"Back Home" would not exist if not for the Mobile Register, chiefly the editorial vision and pragmatic enthusiasm of editor-in-chief Mike Marshall and managing editor Dewey English, their commitment to solid reporting and engaging prose. As publisher, Howard Bronson is a continuously guiding presence in the excellence of the Register. Stan Tiner, now executive editor of the Sun-Herald in Biloxi, and Bailey Thomson, now associate professor at the University of Alabama, were heading up the Register when I arrived, and their contribution to my work will always be deeply felt, and greatly appreciated. Thanks as well to Deborah Howell of Newhouse Newspapers in Washington, D.C.

I am indebted to the editorial help of many others at the Register, among them: Paul Cloos, Dave Helms, Ronni Patriquin Clark, Jim Van Anglen, Roy Brightbill, and Debbie Lord. Dozens of others are part of the long process of moving copy and designing pages, among them Doug Dimitry, Kent Cockson, Matt Irvin, Chris Hall, Charles Croft, Andy Warren, Thom Dudgeon, Jeff Darby, and Chris Brown.

The great photography in the Register, some reprinted in this book, comes from Kiichiro Sato, Kate Reali, John David Mercer, Bill Starling, Glenn Andrews, Mary Hattler, Victor Calhoun, Robie Ray, and Mike Kittrell. Denise Thomas, at the photography desk, dug back through years of images to find the ones I needed in "Back Home."

Part of the life blood of a newsroom comes from the conversations that take place, and none have enriched me more than those with our books editor, John Sledge. The conversation has continued with all my writing colleagues, present and former, among them: Frances Coleman, Sam Hodges, Gene Owens, Jerald Hyche, Cammie East, Byron McCauley, Mike Wilson, Eddie Curran, Mark Holan, Carol Cain, Bill Finch, Danny Cusick, Suzy Spear, Jay Grelen, Matt Teague, Quin Hillyer, Robert Buchanan, Thomas Harrison, Karen Tolkinnen, Jane Nichols, Gary McElroy, Ron Colquitt, Willie Rabb, Rhoda Pickett, Ben Raines, Manuel Torres, George Werneth, Kristen Campbell, Mike Brantley, Lawrence Specker, Renee Busby, David Rainier, Tommy Hicks, John Cameron, and, everybody's favorite guy with cup of coffee in hand, Gary Mitchell. The daily workings of the office are infinitely easier, thanks to Hilda McNair, Michelle Rolls, Judi Rojeski, and Pam Baker. John Sellers and co. have guided me through cyberspace.

The writerly conversation has extended to writer and reader friends from Maine to Manhattan to Atlanta to New Orleans to Texas— Lincoln Paine, Karl Hein, Charles Salzberg, Doug Garr, Eli and Judith Evans, Robert Friedman, Tom Mathison, Karen Braziller, Bill Baker, Phil Patton, Rich Goodman, Tom Quinn, Brian Mori, Bill and Renee Pangburn, Caroline Stewart and Peter Halley, Stephanie and Bernard Perlmutter, Margaret and Ken Leung, Charles and Laura Phillips, Roberta Wright, Charles McNair, Jeanie Thompson, Cindy Coulter, Wayne Greenhaw, Bob Morrell, David Weiner, Andy Antippas, Ann Wakefield and Richard Baudouin.

In Mobile, the Zitsos Cafeteria regulars, among them the Toubianas, the Holbergs, and Jim Tarlton, have joined me and my Dad to discuss religion, travel, and the merits of Greek salad. Ronnie and Michael Hoffman have made our Wednesday Trade Club lunches a round-table chat about issues around town.

At Preservation Magazine, I am indebted to Bob Wilson and Kim Keister; at Southern Living to Dianne Young; at the Brightleaf Review to Dave Perkins; at the New York Times to Alida Becker, Chip McGrath, Neil Genzlinger, Katie Roberts, Connie Rosenblum, and Alex Ward.

At Alabama Public Television, producer Brent Davis and professor Don Noble, of "Bookmark," put these pieces in context for viewers. Ed Mullins, chairman of the department of journalism at the University of Alabama, provided a forum for me to meet students and talk about creative nonfiction.

Thousands of people in Mobile and elsewhere have answered my interviewers' questions; most of whose voices appear in "Back Home." To all of them I say thank you for time and honesty. And to those who provided the information about our city, I am grateful—Mike Thomason and Elisa Baldwin at the University of South Alabama Archives; Jay Higginbotham at the City Archives; George Ewert at the Museum of the City of Mobile; Charlotte Chamberlain and Holly Eckert at the Mobile Public Library.

Countless others have been helpful to me, among them Dr. and Mrs. John Mosteller and family, Rabbi P. Irving and Pat Bloom, Barry Silverman, David Alsobrook, the Walter family in Memphis, the family of Alberta West, Yolande Betbeze Fox, Lulu Crawford, Ruth Lamensdorf, the Oppenheimers, and all the dusk strollers and porch sitters of Williams Court.

But only a handful of people really get tangled into the creative process of a writer—at least, at home.

To my sisters and their families: Sherrell, Charlie, and Aaron; Becky, Lezlee, and Scott; Robbie, John, Marisa, and Sandro—and to my parents, Evelyn and Charlie Hoffman—this book is not only about journeys through my hometown, but part of the longer journey in which this book is a bench to rest on awhile along the way. They are part of every journey I undertake.

My wife, Nancy, and my daughter, Meredith, sometimes appear in this book—but that's deceptive. They are in every page, every word. With their wisdom and humor and love, they help give me a voice when it counts—when the sun has set, the clock is ticking, and it's just me and the keyboard, all on our own.

Permissions

"King Cotton's New Face" was originally published as "King Cotton's Back With a New Face," in the Mobile Register, Sept. 29, 1996.

"The Miller's Tale" was originally published in the Mobile Register, Dec. 22, 1996.

"The Music of 'Pah-cahns'" was originally published in the Mobile Register, Nov. 1, 1999.

PART IV COLORFUL COMPETITIONS

"Baseball in the Blood" was originally published as the baseball stories "Making It Home," in the Mobile Register, Sept. 2, 1997; and "Baseball in the Blood," in the Mobile Register, Aug. 4, 1996.

"Tommie Littleton: Gentleman Boxer" was originally published as "Mobile's Gentleman Boxer," in the Mobile Register, March 8, 1999.

"Men of Steel: Wheelchair Basketball" was originally published as "Men of Steel," in the Mobile Register, Jan. 19, 1997.

"The Great Anvil Shoot" was originally published as "They Shoot Anvils, Don't They?" in the Mobile Register, Oct. 15, 1996.

PART V TANGLED LEGACIES

"Peter's Legacies" was originally published in the Mobile Register, May 3, 1998.

"Search for a Slave Ship" was originally published in the Mobile Register, Jan. 25, 1998.

"Alexis Herman Comes Home" was originally published as "The Old Neighborhood Beams With Pride," in the Mobile Register, Aug. 23, 1997.

"Long Lives the Mockingbird" was originally published in the New York Times Book Review, Aug. 9, 1998. Copyright 1999 Roy Hoffman. Distributed by the New York Times Special Features.

PART VI Newcomers Among Us

"By the Sweat of Their Brows" and "Helping Hands for Children" were originally published in the series "Familias de la Tierra: Families of the Land," which included the following articles in the Mobile Register: "By the Sweat of Their Brows," June 15, 1997; "Alone Across Borders," June 16, 1997; and "Helping Hands for Children," June 17, 1997.

"Khampou's Village" and "Buddhist Temple" were originally published in the series "On the Asian Coast," which included the following articles in the Mobile Register: "Khampou's Village," July 25, 1999; "Survivors of the Sea," August 1, 1999; and "Buddhist Temple," August 8, 1999.

PART VII Intriguing Portraits

"Joe Langan's City Limits" was originally published as "Pushing the Limits: Joe Langan's Mobile," in the Mobile Register, Sept. 15, 1997.

"Albert Murray's House of Blues" was originally published as "House of Blues," in the Mobile Register, May 18, 1987.

"Alma Fisher: Out of Auschwitz" was originally published in the series "Voices of the Holocaust," which included the following articles in the Mobile Register: "Out of Auschwitz," June 19, 1998; "Anguished Journey," June 20, 1997; and "Never Forget," June 21, 1998.

"Dr. James Franklin: Healing Us Still" was originally published as "Healing Us Still," in the Mobile Register, Oct. 13, 1996.

"Ben May: The Quiet Philanthropist" was originally published as "Mobile's Quiet Philanthropist," in the Mobile Register, Feb. 2, 1997.

"U.S. Attorney Armbrecht: A Matter of Will" was originally published as "A Matter of Will," in the Mobile Register, March 29, 1998.

"Morocco to Mobile: Paul Bowles' Secret Journey" was originally published as "Morocco to Mobile: A Journey of Healing," in the Mobile Register, Jan. 5, 1997.

"Monumental Talent: Tina Allen's Heroic Sculptures" was originally published as "Monumental Talent," in the Mobile Register, April 4, 1999.

PART VIII THE SEASONAL ROUND

"Rain Town, U.S.A." was originally published as "Be It Ever So Rainy, There's No Place Like Mobile," in the Mobile Register, June 17, 1997.

"Azaleas at 8 mph" was originally published as "Mobile's Azaleas at 8 mph," in the Mobile Register, March 21, 1998.

"Point Clear P.O." was originally published as "Post Office is the Center of Life in Tiny Point Clear, 36564," in the Mobile Register, April 12, 1998.

"In My Parents' Dancesteps" was originally published as "Big Shoes to Fill on the Dance Floor" in Newsday, "Viewpoints" section, June 17, 1994. Copyright Roy Hoffman.

"The End-of-Year Recital" was originally published as "Growing Up Gracefully," in the Mobile Register, May 22, 1999.

"Summer Heat" was originally published as "In the Sultry Mobile Summer," in the Mobile Register, June 20, 1998.

"The First Music of Fall" was originally published as "Playing Around," in the Mobile Register, Sept. 20, 1998.

"Already Home for the Holidays" was originally published as "Holidays Mean Home in a Distant Airport," in the Mobile Register, Nov. 29, 1998.

"Snow!" was originally published as "Flurries Fuel Rare Moment in Time," in the Mobile Register, Dec. 19, 1996.

"Holiday Lights" was originally published as "Reflections on the Brilliance of the Season," in the Mobile Register, Dec. 25, 1998.

"Marking Time" was originally published as "Clocks Remind that Time Trips on Ever Faster," in the Mobile Register, Dec. 31, 1996.

PART IX MARDI GRAS DRUMS

The introduction to this section was originally published as "A Drum Roll, Please, for Carnival Cadence," in the Mobile Register, Feb. 11, 1997.

"Let the Good Times Roll" was originally published as "Mobile at Mardi Gras," in Brightleaf: A Southern Review of Books, Spring 1999. Copyright Roy Hoffman.

"Welcome Millennium" was originally published as "A Millennium History Lesson," in the Mobile Register, Jan. 1, 2000.

About the Author

ROY HOFFMAN is Writer-in-Residence for the Mobile Register. His writings have appeared in the New York Times, the Washington Post, Fortune, the Oxford American, and Esquire. He is also the author of the Lillian Smith Award–Winning novel "Almost Family" (University of Alabama Press, 2000).